SPITFIRE
LIFE OF THE LEGEND

SPITFIRE
LIFE OF THE LEGEND

ROBERT JACKSON

Foreword by Air Marshal C R Spink CB CBE FCMI FRAeS RAF (Rtd)

METRO BOOKS
NEW YORK

CARNEGIE BUILDING
1 LaGrange Street
Newnan, GA 30263

METRO BOOKS
New York

An Imprint of Sterling Publishing
387 Park Avenue South
New York, NY 10016

© 2010 by Elephant Book Company Limited

Editorial Director: **Will Steeds**
Project Editor: **Kevin Wiltshire**
Designer: **Mark Holt**
Copy Editor: **Karen Stein**
Photographers: **Mark Winwood; Neil Sutherland**
Production: **Robert Paulley**
Proofreader: **Alison Candlin**
Color reproduction: **Modern Age Repro House Ltd, Hong Kong**

ISBN: 978-1-4351-2607-7

For information about custom editions, special sales, and premium and corporate purchases, please contact Sterling Special Sales at 800-805-5489 or specialsales@sterlingpublishing.com.

Manufactured in China

2 4 6 8 10 9 7 5 3

www.sterlingpublishing.com

Elephant Book Company and the editors particularly wish to thank the following for their help in preparing this book: Peter Arnold; Barrie Smith and Peter Verdemato, RAF Spitfire and Hurricane Memorial Trust; Phil Jarrett; Ewen Cameron and Ian Alder, RAF Museum; The Spitfire Society; Tangmere Military Aviation Museum; Alan Mansell, Solent Sky Museum; Ian Blair; Karen Crick, Royal Air Force Museum, Cosford; Col Pope, ARCo. Museum details in the Acknowledgments section on page 160.

JACKET AND FRONT COVER ILLUSTRATION *Achtung Spitfire* © Roy Grinnell, altered by permission of the artist. (website: www.roygrinnell.com).

ENDPAPERS This Mk II, almost certainly on delivery with an ATA pilot, dates by the livery from August–November 1940.

HALF TITLE A Spitfire Mk XIV, with Supermarine chief test pilot Jeffrey Quill at the controls, rolling for the benefit of Supermarine photographer F.H. Burr.

FULL TITLE Spitfires of No. 19 Squadron, the first unit to receive the type, seen at RAF Duxford with ground crews (and mascot) before the outbreak of World War II.

IMPRINT AND CONTENTS Spitfire Mk IAs of No. 65 Squadron, sporting new three-blade propellers, on parade at RAF Hornchurch, Essex, on June 8, 1939.

CHAPTER 1 The Supermarine S.6B floatplane was the unopposed winner of the 1931 Schneider Trophy contest, securing the coveted trophy for Great Britain for all time.

CHAPTER 2 Two German soldiers pose for a propaganda photograph, perched on a Spitfire brought down during the Dunkirk evacuation.

CHAPTER 3 Spitfire Mk VB R6923 of No. 92 Squadron, a converted Mk I, was shot down over the English Channel by a Messerschmitt 109 in June 1941.

CHAPTER 4 From February 1943, rocket-assisted take-off gear (RATOG) became a standard fit for all Seafires.

CHAPTER 5 Griffon-engined Spitfire Mk XIV RB146 was a trials aircraft, and among other refinements was fitted with a five-blade propeller.

CHAPTER 6 Spitfire Mk VIIIs of No. 136 Squadron in the Cocos Islands, late 1945. The squadron re-armed with Spitfire XIVs in February 1946.

CHAPTER 7 Last of the Spitfires: a Spitfire Mk 24 is flanked by a Mk 21 and Mk 22. The Mk 21 was the first to feature a new wing shape.

Contents

Foreword

There are few greater privileges afforded a pilot than to fly a Spitfire—in this I count myself very lucky indeed, having flown many marks of this wonderful aircraft over the past 20 years. But I was given this opportunity in peacetime and only when weather and conditions were the most favourable to fly these precious aircraft. This book gives a wonderful insight into the difficult times that existed when this iconic machine was designed, built and flown—when pilots flew in the most arduous conditions that tested both man and machine. With new material that gives the reader a fresh perspective on these dangerous times, the author has constructed a most informative and readable book, which underlines the importance of the Spitfire to this country in the critical days of 1940.

The Spitfire is quite simply the most wonderful aircraft to fly, and its graceful lines and symmetry are testimony to the genius of R. J. Mitchell and his successors in the Supermarine Company. But this beautiful aircraft had teeth, and it was the performance of the aircraft that allowed the brave "Few" to take on the might of the Luftwaffe and win the day. The Hurricane was in the majority during the Battle of Britain and did quite sterling service, but it was always tested by the faster Bf 109, so it was the Spitfire that was used to combat the fighter threat. And it was the Spitfire that went on to be developed in many versions, with the outstanding Rolls-Royce Merlin engine eventually giving way to the larger RR Griffon.

The Spitfire will no doubt go down in aviation history as one of the greatest fighter aircraft of all time—and it is—but we must remember that it was the courage and skill of the young men that won the day; and they will tell you that they had the most capable machine with which to do the task.

The Spitfire is quite deservedly a legend, and this book significantly adds weight to that reputation.

Air Marshal C R Spink CB CBE FCMI FRAeS RAF (Rtd)

Introduction

No fighter aircraft in history has evoked such enthusiasm as the Supermarine Spitfire. A machine of grace and beauty, beloved by all who flew it, the Spitfire and its naval version, the Seafire, fought in every theater of war. In fact, the Spitfire was the only Allied fighter aircraft to see continual front-line service from 1939 to 1945, a testament to the vision and strength of the original design. It saw action over the snows of Russia and the desert sands of North Africa; it fought off savage enemy attacks on the gallant island of Malta in 1942; and it took the war deep into the heart of Germany during the final Allied offensive against the Third Reich in 1944–45. In the Pacific theater, Spitfires battled with Japanese fighters and bombers in the air defenses of Australia, while the naval version of the Spitfire, the Seafire, took the war to the Japanese home islands as part of the Royal Navy's Task Force 57.

This superbly illustrated and highly evocative book charts the Spitfire's evolution through its combat career across the world, from its earliest skirmishes against the Luftwaffe over the North Sea to its final actions in World War II against the Japanese in Burma, and also includes operations by the Royal Navy's Seafires in European and Far Eastern waters.

Through the eyes of pilots, readers will discover what it was like to fly unarmed photo-reconnaissance missions over Germany, dodging enemy fighters at the edge of the stratosphere, and to engage V-1 flying bombs over south-east England. Each chapter also provides a comprehensive account of the Spitfire's ongoing development and its combat career in the various roles it had to perform under the stresses and demands of war.

For the Spitfire the war did not end in 1945: in 1948–49, Israeli and Egyptian Spitfires battled with one another over the Sinai Desert, where they played a vital part in assuring the infant Israeli Air Force's air supremacy over its Arab foes. Meanwhile, RAF Spitfires hammered communist terrorists in Malaya and French-flown ones were used in Indo-China during the early phase of what was to escalate—more than a decade later—into the Vietnam War.

But the Spitfire's finest hour, for which it will be forever remembered, was during 1940. This was the year in which the British people, in the months after Dunkirk, developed a new spirit in the realization that they stood alone against an implacable enemy who seemed unstoppable and whose war machine now stood poised a stone's throw away across the English Channel; an enemy who was about to unleash the might of his air force against Britain's cities, just as it had done against Warsaw and Rotterdam.

Between that enemy and subjugation, with its associated misery and the horror of occupation, there stood the Spitfires and Hurricanes of the Royal Air Force, and a few hundred fighter pilots; upon their shoulders rested the hopes of the free world. On average, they were 20 years old.

Robert Jackson

1 Spitfire: The genesis

The provenance of the Spitfire

On the morning of March 5, 1936, the prototype of a sleek, new monoplane fighter, the Supermarine Type 300, lifted off the grass at Eastleigh Aerodrome, near Southampton, and climbed away on its maiden flight.

Silver in color and highly polished, to many of the spectators who had helped to bring this moment to fruition, the little aircraft was sheer poetry in flight. Soon to be named Spitfire, its progeny—together with its contemporary, the Hawker Hurricane—would form the first line of Britain's air defenses, then the most sophisticated in the world.

For those witnessing this maiden flight, it would have been hard to believe that less than 20 years earlier Britain's air defenses had been virtually nonexistent, and that the Royal Air Force had stood on the brink of extinction.

The four years of World War I had witnessed an astonishing technological leap forward in military hardware. And yet, almost before the guns had ceased firing, the victorious Allies began dismantling their respective military assets seemingly without much thought for the needs of tomorrow. In Britain's case, powerful lobbies in the Admiralty and the War Office almost succeeded both in engineering the demise of the Royal Air Force as an independent organization and in subordinating British air power to the Army and Navy; that they failed to do so was mainly due to the determination of the chief of the air staff, Air Chief Marshal Sir Hugh Trenchard.

By 1921 the strength of the RAF was at a very low ebb, with only 24 squadrons of all types at home and abroad (including a solitary fighter squadron in the United Kingdom). But in April 1922 a defense subcommittee recommended the force's expansion to 52 squadrons, totaling some 500 aircraft—which would later be increased to 600—for home defense. The reequipment program had to start from scratch, and to fulfill the air defense role it was decided to standardize the Sopwith Snipe, the fighter designed during the closing months of World War I to replace the Sopwith Camel.

The first squadron to equip fully with Snipes was No. 29, which reformed at Duxford on April 1, 1923. By the end of the year the fighter strength available for the air defense of Great Britain stood at 11 squadrons, equipped predominantly with

ABOVE LEFT Marshal of the Royal Air Force Sir Hugh Trenchard fought hard to preserve the integrity of the RAF when both Army and Navy tried to subordinate it to themselves.

LEFT The Sopwith Snipe was a nimble successor to the Sopwith Camel of WWI fame, and was the RAF's standard fighter equipment in the early post-war years.

OPPOSITE TOP The Hawker Woodcock was the first new British fighter to enter production after WWI. The RAF received a total of 67.

OPPOSITE BOTTOM The Pemberton Billing PB.9 had excellent reports from the pilots who tested it, but was not selected for production.

One of them, No. 25 Squadron, became famous for performing spectacular aerobatic displays in the mid-1920s. Despite early problems with wing flutter, the Grebe was a highly maneuverable and robust little aircraft, and it was the first British machine to survive a terminal velocity dive, reaching 240mph (386km/h).

Although the Grebe replaced the Sopwith Snipe in some first-line RAF squadrons, the true successor to the Snipe was the Hawker Woodcock, the H.G. Hawker Engineering Company having reestablished Sopwith's former aviation enterprises. The Hawker company's early activities involved refurbishing Snipes and Camels for sale overseas. The first of its own designs, the Duiker parasol-wing monoplane, was unsuccessful, but the Woodcock single-seat fighter was accepted after lengthy trials. It was delivered to No. 3 Squadron in May 1925, becoming the first new British fighter to enter production after the end of World War I.

Snipes; this was still a long way from the planned total of 52 squadrons. It was also clear that the Snipe, although invaluable as an interim aircraft, was quickly approaching obsolescence, and steps were taken to rearm the fighter squadrons with post-war designs at an early date.

The first such design was the Gloster Grebe, a product of the Gloucestershire Aircraft Company (which would change its name to Gloster in 1926). Gloucestershire Aircraft Company's chief designer, H. P. Folland, had previously worked for the Nieuport & General Aircraft Company, which had been set up in Britain late in 1916 to license-build the fighter designs of the French company. The Grebe prototype was originally ordered as a Nighthawk; it made its first public appearance at the RAF Air Pageant, Hendon, in June 1923, and entered RAF service with No. 111 Squadron in October that year, subsequently equipping five more RAF fighter squadrons.

However, there was another company that had yet to make its mark in the field of landplane fighters, even though it had attempted to do so years earlier. Its story began on August 12, 1914, when a sturdy little fighter biplane took off on its first flight from a small field at Woolston, near Southampton. Its pilot, Victor Mahl, reported that it had had a creditable performance, having a top speed of 78mph (126km/h) and a rate of climb of 500ft per minute (152 meters per minute).

The aircraft, the PB.9, was the brainchild of perhaps the most eccentric and certainly one of the most talented of Britain's early aircraft designers, Noel Pemberton Billing. The PB.9 was the progenitor of a line of combat aircraft that, two decades later, would develop into a fighter that proved to be crucial to Britain's survival in one of the darkest periods of the nation's long history. From such humble beginnings, the legendary Spitfire was born.

Supermarine: From flying boats to fighters

One of inventor and aircraft designer Noel Pemberton Billing's closest friends was Charles Grey, founder and for many years editor of the prestigious aviation journal *The Aeroplane*; Grey wrote the following about Billing's PB.9:

"Perhaps the most remarkable machine that PB ever built was a little fighting scout that broke all records for its power in 1914. It became known as the 'Seven-Day Bus' because it was designed, built and flown in six days and ten hours. PB chalked-up the outlines on the walls of this works one night as soon after the declaration of war as he could . . .

Work began next morning, and no one left that factory until the PB.9 was finished. The only engine available was a very old 50hp Gnome, which developed no more than 18hp on the bench. With that it did 78mph [126km/h] and climbed 540ft [165m] in a minute."

Despite its potential, the PB.9 was not accepted for production, the sole example being sent to Hendon for use as a trainer by the Royal Naval Air Service.

Pemberton Billing was undoubtedly a man of extraordinary vision and ability; in 1912 he entered into a wager with another aviation pioneer, Frederick Handley Page, that he would learn to fly and gain his Royal Aero Club Aviator's Certificate within 24 hours. In fact, instructed by Harold Barnwell of the Vickers Flying School at Brooklands, flying a Bristol Boxkite, he did it between 05:45 and breakfast time one summer morning.

Billing's first venture into aircraft construction—apart from a man-lifting glider, built in 1904—involved a small flying boat he called the Supermarine PB.1. In doing so he unknowingly gave birth to a name that was to become world famous. The PB.1 was a comparatively streamlined design, and it aroused great interest when it was displayed at the International Aero Show at Olympia in London in 1914. Other pre–World War I flying boat designs included the PB.2, PB.3, and PB.7, the last two being designed so

that their wings and tail units could be removed and the hulls used as cabin cruisers. With the outbreak of World War I, PB, as he had become known, designed a series of landplanes for the RNAS, starting with the PB.9; however, only one, the PB.25 Scout—known as the "Push Prodge"—went into production, and it did not enter service. The PB.25 featured a perfectly streamlined nacelle and was the world's first fighter in which the gun was fixed, the pilot using the aircraft as an aiming platform. Other designs included the PB.29E "Zeppelin Destroyer" and the PB.31E "Nighthawk," the latter armed with a recoil-less gun firing a 1.5lb (0.67kg) shell; both were twin-engine designs with four wings.

On March 10, 1916, Pemberton Billing sold his company at Woolston to Hubert Scott-Paine, who had managed the works since December 1914. Scott-Paine retained the name "Supermarine," which had featured in the firm's telegraphic address, and the company now became known as the Supermarine Aviation Works Ltd. Pemberton Billing was now free to fight the cause of British aviation as an MP in the House of Commons. He was outspoken in his criticism of the failure of both the Royal Naval Air Service and the Royal Flying Corps to place an order for the PB.25 at a time when the Fokker Monoplane, with its synchronized forward-firing machine gun, was wreaking havoc on the Western Front.

However, Pemberton Billing's main legacy was the Supermarine Works, which remained under government control until the end of World War I, and which was managed during that period by Hubert Scott-Paine.

The factory's main activity during the war was to carry out repair and experimental work on behalf of the Admiralty, which predictably led to a focus on seaplanes. The first of these were

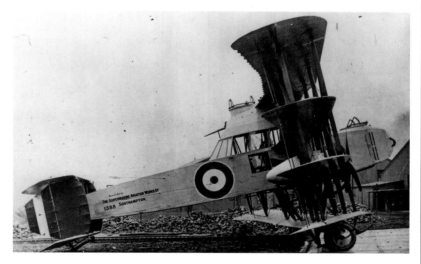

based on designs submitted by the Air Department of the Admiralty and were known as the "AD" designs. One of them, the AD Boat, was already being flight tested when Pemberton Billing left and the new company was registered. It was followed by two more, the AD Navyplane and the N.1B Baby.

The Navyplane was a two-seat floatplane with a pusher engine. A biplane, it first flew in 1915; however, only one prototype was built. The Supermarine Baby, tested in 1918, was the first British fighter flying boat, but only one Baby was completed and the type never went into production. Nevertheless, the concept led directly to the development of two more designs: the Sea King and Sea Lion, both important threads in the tapestry of the Spitfire story.

Much of the design work on the Sea King and Sea Lion was undertaken by a young man who had joined the firm in 1916; his name was Reginald J. Mitchell.

Architects of the Spitfire: Mitchell and the Supermarine team

Reginald Joseph Mitchell, the man whose name will be forever associated with the Spitfire, was born on May 20, 1895, in the village of Talke, near Stoke-on-Trent in Staffordshire. His father was headmaster of a local school but later gave up teaching to found a printing business. At the age of 16, Mitchell, having completed his high-school education, joined the Kerr, Stewart & Co. Ltd. locomotive works at Stoke as an engineering apprentice.

After his apprenticeship, Mitchell worked in the firm's drawing office, continuing his education by attending night school, where he studied engineering and mechanics, higher mathematics, and technical drawing. In 1917 he applied for a job at the Supermarine Aviation Works in Southampton, and he was given the post of assistant to the manager, Hubert Scott-Paine. Scott-Paine was quick to recognize that Mitchell was an engineer of considerable talent, and in 1919 transferred him as assistant to Mr. Leach, the works manager. However, he did not remain Leach's assistant for long; in 1919, with the departure of Supermarine's chief designer, F. J. Hargreaves, Mitchell returned to the drawing office to fill the vacant post. Further advancement followed, and in 1920 the 25-year-old Mitchell, then recently married, was appointed chief engineer and designer on projects concerned primarily with military flying boats.

Mitchell had a hand in the design of both the Supermarine N.1B Baby—although the principal designer was F. J. Hargreaves—and the Navyplane.

ABOVE Reginald Mitchell, pictured toward the end of his working life. By this time, he was busy with other projects.

LEFT Mitchell's engraved cigarette case. His untimely death—at the age of just 42—was caused by rectal cancer.

He subsequently set about refining these designs, and his influence was apparent in their successors, the Supermarine Sea King and Sea Lion.

Like the Baby, the Sea King I began life as a fighter flying-boat project. It was powered by a 160hp Beardmore engine, and attracted a considerable amount of interest when it appeared at the 1920 Olympia Aero Show; unfortunately, it failed to attract any customers. A developed version, the Sea King II, with a 300hp Hispano-Suiza engine, did not fare any better.

But in the meantime, Supermarine had produced a design along broadly similar lines, and this, powered by a Napier Lion engine, became the Sea Lion. It was one of three British seaplanes entered in the 1919 Schneider Trophy Contest, the others being Fairey and Sopwith floatplanes. The Schneider Trophy—or La Coupe d'Aviation Maritime Jacques Schneider, to give its correct title—had begun in 1912, when Schneider, a French financier and aviation enthusiast, had put up the award to be competed for by seaplanes over a course of at least 150 nautical miles (278km). Britain, having won the trophy with a Sopwith Tabloid in 1914, was the host nation for the 1919 event, there having been no contest during the war years. Bournemouth, on the south coast, was the focal point of a ten-lap course totaling 200 nautical miles (370km).

The Sea Lion performed well, but its hull was holed by an obstacle on takeoff, and the pilot, Squadron Leader Basil Hobbs, lost his bearings in fog. When he touched down at the first marker point, as required by the rules, the hull filled with water and the aircraft sank (it was later salvaged). However, the other competitors also had problems, and the race was declared void. As a gesture of goodwill to the Italian team, whose pilot had circumnavigated the course but missed a turning point, the Royal Aero Club (the organizing body) consented to hold the following year's contest in Venice.

The Italians won the 1920 competition outright in a Savoia S.19, and again in 1921 with a Macchi M.7. In 1922 the contest was held at Naples, and on this occasion the Italians entered three

aircraft, the French two, and the British one: the Supermarine Sea Lion II, powered by a 450hp Napier Lion engine. It was this last aircraft, Reginald Mitchell's brainchild, that won the contest, although the triumph was short lived: in the following year the trophy went to a US Navy entrant, the Curtiss CR-3 floatplane.

In 1928 Supermarine was taken over by Vickers, and shortly afterward Mitchell was appointed director and chief designer. The qualities of Mitchell, the man, were summarized by Joseph Smith, who would later succeed him as chief designer:

"R. J. was a well-built man, pleasant-faced, of medium height and fair colouring, with a very determined chin. He possessed great charm, an engaging smile which was often in evidence and which transformed his habitual expression of concentration. He was rather shy with strangers, although preserving an outwardly easy manner, and only when one came to know him well did his chief characteristics become evident. Foremost among these characteristics was a clear-thinking ability to create, which made him a designer in the truest sense of the word. This creative ability was the driving force of his life."

Yet as the turbulent 1930s dawned, Reginald Mitchell's greatest creation was to come.

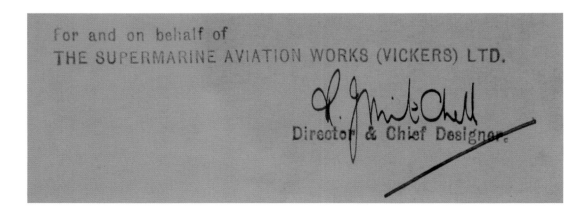

ABOVE The Supermarine Sea Lion I was one of four British seaplanes which were available to compete in the 1919 Schneider Trophy contest.

LEFT Reginald Mitchell's signature. The handwriting shows both determination and strength of character, which Mitchell had in abundance.

The Schneider Trophy racers

Following the American victory in the 1923 Schneider Trophy contest, Mitchell and his team at Supermarine began the design of a new single-seat high-speed flying boat. This was the Sea Urchin, which was to have been powered by a 600hp Rolls-Royce Condor engine, giving it an estimated maximum speed of 200mph (321km/h). The project had Air Ministry support, but the Sea Urchin was never completed, mainly because of problems with the engine.

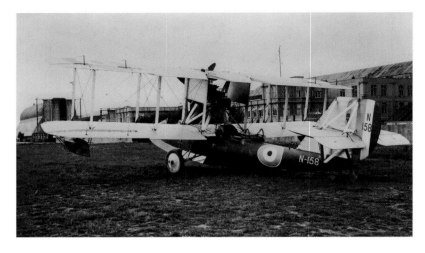

ABOVE The Supermarine Seagull was a modified version of the Supermarine Seal II. N-158, seen here, was one of two aircraft tested at Martlesham Heath.

Mitchell's next design, the Supermarine S.4 floatplane, was much more revolutionary. It was a cantilever monoplane, and set a pattern in aircraft design that was to remain virtually unchanged for two decades. The S.4 was one of three British aircraft prepared for the 1925 Schneider Trophy competition, the others being two Gloster-Napier IIIs. All three were powered by 700hp Napier Lion engines, and were designed to Air Ministry Specification 2/25.

The S.4 made its first flight at Southampton on August 25, 1925, in the hands of Supermarine's chief test pilot, Captain Henri Biard, a Channel Islander who had piloted the winning 1922 entry. It was shipped subsequently with the other two competitors to Chesapeake Bay, Baltimore, where the 1925 race was to be held. The S.4 was firm favorite to win, but on October 22—the day before the race—it developed wing flutter in a turn and went out of control, plunging into the sea; the aircraft was a total loss and Biard narrowly escaped with his life. The race was won by a Curtiss R3C2 biplane flown by Lieutenant Jimmy Doolittle of the US Army Air Corps.

There were no British entries in the 1926 event, which was won by an Italian team, but for the 1927 contest Supermarine fielded an improved S.4 design, the S.5, again powered by a Napier Lion. For the first time, the British entry was an all-RAF affair, and a unit known as the High Speed Flight was formed for the occasion. Two S.5s were shipped to Venice, the venue for the 1927 race, in which they secured first and second places.

There was no contest the following year, but high-speed development work was continued by the High Speed Flight, and in February 1929 the Air Ministry once again decided to enter a team for that year's Schneider Trophy race. Reginald Mitchell's team set about developing a new aircraft, the S.6, which was somewhat larger than the S.5. By this time, considerable progress had been made in aero-engine design.

During the 1920s, the companies that were at the forefront of engine development in the United Kingdom were Bristol, Armstrong Siddeley, Napier, and Rolls-Royce. The first generation of post-war British fighters—types such as the Armstrong Whitworth Siskin, Gloster Grebe, and Fairey Flycatcher—were powered by the Armstrong Siddeley Jaguar, a heavy, complex, and cumbersome two-row radial that suffered from a short running life and lubrication problems. The situation improved in 1925, with the introduction of the Bristol Jupiter; this powered the nimble little Gloster Gamecock, the first really viable British fighter of post-war design, and the later Bristol Bulldog. Its successor, the Mercury, was installed in the Gloster Gauntlet and Gladiator, the last of the RAF's biplane fighters.

From the Rolls-Royce stable came the Kestrel, which was selected to power the Hawker Hart light bomber and Hawker Fury fighter. The performance of Rolls-Royce engines was a powerful factor in persuading the Directorate of Technical Development (a division of the Air Ministry) that Rolls-Royce had established a firm lead in the design of high-performance, liquid-cooled power plants. As a result, the decision was made to fit the company's latest racing engine, the 1900hp Rolls-Royce "R," in the Supermarine S.6, two examples of which were built. One of them went on to win the contest outright, the Napier-powered Gloster VI entries having been withdrawn because of engine trouble.

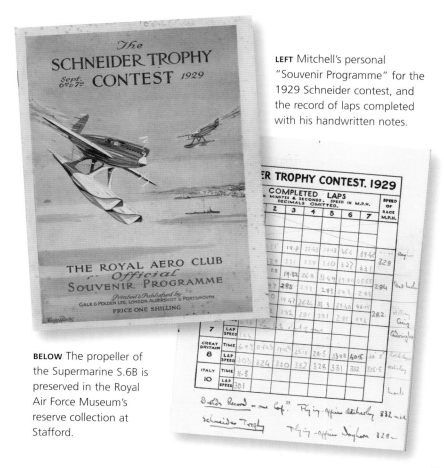

The Schneider Trophy contest was now being held every two years. However, the British government refused to support the 1931 British entry on grounds of cost, but a great patriot, Lady Houston, stepped into the breach with an offer of £100,000 ($454,000). Mitchell first of all modified the two existing S.6s by fitting them with enlarged floats and redesignating them S.6As. He then built two new machines, based on the existing airframe but incorporating much more powerful 2350hp Rolls-Royce "R" engines. The new aircraft were designated S.6B.

The S.6B won the 1931 race without competition, since the Italians were not able to produce a suitable aircraft in time and the French entry was accidentally destroyed during trials. In the 1931 race, not only did Mitchell's Supermarine racers bring the coveted Schneider Trophy back to Britain for all time (the competition was not held again), with three successive victories, but they also smashed a number of world air speed records in the process.

Even more important, they had made an unparalleled contribution to the development of high-speed aerodynamics. Within five years, this expertise would merge with further Rolls-Royce engine developments to produce an outstanding combat aircraft that would help the nation survive its hour of greatest peril.

BELOW The victorious 1931 Schneider Trophy team with Lady Houston, the great patriot whose donation of £100,000 made victory possible.

BELOW The powerful 2350hp Rolls-Royce "R" engine being lowered into position in the airframe of the Supermarine S.6B.

The Merlin engine and the monoplane fighter

In the early 1930s development work was in progress at Rolls-Royce on three power plants (engines): the PV.12, Peregrine, and Vulture. The PV.12 was a progressive and larger development of the Rolls-Royce Kestrel, which had powered the excellent Hawker Hart series of multipurpose biplanes. Tests with the first completed model on October 15, 1933, had left Rolls-Royce optimistic: the company informed Hawker that the new engine could be expected to provide an increase of 40 per cent in takeoff power.

Also, with single-stage supercharging, the PV.12 would produce an increase of 60 per cent at altitude over the Kestrel. After further ground running and flight testing on specially adapted test beds—two Hawker Horsleys, a Hawker Hart and the Hawker High Speed Fury, a private venture development of the Fury fighter biplane—the installation of the PV.12 was approved by the Directorate of Technical Development at the Air Ministry. It was to be installed in a new monoplane fighter then being developed by the Hawker Aircraft Company, the Fury Monoplane, later to be called the Hurricane. Similarly, it was the PV.12 that was chosen to power Supermarine's monoplane fighter, designed to Air Ministry Specification F.7/30.

Supermarine's answer to F.7/30 was an all-metal monoplane, the Type 224, featuring a thick, inverted gull wing and short cantilever fixed undercarriage. It was powered by a Rolls-Royce Goshawk engine, a not very successful derivative of the Kestrel IV. The F.7/30 was Mitchell's first attempt to apply the aerodynamic knowledge gained from the Supermarine racing floatplanes to a landplane fighter design, but he was not happy with the result. Nevertheless, work went ahead, the aircraft was built, and, on February 19, 1934, it was flown by Vickers-Supermarine Chief Test Pilot Joseph "Mutt" Summers. Then it went to the Aeroplane and

Armament Experimental Establishment at Martlesham Heath for comparative trials alongside other contenders. It was not a success, and neither were the others; the Air Ministry was left with no alternative but to fill the fighter gap with the Gloster Gladiator, the last of the RAF's biplane fighters.

Despite his disappointment in the Type 224, Mitchell continued to work on the design, making improvements that included straight, thinner wings and a retractable undercarriage. With these, he calculated that he could raise the F.7/30's maximum speed of 230mph (370km/h)—achieved during trials at Martlesham Heath—to 265mph (426km/h). But the developed version was never built, although in concept it was much closer to the aircraft that would eventually become the Spitfire.

Meanwhile, at Rolls-Royce, some weaknesses had been revealed during early running of the PV.12, and it was not until July 1934 that the usual 100-hour type test could be attempted. This exposed further issues: the cylinder blocks were prone to cracking and the double-helical reduction gear failed, necessitating the substitution of straight spur gears to the same ratio. However, all these problems were smoothed out in due course, and the PV.12 went on to take its place as the latest in Rolls-Royce's traditional "birds of prey" series of aero-engines; they called it the Merlin.

On November 16, 1934, the Air Ministry issued Specification F.5/34 in connection with the proposed monoplane fighter, and in the following month Supermarine received a contract to build a prototype, which was designated Type 300. It was covered by yet another specification, F.37/34 (a parallel specification, F.36/34, covered the monoplane fighter designed by Hawker, originally known as the Fury Monoplane but later to be named the

BELOW Installation of the Merlin engine in the Spitfire. The Merlin was a very compact design, with plenty of scope for further development.

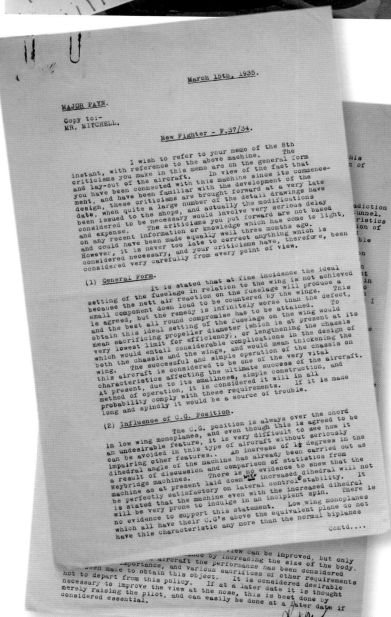

ABOVE LEFT Wool tufts attached to the wing of the F.7/30 Type 224 during the flight test phase. These were used to measure the characteristics of the airflow.

ABOVE Mitchell's choice of an elliptical wing for the Spitfire was not an innovation; Heinkel had already used it in the design of the He 70 fast mail aircraft.

LEFT Supermarine inter-office internal documents voicing Major Payn's concerns and criticisms of the Type 300, and Mitchell's response to those concerns.

Hurricane). [A specification was issued by the Air Ministry to cover each new aircraft project. For example, F.37/34 signifies Air Ministry fighter project No. 37, issued in 1934—author]

The prototype Supermarine 300, gradually taking shape in the Woolston factory during 1935, had not been officially named. Sir Robert McLean, chairman of Vickers-Supermarine, suggested that it should begin with an "S" and sound venomous. "Shrew" and "Shrike" had been put forward for the F.7/30 monoplane. So had another, more exotic name—"Spitfire"—and it was this designation that was suggested for the Type 300. McLean particularly liked it, although neither Mitchell nor the Air Ministry agreed. Mitchell's objection to it has been the subject of much speculation, but his son, the late Dr. Gordon Mitchell, gave the real explanation in correspondence with the author:

"My father's concern about the name Spitfire was not the name per se, but that he felt it was bloody silly to give it the same name as the F.7/30, which was a disastrous failure and for which the name Spitfire had been briefly considered!"

But the Spitfire name stuck, and it was formally adopted after the Type 300's maiden flight. Somehow it seemed ideal for an aircraft that could only be described as beautiful, its lines blending into one another in a way that was almost poetic. Everything—airframe and engine—evolved right at the appropriate moment, a rare event in aircraft and engine design.

Four guns or eight guns?

During those crucial years of the early 1930s, only a handful of senior officials at the Air Ministry seemed fully aware of how critically deficient in first-line equipment the RAF really was. One of them was Squadron Leader Ralph Sorley (later Air Marshal Sir Ralph Sorley, KCB, OBE, DSC), who joined Flying Operations 1 (FO1) at the Air Ministry in 1933, fresh from a tour of duty in Aden:

"I . . . occupied one small room with two others, Wing Commander A. T. Williams and Squadron Leader Jock Andrews [Sorley said]. A. T. and Jock devoted most of their efforts to defining the scope and geographical layout of a recognised system of air defence for the RAF in Britain, which eventually developed into Fighter and Bomber Commands, while I devoted my time to drawing up requirements for new types of aircraft which were badly needed."

He soon developed some very definite beliefs on how the design of future fighters should progress.

"Seeing the trend of German aircraft design towards twin-engined monoplane bombers there was plenty of need and scope for some drastic change in our operational requirements, and without doubt the prime necessity was for a monoplane fighter with sufficient need and hitting power to ensure the destruction of such potential German attackers [he wrote]."

Sorley considered the various armament options.

"The choice lay between the .303 gun, the .5 gun and a new 20mm Hispano gun . . . During 1934, this gun was experimental, and details of its performance and characteristics were hard to establish. On the other hand, designs of better .303 guns . . . had been tested over the preceding years, with the result that the American Browning from the Colt Automatic Weapon Corporation appeared to offer the best possibilities from the point of view of rate of fire . . . the .5-inch on the other hand had developed little, and although it possessed a better hitting power the rate of fire was slow and it was a heavy item, together with its ammunition, in respect of installed weight."

ABOVE HM King Edward VIII, who reigned for only six months before abdicating, inspects the prototype Spitfire at Martlesham Heath on July 8, 1936. R. J. Mitchell stands next to the propeller.

LEFT Squadron Leader (later Air Marshal Sir) Ralph Sorley, who vigorously pursued his recommendation that the Spitfire and Hurricane should be armed with eight machine guns instead of four.

BELOW The Colt-Browning 0.303in machine gun, fitted with cooling fins. A one-second burst of fire from the Spitfire's eight guns delivered 10lb (4.5kg) of metal to the target.

OPPOSITE TOP The Hawker Hurricane's wing structure was much deeper than the Spitfire's, and was more readily able to accommodate eight machine guns or four cannon, as seen here.

At this time, powerful voices in the Air Ministry were still advocating for the use of no more than four machine guns in the new generation of monoplane fighters; Sorley did not agree.

"The solution . . . lay in making the best assessment possible of the decisive lethality which could be expected in the very short firing time available. By using eight Browning guns it should be possible to build up a density of 256 rounds in that time."

He was also conscious of the fact that mounting the guns in the fuselage would mean an increase in the latter's cross-sectional area, producing more drag and thereby reducing speed.

"The monoplane wing offered a space in which they might well be mounted [Sorley concluded]. This would entail mounting a battery of four guns in each wing, which in turn would demand a rigid mounting and the provision of many new features.

"The controversy was something of a nightmare during 1933–34 [Sorley later admitted]. It was a choice on which the whole concept of the fighter would depend, but a trial staged on the ground with eight .303s was sufficiently convincing and satisfying to enable them to carry the day."

As it was, Sorley pointed out that . . .

" . . . squadron or flight formation attacks were necessary in order to produce a concentration of fire by fighters armed with only two or even four guns each. They required a high degree of skill and extensive training of pilots. This factor, in conjunction with the greatly increased speed to be expected, and the very short time for decisive action, pointed to new tactical methods, but too little thought was put into this aspect . . . "

However, there were further problems to be considered, as Sorley explained:

"The Supermarine and Hawker aircraft differed essentially in one important feature. The Supermarine was designed for a thin wing whereas the Hawker design used a thick one. As a result, the installation of the guns in the Hawker aircraft was a somewhat easier problem, enabling four guns to be grouped together in each wing. In the

Supermarine the depth of the wing entailed the guns being installed separately; in fact the outer guns of the four on each side were well out towards the tip of the wing."

In the end, it was the Air Ministry who set the seal on the matter, in the opening paragraph of Specification F.5/34, issued in connection with the proposed monoplane fighters:

"The speed excess of a modern fighter over that of a contemporary bomber has so reduced the chance of repeated attacks by the same fighters essential to obtain decisive results in the short space of time offered for one attack only. This specification is issued, therefore, to govern the production of a day fighter in which speed in overtaking an enemy at 15,000ft [4,572m], combined with rapid climb to this height, is of primary importance. The best speed possible must be aimed for at all heights between 5,000ft [1,524m] and 15,000ft [4,572m]. In conjunction with this performance the maximum hitting power must be aimed at, and eight machine guns are considered advisable."

Eight guns it would be. And the Spitfire and Hurricane would be properly equipped to fight a desperate air war.

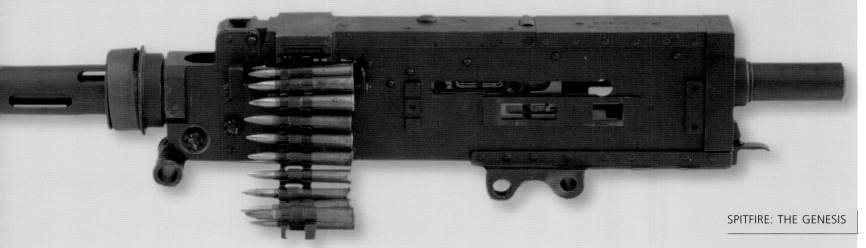

Testing the Spitfire

The hand-built airframe of the Supermarine Type 300, which had been allocated the serial number K5054, was completed in January 1936, having undergone a number of modifications as it developed. The engine had been installed the previous November, so all was now set for the first flight. This took place on the morning of March 5, 1936 from Eastleigh Airport. At the controls was "Mutt" Summers, who elected to take off 35 degrees across wind.

Experience with the racing seaplanes had revealed a strong tendency to swing to port because of the high torque. (In fact, although there was a tendency to swing, it was easily checked by the application of opposite rudder.) The aircraft seemed to drift into the air, and the maiden flight, which was made with the undercarriage locked down, was effortless—so much so that, when Summers landed, he told the engineers and designers not to touch anything.

The only item that was subsequently altered, in fact, was the propeller. For its maiden flight K5054 had been fitted with a fine-pitch propeller to generate more rpm and therefore more power on takeoff; this was replaced by a normal-pitch one for the second and later flights, as Supermarine test pilots George Pickering and Jeffrey Quill now joined Summers in the test program. Quill's name was to become synonymous with that of the Spitfire, since he assumed responsibility for most of the test flight work.

ABOVE A Supermarine "family affair". Left to right: J. "Mutt" Summers, Major H.J "Agony" Payn, R.J. Mitchell, S. Scott-Hall, Jeffrey Quill.

LEFT Jeffrey Quill at the controls of K5054, the Supermarine Spitfire prototype. Quill carried out most of the test flying in this aircraft.

BELOW The knee pad used by Supermarine test pilot Jeffrey Quill during his many test flights in the Spitfire prototype.

After some minor modifications, including the addition of undercarriage fairings and the sealing of some oil leaks, George Pickering flew K5054 to Martlesham Heath in Suffolk on March 26 for evaluation by the Aeroplane and Armament Experimental Establishment. During high-speed trials, the aircraft reached a speed of 430mph (692km/h) Indicated Air Speed (IAS) in a dive, which gave some indication of its potential. On June 10 the Air Ministry wrote to Supermarine, approving the name Spitfire, and on June 18 the aircraft returned to Eastleigh to be demonstrated before an invited audience of 300 people from the aircraft industry. The performance was impressive, although it had to be cut short when an oil connection broke.

After spinning trials at Farnborough and further flight testing at Eastleigh, the aircraft went back to Martlesham for full handling trials on February 23, 1937. Performance figures logged during these trials included a True Air Speed (TAS) ranging from 330mph (531km/h) at 10,000ft (3,050m) to 349mph (562km/h) at 16,800ft (5,124m), the TAS falling to 324mph (521km/h) at 30,000ft (9,150m). Time to 20,000ft (6,100m) was 8 minutes 12 seconds at 1,770ft (540m) per minute, while rate of climb at sea level was 2,400ft (732m) per minute. All these values far exceeded those demanded by the Air Ministry specification.

During this period, a number of modifications were incorporated. The original Rolls-Royce Merlin C engine was replaced by a Merlin F, developing 1045hp; a reflector sight was installed and a tailwheel fitted, replacing the simple skid that had been used so far. The aileron controls were also modified, but on March 22, 1937, while the effectiveness of these was being tested, oil pressure was lost, the engine threatened to seize, and the pilot, flight lieutenant J.F. McKenna, made a belly landing on a heath. However, the aircraft sustained only minor damage and was soon flying again.

On July 11, 1937, Reginald Mitchell, who had been diagnosed with rectal cancer four years earlier—a fact kept secret from all except his family and a few of his closest friends—died at the age of 42, leaving his wife, Florence and son, Gordon. Although he had labored under a great deal of pain, the popular notion that he had virtually worked himself to death in order to get the Spitfire design finished is a myth; he was still working at the time of his death, but on a bomber project. Mitchell's place as Vickers-Supermarine's chief designer was taken by Joseph Smith, who had

been his assistant; Smith was to be responsible for all subsequent Spitfire design developments.

By September 1937, K5054 had been fitted with its eight-gun armament and had been brought up to Spitfire Mk I production standard. On October 23, it was taken on RAF charge at Martlesham Heath. In March the following year it suffered damage in two accidents, the first when it nosed over in soft ground after the pilot overshot the runway during a night flying test, and the second when it bounced after a heavy touchdown, forcing the port undercarriage leg up into the port wing. Repaired, it returned to Martlesham on May 12, 1938, for full armament trials.

In November 1938, K5054 went to Farnborough, where it continued to work hard on various flight test programs until September 4, when it was written off in a fatal landing accident.

But by this time, the first Spitfire squadrons were firmly established in Fighter Command's Order of Battle—and Britain had been at war with Germany for 24 hours.

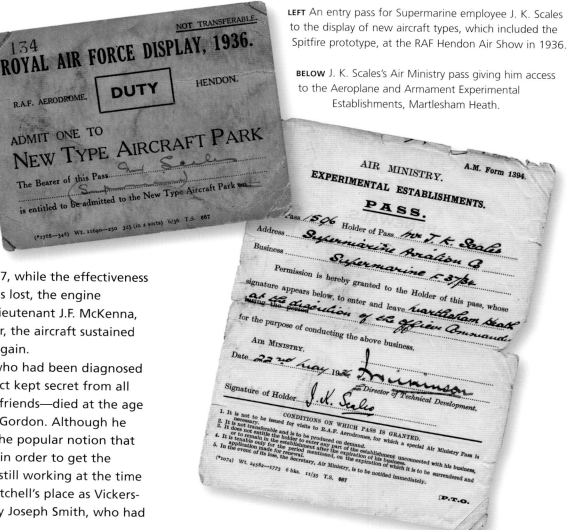

LEFT An entry pass for Supermarine employee J. K. Scales to the display of new aircraft types, which included the Spitfire prototype, at the RAF Hendon Air Show in 1936.

BELOW J. K. Scales's Air Ministry pass giving him access to the Aeroplane and Armament Experimental Establishments, Martlesham Heath.

Spitfire K5054

The Spitfire prototype K5054 had a number of features that were not repeated in production aircraft. For example, the exhaust was flush and set at 90 degrees to the direction of flight, the windscreen was a simple wrap-around type with no armor plating or optical flatness, and the overlapping design of the wing skin was derived directly from the type used on flying boats. The horn of the rudder shown right, is in its modified form.

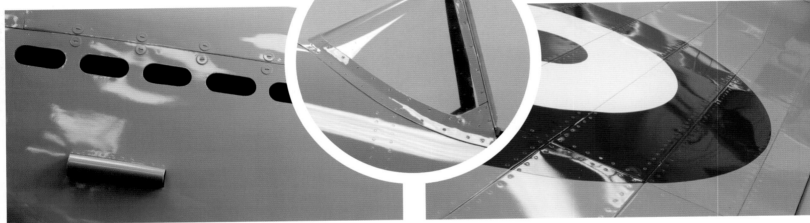

K5054 was damaged beyond repair in September 1939; this is a facsimile, signed by Jeffrey Quill in 1992, who as President of the Spitfire Society instigated the build. It is seen here on display at Tangmere Military Aviation Museum. Although this is a good replica, the cockpit lacks some instruments, see inset picture of the original, and some parts, above, may not be as the original. The wheel flap, right—fitted only to K5054—was designed to fold in the up position to close the wing for aerodynamics.

Spitfire Mk I and II

Early production Spitfire Mk I aircraft were fitted with a ring-and-bead gunsight, replicated here on this aircraft restored to early Mk I pre-war standard. The ring was to aid deflection shooting; the bead can be seen in red. The exhaust was now directed backwards on production machines, delivering a slight increase in speed. The cockpit gained an optically flat windscreen and a curved canopy, replacing the original flat one.

The perspex flat-sided cockpit canopy has been "ballooned" to give more headroom for the pilot, and includes a "clear-view" side panel, designed to allow the pilot to see in case of ice. There is no armor plating on the screen or behind the pilot, which meant he was vulnerable to head on and rear attack; this was addressed in the Mk II (opposite). Note that the vertical speed indicator in the cockpit—just under the gunsight—has green figures on it; this indicates this version is post 1944.

Mk IIs incorporated 73lb (33kg) of armor plating in production; the triangular 0.25 inch (63mm) plate can be seen in the center photo behind the pilot's head cushion, and the 1.5 inch (3.8cm) thick external armored glass windscreen is visible left and top left. The elevator horn—top right—is in its earlier form; it was later reduced in size. However, the wheels in the picture above are 10.25 inch (26cm) Dunlop wheels; the originals would have been 10 inch (25.5cm) with five apertures.

Spitfires into service

On June 3, 1936, Supermarine received an initial production order for 310 Spitfires under the RAF's Expansion Scheme F, which called for a frontline force of 1,736 aircraft to be in place by 1939, the total to include 30 home-based fighter squadrons. The first two production aircraft, K9787 and K9788, were retained for trials, but on August 4, 1938, the third aircraft, K9789, went to RAF Duxford, near Cambridge, where No. 19 Squadron had been selected to pioneer the fighter's entry into service.

Over the following six weeks, K9789 was put through 300 hours of intensive flying, after which it went back to the Supermarine works to be stripped down and subjected to a detailed examination. The first Spitfire to be taken on RAF charge was actually K9792, which was allocated to the Central Flying Establishment at RAF Cranwell for evaluation by instructors.

No. 19 Squadron received its first Spitfire before the end of August, and after that deliveries continued steadily, albeit slowly, at the rate of about one a week. Previously the squadron had been equipped with Gloster Gauntlet biplanes, and pilots were euphoric about the new fighter, although there were some criticisms, the principal one focusing on the manual undercarriage pump lever. Raising and lowering the undercarriage involved pumping this rapidly up and down, often resulting in the pilot's knuckles coming into painful contact with the side of the cockpit, and the whole aircraft wobbling dangerously during the process. Thankfully, a powered retraction system was introduced in the Mk II Spitfire.

However, pilots were delighted with most aspects of the Spitfire, including the Barr and Stroud GD5 reflector sight, which replaced the old ring-and-bead sight installed in the

ABOVE The eyes of Fighter Command: a "Chain Home" radar mast on the English coast. Radar was originally known as RDF (Radio Direction Finding).

LEFT A Royal Air Force officer's cap band and badge, showing the eagle and King's crown, with the pilot's brevet: the coveted 'wings', worn on the left breast of the tunic.

ABOVE King George V is shown the cockpit of a Spitfire at Duxford in 1938. The King took a keen interest in Fighter Command's modern equipment.

earlier biplane fighters. The reflector sight consisted of a system of lenses that projected the image of a gun sight onto a small glass just behind the windshield inside the cockpit; the image intensity was adjustable for varying combat conditions. At the center of the display, projected by a lamp, was a faint red circle with a dot in the middle. Running across the circle were two horizontal lines that could be adjusted inward or outward by turning a milled ring, graduated to represent the wingspans of various types of aircraft. When the target's wings filled the gap between the two lines, it was within range. The sight's brightness could be adjusted by a dimmer switch. The sight was a key element in the Spitfire's offensive capability, but despite its

effectiveness, shots would still go astray when the fighter was allowed to slip or skid during air combat.

Inevitably there were accidents. No. 19 Squadron suffered its first training accident on September 30, when Pilot Officer G. L. Sinclair, making his first flight in the new type, flared out a little too high and stalled; the aircraft hit the ground hard, bounced, and turned over. Luckily, the pilot escaped with nothing more than a severe shaking.

In October 1938 the other Duxford-based fighter unit, No. 66 Squadron, also began to re-arm with Spitfires. At this time, Operational Training Units (OTUs) were still two years away—they would begin to form in March 1940—so pilots learned to fly and fight their new aircraft on the squadron. The squadrons were allocated a Fairey Battle light bomber to give pilots experience with a Merlin-engined monoplane. In the spring and summer of 1939, with the virtual certainty that war with Germany was a matter of months, perhaps even weeks, away, the Spitfire-equipped squadrons trained intensively, concentrating on air-to-air gunnery, dog-fighting, formation flying, and formation attacks.

Spitfires participated in Anglo-French air exercises in 1939. On August 17, following an "attack" on Paris by Vickers Wellingtons of RAF Bomber Command, a small force of French Bloch 200 bombers made a simulated raid on Birmingham under cover of darkness, and Spitfires of No. 19 Squadron were sent up to intercept them. The RAF pilots made a couple of sightings, but the exercise proved only one thing: that single-engine day fighters such as the Spitfire and Hurricane were totally unsuited to night operations.

Air exercises apart, the real value of the 1938–39 "breathing space" to RAF Fighter Command was that it enabled the Spitfire and Hurricane squadrons to become fully integrated with the Air Defence Control and Reporting System, which depended on radar, or radio direction finding (RDF), as it was then known. By September 1939 a planned chain of 20 radar stations at home—the Chain Home (CH) stations—had been completed, stretching from Southampton in the south to Newcastle-upon-Tyne in the north.

At the outbreak of war on September 3, 1939, nine RAF squadrons were fully equipped with Spitfires and a tenth, No. 609 Squadron, had just begun to equip. During September, No. 603 Squadron at Turnhouse, near Edinburgh, also began to receive Spitfires, and it was the two Scottish-based Auxiliary Air Force squadrons, Nos. 602 and 603, that were the first Spitfire units to make contact with the Luftwaffe.

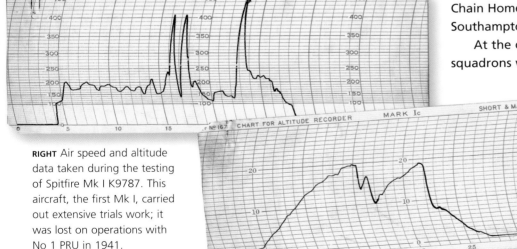

RIGHT Air speed and altitude data taken during the testing of Spitfire Mk I K9787. This aircraft, the first Mk I, carried out extensive trials work; it was lost on operations with No 1 PRU in 1941.

Pilots' experiences

Although pilots took a little while to get used to the Spitfire's exhilarating performance, some had difficulty in mastering the fighter's technical aspects, in particular the retractable undercarriage.

"It soon became surprisingly obvious [wrote Australian Spitfire pilot John Vader] that pilots used to fixed undercarriage aircraft needed the reminder horn which blew when the throttle was cut back while the undercarriage was still in the 'up' position. The first two squadrons equipped with Spitfires were used to the fixed-undercarriage Gloster Gauntlet, and several pilots suffered the indignity of their new aircraft skidding across the field in an unintentional belly landing, airscrews splintering as they wondered why the horn kept blowing."

In fact, the warning horn was affected by vibration and often sounded at much higher speeds than it was designed to do. One No. 19 Squadron pilot, who inadvertently belly-landed Spitfire K9798 on April 18, 1939, told the subsequent Court of Inquiry that the horn sounded so frequently that he had forgotten what it was for.

The cockpit was also completely different from that of the relatively simple biplane fighters that the Spitfire replaced.

"At first sight the cockpit seemed to be laid out in a very confused order [says John Vader] but after a few hours' familiarisation, pilots found the instruments easy to read and conveniently grouped, and the levers, switches and buttons placed in handy positions, a vital point because in a 'scramble'—quick start and takeoff—it was necessary to manipulate the various levers, switches and buttons without looking."

Takeoff could be a little tricky, as Sergeant (later Flight Lieutenant) Jim Rosser, who was later to become a Spitfire production test pilot at Castle Bromwich, explains:

"The Spitfire Mk I had a pump-up undercarriage, so to begin with the initial climb from takeoff was very undulating, as the left hand holding the stick kept pace with the right hand holding the pump. Each aircraft had a facility for transmitting an IFF (Identification Friend/Foe) signal; one aircraft only in a squadron or flight operated this for 15 seconds in each minute, and for that 15-second period he could not be warned if the formation came under attack, as he could not receive any R/T [radio telephony] messages while transmitting.

"As a matter of interest, the first takeoff in a Spitfire was disappointing in a way, because there was no thump in the back on opening the throttle, as

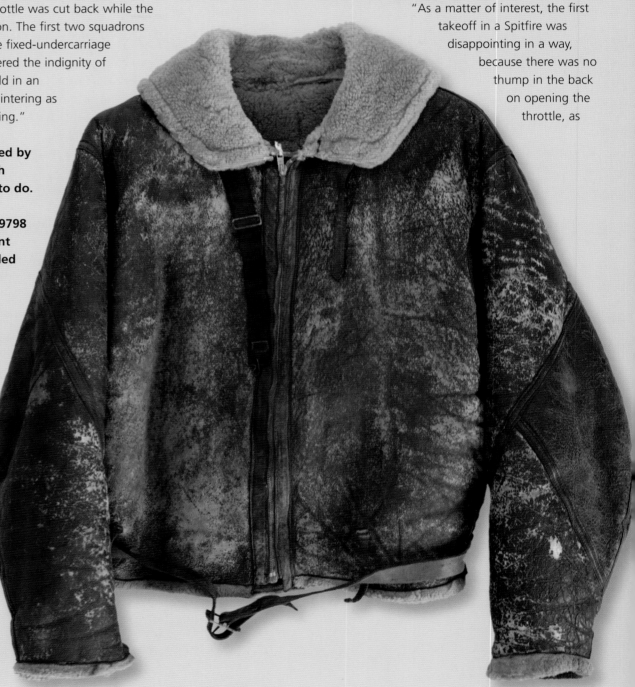

OPPOSITE A typical fleece-lined flying jacket as worn by a Spitfire pilot. Pilots—especially photo-reconnaissance pilots—went to great lengths to keep warm, but seldom succeeded.

RIGHT The cockpit of a Spitfire presented a bewildering array of instruments to pilots used to flying the biplane fighters that previously equipped the squadrons.

BELOW The illuminated undercarriage warning indicator had a pull-down blind, which was designed to prevent the pilots from being dazzled by the light during night flying.

with the Miles Master on which I had trained. The latter had a Rolls-Royce Kestrel engine in a very light wooden frame. The Spitfire's performance after takeoff, of course, was very different from the Master's.

"The Spitfire's long nose restricted the pilot's view ahead, and he had to weave the aircraft from side to side while taxiing in order to clear the blind spot. Night flying in a Spitfire was also very difficult because the blue flames and sparks emitted from the engine through the exhausts, on either side of the nose, were likely to dazzle the pilot, a hazard which did not occur during the daytime except in conditions of very poor visibility. Although Spitfires rarely flew at night, being designed for the day-fighter role, they often flew through cloud, where the leader relied on instruments and the rest of the flight flew in close visual contact. If this contact were broken, formating pilots not only had to fly carefully on instruments, but also found it necessary to keep a lookout to avoid a potential collision.

"To help preserve the pilot's night vision, the instruments were illuminated with lamps which gave off a red glow, a colour which does not lessen the ability to see in the dark. The Spitfire's port and starboard navigation lights were recessed in the wings just forward of the tips, the tail navigation light below the trimming tab on the rudder and the upward identification lamp on the fuselage behind the radio mast.

"At elementary training schools all pilots learned to land without lights, judging with practice the relative positions of the marker beacons along the flarepath during approach and touchdown. This exercise was particularly useful to Spitfire pilots landing their aircraft with the long nose blanking out forward vision in the three-point landing attitude. It was much safer to land faster with the tail up and the runway ahead clearly visible, until the aircraft slowed down and the nose rose as the tail dropped.

"As well as bright exhaust dazzle, which was later reduced by baffles on the exhausts, the reflector sight could also be slightly dazzling if turned up too bright at night or in dusk conditions."

Mastery of the Spitfire came with experience. How this experience would translate into the fighter tactics that would spell the difference between life and death in air combat was quite a different matter.

Britain's invisible shield: The radar defenses

In order to meet the expected German air offensive, RAF Fighter Command had set up a tightly knit defensive warning network where control and standardization were the keywords. This system, the first of its kind in the world, was attributable in no small measure to the energetic leadership of one man: Air Chief Marshal Sir Hugh Dowding, Commander-in-Chief of Fighter Command. There was no room for compromise in Dowding's world; it was not for nothing that his subordinates nicknamed him "Stuffy."

Dowding's approach to the requirements of Fighter Command was essentially a scientific one. He believed that Britain's air defenses should have the benefit of the latest technological developments, and this was reflected in Fighter Command's network of operations rooms, linked with one another by an elaborate arrangement of telephone and teleprinter lines to provide an integrated system of control. This enabled fighter aircraft to be passed rapidly from sector to sector and from group to group, wherever they were most needed.

Nowhere was technology more apparent in Britain's air defenses than in the use of radar—or Radio Direction-Finding (RDF), as it was originally known. This use of

radar was developed by a team of scientists led by Dr. Robert Watson-Watt in earlier experiments in thunderstorm detection by the use of radio waves. The integral part that it played in the British air defense system was largely the fruit of Dowding's initiative; he had worked with Watson-Watt during the 1930s, and had not been slow to recognize the potential of the new invention.

By September 1939, the planned chain of 20 radar stations at home—the Chain Home (CH) stations—had been completed. Each had twin masts, the taller—350ft (107m)—for transmitting, and the

ABOVE Everything in the RAF had a manual associated with it. Going "by the book" was supposed to leave little room for error, and such documents were expertly compiled.

FAR LEFT A pair of Spitfires coming in to land. The fighter's narrow-track undercarriage is apparent in this photograph.

LEFT Dr Robert Watson-Watt, whose team of scientists developed radar from earlier experiments in thunderstorm detection by the use of radio waves.

shorter—240ft (73m)—for receiving. The CH stations, known for security reasons as Air Ministry Experimental Stations (AMES) could detect aircraft up to 100 miles (160km) away and could give the bearing and an approximate indication of height and number of an approaching formation. The main stations were supplemented by another series, Chain Home Low (CHL), which were designed to detect aircraft flying below 3,000ft (915m).

These electronic eyes of Britain's defenses were backed up by the human ones of the Observer Corps. While the radar stations were responsible for tracking enemy aircraft before they reached the British coast, the volunteers of the Observer Corps (later called the Royal Observer Corps) were responsible for tracking and reporting on them once they had crossed it. By mid-1940 there were 31 Observer Corps groups in Britain, each group incorporating between 30 and 50 posts that were manned around the clock.

Information from these reporting agencies, and later from signals intelligence gathered by the RAF's "Y" listening service, was passed by landline to HQ Fighter Command at Bentley Priory. From there, it was rapidly filtered and processed for retransmission to the sector airfield operations rooms at key locations, such as Biggin Hill and Hornchurch, which in turn passed it on to the fighter squadrons at readiness on their forward airfields, that is those that were closest to the Channel coast.

Speaking after the war, General Adolf Galland, the renowned German fighter leader, paid this tribute to the system:

"From the first the British had an extraordinary advantage, never to be balanced out at any time in the whole war, which was their radar and fighter control network and organization. It was for us a very bitter surprise. We had nothing like it. We could do no other than knock frontally against the outstandingly well organized and resolute direct defense of the British Isles."

Generally, the so-called "Dowding System" worked very well, especially after constant practice under operational conditions had smoothed away the rough edges, but inevitably there were

ABOVE A Chain Home Low (CHL) radar array. Designed to detect enemy aircraft flying below 3000ft (915m), the CHL stations supplemented the main Chain Home (CH) network.

LEFT German fighter leader Adolf Galland confessed that the effectiveness of Britain's radar contributed immeasurably to the RAF's victory in the Battle of Britain.

teething problems. During the first week of the war there were several false alarms generated by "intruders" that turned out to be civil aircraft coming in from the continent. A more tragic mistake, though, occurred just after dawn on September 6, 1939, a searchlight battery on Mersea Island in the Thames Estuary alerted No. 11 Group HQ to the presence of some incoming aircraft that were thought to be hostile. Various fighter squadrons were scrambled and became tangled with one another over the Thames Estuary; in the confusion two Hurricanes from the No. 151 Squadron were shot down by Spitfires of the No. 74 Squadron, and one of the pilots was killed. This unfortunate incident, which went down in history as the Battle of Barking Creek, was later said to have been sparked by a malfunction at the radar station at Canewdon on the Thames Estuary; a much more likely cause was an excess of zeal mingled with the inevitable high tension.

2 # The dangerous year

First contact

Although the sirens of Britain's air-raid defenses sounded on numerous occasions during the early weeks of World War II, the expected attacks on Britain's cities didn't materialize right away. In fact, it would have been impossible for the Luftwaffe to mount such attacks, as its Germany-based bombers did not have the range to do so. The onslaught would not begin until months later, when the capture of France's airfields brought British targets well within the combat radius of the German air fleets.

It was not until October 16, 1939, that German bombers ventured into British airspace for the first time. They were nine Junkers Ju 88s of I Gruppe, Kampfgeschwader 30 (I/KG 30), operating at the limit of their range from Westerland on the North German island of Sylt. Their targets were the warships of the British fleet, at anchor in the Firth of Forth, a few miles from Edinburgh. The German formation was led by Hauptmann Helmut Pohle, the group commander.

At 14:22, Blue Section of No. 603 Squadron, led by Flight Lieutenant George Pinkerton, was ordered into the air from Drem, south of the Forth estuary, and ten minutes later Yellow Section was ordered to patrol Turnhouse at 10,000ft (3,050m) in response to an unconfirmed report that a formation of unidentified aircraft was heading in toward the Forth Bridge. Climbing hard, Pinkerton and his pilots sighted Pohle's nine Ju 88s dive-bombing warships off Rosyth and gave chase, pursuing the lead bomber as it pulled out of its dive and raced away over May Island. The bomber, Pohle's aircraft, was attacked by each of the three Spitfires in turn. Their gunfire killed Pohle's flight engineer and mortally wounded the

navigator. First one engine failed as bullets tore into it, and then the other. Pohle spotted a trawler and turned toward it, using all his skill to keep the Junkers airborne, but the bomber plowed into the sea and he lost consciousness. A few minutes later the trawler crew pulled him from the sinking aircraft, severely concussed. He woke up five days later in Port Edwards hospital.

Meanwhile, Red Section of No. 603 Squadron, led by Squadron Leader E. H. Stevens, had pursued a twin-engine bomber north of Dalkeith. It turned out to be another Junkers 88. Other Spitfires from No. 603 Squadron joined in the chase, and between them they sent the Junkers down into the sea off Port Seton. Three crew members—shocked but unhurt—were picked up by the trawler Dayspring; the fourth was missing. The Ju 88 was later salvaged.

Arguably, if Hurricanes instead of Spitfires had been in pursuit of the Ju 88s, the German bombers might have got away, as the Hawker fighter was only marginally faster; the Spitfire's higher speed was undoubtedly an important factor in these encounters.

The Spitfires were in action again the next day, October 17. This time, the attacking aircraft belonged to No. 41 Squadron, based at Catterick in North Yorkshire, and the victim was a

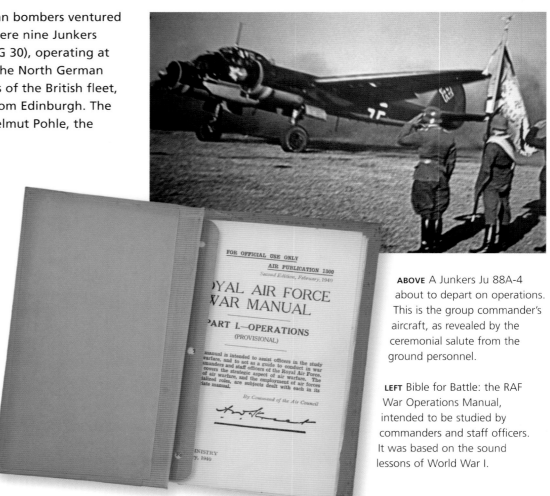

ABOVE A Junkers Ju 88A-4 about to depart on operations. This is the group commander's aircraft, as revealed by the ceremonial salute from the ground personnel.

LEFT Bible for Battle: the RAF War Operations Manual, intended to be studied by commanders and staff officers. It was based on the sound lessons of World War I.

tail surfaces. McKellar drew away to make another firing pass but was beaten to it by three Spitfires of No. 603 Squadron, whose fire hit the bomber's starboard wing and cockpit area. The Heinkel crash-landed in a field at Kidlaw, near Haddington, killing both gunners and wounding the pilot; only the navigator was unhurt.

This Heinkel, which belonged to Kampfgeschwader 26, was the first enemy aircraft to fall on the British mainland in World War II, and as a result it attracted a great deal of publicity. More important, it was dismantled and taken to Farnborough, where a lengthy technical report was made. Unfortunately, the report was not issued until August 1940, by which time the RAF's fighter pilots had learned all about the Heinkel's defensive capabilities in the hard school of combat.

Although the two Auxiliary Air Force Spitfire squadrons in Scotland had several more skirmishes with the enemy in the winter months of 1939–40, results were mostly inconclusive, although on December 7, two Heinkels of KG26 were destroyed off the Tay estuary by the Spitfires of Nos. 603 and 72 Squadrons, the latter temporarily based at Drem.

reconnaissance Heinkel He 111 of I(F)122, which they had caught on its way home from photographing the Scottish port of Dundee. In the skirmish they shot it down into the sea 20 miles (32km) off Whitby. Two of the crew survived and were taken prisoner. On October 22, the same German unit lost a second Heinkel, shot down off Berwick by the Spitfires from No. 603 Squadron.

On October 29, Red Section of No. 602 Squadron was scrambled to intercept a Heinkel He 111 over the Firth of Forth. The bomber was sighted by Flying Officer Archie McKellar, who drew ahead of his section and dived to the attack, opening fire at 200 yards (183m) and giving the Heinkel two bursts. The first struck the bomber's wing root and killed its dorsal gunner; the second riddled its

Then, early in 1940, a marked increase of enemy air activity brought further action for the RAF fighter squadrons based in the north; it was the prelude to the German invasion of Norway.

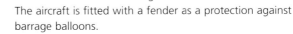

TOP Spitfires of No 72 Squadron over the coast of Northumberland. This was a posed photograph, taken for the benefit of US war correspondents.

ABOVE This piece of metal, recovered from a Spitfire crash site, is the top for "Frame 11," a structural part of the fuselage monocoque.

LEFT A Heinkel He 111 brought down on British soil. The aircraft is fitted with a fender as a protection against barrage balloons.

Luftwaffe vs. home fleet

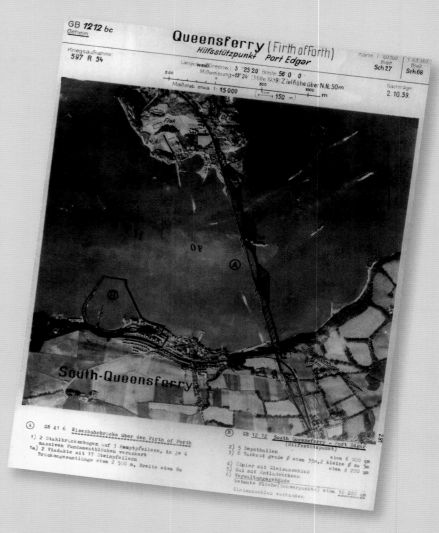

The raid of October 16, 1939, unequivocally demonstrated to Germany that its bombers could not hope to operate in British skies with impunity, especially in daylight. Later, Helmut Pohle described his own experience:

"It was October 16, 1939. On that day HMS *Hood* was on her way to Rosyth in the early hours of the morning and being shadowed by German maritime reconnaissance. When I arrived over the Firth of Forth in my Ju 88, having taken off from Westerland, HMS *Hood* was already in dock. A perfect target for dive-bombers! But the order was quite definite: 'Do not attack when she is in dock.' The powers in Germany at that time were still hoping that there could be an agreement with England and civilian casualties should in no circumstances aggravate propaganda. However, in the Forth lay HMS *Southampton* and HMS *Edinburgh* at anchor, and these we dive-bombed . . . I was flying one of the first Ju 88s to go into attack but during the dive the top part of the canopy came off. Although I was now flying with my crew in a half open plane, I nevertheless remained in the area to observe the results of the other aircraft. However, I was surprised by a Spitfire which I could not get away from. Also, we could not defend ourselves with the rear top gun as this had gone with the canopy. After other attacks, during which two of my crew were killed, one of the engines failed. Flying on with one engine I managed another 20km when, some distance off the Scottish coast, and flying in an easterly direction, I saw a trawler through the slowly lifting mist. There was no sign of any crew, but I thought it might be Norwegian—then a neutral country. I was just able to clear the trawler before ditching the Junkers, although the sea was running at strength four. The crew of the trawler did not rescue me; instead I was picked up by a Navy destroyer, as well as my badly injured fourth crew member. However, I collapsed on the deck with concussion and facial injuries. My crewman died from his injuries the next day.

"A few days later I regained consciousness. I [saw a] white bed and a nurse. I thought that I was in Norway, and for some reason I asked if I could make a telephone call to Italy. However, I was in the Royal Navy Hospital at Port Edward, near Edinburgh. At the head of my bed stood an RAF Intelligence Officer. About ten days later I was transferred to a military hospital in Edinburgh Castle. After that, and shortly before Christmas, I was taken to the Tower of London and finally off to No. 211 PoW Camp at Grizedale Hall."

OPPOSITE TOP A 1939 Luftwaffe reconnaissance photograph of Queensferry in the Firth of Forth. Attacks on the British Home Fleet were given high priority.

OPPOSITE BOTTOM LEFT The battlecruiser HMS *Hood* was one of the Luftwaffe's principal targets in the early months of the war. She was sunk by the battleship *Bismarck* in May 1941.

OPPOSITE BOTTOM RIGHT The cruiser HMS *Southampton* survived German bombing attacks in 1939, but was sunk by dive-bombers in the Mediterranean in 1941.

RIGHT Aircraft identification booklets like this one became best-sellers. This one, produced by *The Aeroplane* magazine, included a Junkers Ju 88.

For Flight Lieutenant Hodge, who led Yellow Section of No. 602 Squadron to intercept the raid of October 28, events very nearly took a tragic turn when he mistook an Avro Anson for an enemy bomber and attacked it.

"At 10.45 E/A [enemy aircraft] passed over Drem and OC 602 ordered Yellow Section to take off in pursuit. By the time Yellow Section had left ground E/A had been lost sight of. At 10.55 ordered by R/T [radio telephony] from Turnhouse to investigate one unidentified A/C [aircraft] height unknown 3 miles [4.8km] east of May Island. On arrival reported having seen Spitfires and almost immediately sighted Anson which I mistook for E/A. I then put section into line astern and attacked. Having given a short burst I realised my mistake and put section back into vic formation. I then continued to patrol until ordered to pancake."

The Anson and its crew survived, despite its pilot being wounded in the jaw by Hodge's gunfire.

On the same sortie, it was anti-aircraft fire that drew Archie McKellar of 602 Squadron to the real target, as his combat report reveals.

"Patrolling Turnhouse at 16,000ft [4,977m] I noticed AA [anti-aircraft] fire north of my position. Saw one A/C heading SE at 14,000ft [4,267m] approx. Being doubtful of identity asked Turnhouse for information. Put section into line astern full boost and followed. Identified as hostile. Carried out No. 2 attack. My No. 2 followed with No. 1 attack. E/A dodged into cloud and I followed him. He appeared again when I and No. 2 attacked. Noticed port engine disabled with smoke issuing. Machine started to circle. Reported Turnhouse E/A appeared to be going down. Three other Spitfires then came in and attacked. Saw machine land . . ."

McKellar went on to become a leading RAF ace, being officially credited with the destruction of 20 enemy aircraft during the year that followed. He achieved most of his victories while flying Hurricanes. He was killed while flying with No. 605 Squadron on November 1, 1940.

By day and night

On April 3, 1940, the RAF lost its first Spitfire to enemy action. Its pilot was Flight Lieutenant Norman Ryder of No. 41 Squadron, who took off from RAF Catterick in response to an alert, found a Heinkel He 111 off England's northeast coast between Redcar and Whitby and shot it down. However, his Spitfire was hit in the engine by return fire and he was forced to ditch in very rough conditions about half a mile (0.8km) from a trawler. The impact knocked him unconscious, and he was some distance below the surface in the sinking aircraft when he came to. After considerable difficulty, Ryder freed himself from his parachute harness and, exhausted by his efforts, was picked up by the trawler crew.

On May 10, 1940, with the campaign in Norway still in progress, the Germans attacked France and the Low Countries (an area that now includes the Netherlands, Belgium, Luxembourg, and parts of west Germany and north France), and on that day the Spitfire squadrons based in southern England, which had so far seen very little action, were authorized to carry out offensive patrols across the Channel. The Duxford Wing was particularly active, being well placed to cover the Dutch coast from the East Anglian airfields of Coltishall and Horsham St. Faith. It was here to which No. 66 Squadron deployed in May from its main base at Duxford, while its sister squadron, No. 19, deployed south to Hornchurch in Essex. By the end of the first week of operations, mainly in The Hague area, No. 66 Squadron had claimed the

ABOVE The operations room at Fighter Command HQ, Bentley Priory, with symbols gathering on the plotting table as a raid begins to develop.

LEFT A Luftwaffe reconnaissance photograph of RAF Duxford, the first Spitfire base. Luftwaffe intelligence was often inaccurate.

destruction of four enemy aircraft, with three more damaged. The defeat of France in June 1940 was followed by a growing number of incursions into British air space by enemy aircraft at night. Many of these raids were intercepted by both day fighters and Blenheim night fighters. At 00:50 on June 19, for example, a Heinkel He 111H-4 of 2/KG54 was shot down into the sea off the Norfolk coast by Flight Lieutenant R. M. B. Duke-Woolley in a Blenheim of No. 23 Squadron, and the German crew was captured; on the same night two Heinkels of 4/KG4 were also destroyed, both at 01:15. The first was shot down off Felixstowe by Flight Lieutenant A. G. Malan, a South African flight commander with No. 74 Squadron. Nicknamed "Sailor" because of his pre-war service in the Merchant Navy, he was already one of the RAF's foremost combat tacticians. His combat report tells the story.

"During an air raid in the locality of Southend various E/A were observed and held by searchlights for prolonged periods. On request from Squadron I was allowed to take off with one Spitfire. I climbed towards E/A which was making for coast and held in searchlight beams at 8,000ft [2,438m]. I positioned myself astern and opened fire at 200 yards [183m] and closed to 30 yards [27m] with one burst. Observed bullets entering E/A and had my windscreen covered in oil, broke off to the left and immediately below as E/A spiralled out of the beam. Climbed to 12,000ft [3,657m] towards another E/A held by searchlights on Northerly course. Opened fire at 250 yards [229m] taking care not to overshoot this time. Gave five two-second bursts and observed bullets entering all over E/A with slight deflection as he was turning to port. E/A emitted heavy smoke and I observed one parachute open very close. E/A went down in spiral dive. Searchlights and I following him right down until he crashed in flames near Chelmsford. As I approached target in each case I flashed succession of dots on downward recognition light before moving in to attack. I did not notice AA gunfire after I had done this. When following second E/A down I switched on navigation lights for short time to help establish identity."

The second Heinkel was shot down jointly by a Spitfire of No. 19 Squadron and a Blenheim of No. 23 Squadron at Fleam Dyke, Cambridgeshire. Unfortunately, the Spitfire pilot, Flying Officer Petra, was forced to bail out during the combat after his aircraft was hit, while the Blenheim pilot, Squadron Leader O'Brien, bailed out after losing control. Both his crew members were killed. The third victory of the night was achieved at 02:15 by Flying Officer G. E. Ball of No. 19 Squadron, who shot down a Heinkel 111H of 6/KG4, which fell into the sea off Margate. Three more Heinkels were destroyed in the early hours of June 26. The first, a Heinkel He 111P-2 of 3/KG4, was shot down into the sea off Hull by Pilot Officers R. A. Smith and R. Marples of No. 616 Squadron—whose Spitfires were based at Leconfield in Yorkshire—at 00:17, while two He 111H-3s of 3/KG26 were shot down by pilots of Nos. 602 and 603 Squadrons off the Scottish coast. Interceptions of this kind were aided by the clear conditions of the summer nights, with their attendant good visibility.

When the darkness of winter came, and the Luftwaffe began its night offensive, the RAF's need for a dedicated night fighter would become critical. It would eventually be met by the powerful twin-engine Bristol Beaufighter, equipped with airborne interception (AI) radar and a devastating armament of four cannons and six machine guns.

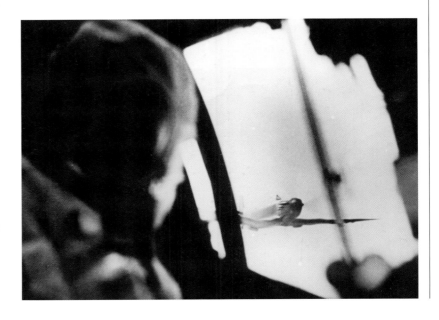

ABOVE The hand grip from a Spitfire's control column, with the early circular gun button and its Dunlop pneumatic attachments.

LEFT Adolph Gysbert "Sailor" Malan, pictured as a group captain later in the war.

RIGHT A Spitfire comes up on the port side of a Heinkel He 111 in what is almost certainly a posed shot by German propagandists.

Dunkirk: Battle over the beaches

By May 23, 1940, the battle for Norway had been lost, Holland had been overrun, Belgium was close to surrendering, and France's armies in the north were on the point of collapse. The British, sensing that the situation might lead to their own army being trapped, had ordered the evacuation of the British Expeditionary Force from the northern French port of Dunkirk.

Spitfires had played no part in the Battle of France, where the RAF's fighter contribution had been made by the few squadrons of Hawker Hurricanes deployed in support of the BEF (British Expeditionary Force), reinforced as necessary by aircraft drawn from the Hurricane squadrons based in England. Now, on May 23, the Spitfires of No. 11 Fighter Group, based in southeast England, made their first major contact with the Luftwaffe as they crossed the Channel to provide air cover for the British garrison still fighting in Calais.

This was the first occasion on which Spitfires encountered Messerschmitt 109 and 110 fighters, and the RAF pilots later made some quite outrageous claims about the battle, as doubtless did their opponents. No. 92 Squadron, for example, claimed to have destroyed 17 Bf 110s and 6 Bf 109s during a series of patrols between Calais and Dunkirk; the Germans admitted to losing two of each type, while No. 92 Squadron lost three Spitfires.

As the tempo of the evacuation increased, so did the fury of the air battles that raged overhead. Sixteen fighter squadrons of No. 11 Group were assigned to provide continuous air cover over the evacuation areas. The fighters were highly active on May 26, when Dunkirk was

ABOVE British troops being evacuated from Dunkirk. The soldiers, unaware that savage dogfights were taking place out of their sight, unjustly criticised the RAF for failing to provide air cover.

LEFT Major Werner Kreipe served with KG2 until June 1940, when he was appointed Operations Officer of Luftflotte 3. He survived the war.

OPPOSITE TOP The "scramble bell." Hanging outside the readiness room, it was rung furiously when the order to scramble was received. This one is the largest model with the largest logo.

OPPOSITE BOTTOM A Dornier Do 17 bomber, on a reconnaissance mission, brought down by RAF fighters during the battle of France. The Dorniers suffered serious losses in carrying out their task.

subjected to a series of heavy air attacks and the 16 fighter squadrons patrolled the Dunkirk-Calais area in relays. Between 04.30 and 19.30, 22 patrols were carried out at squadron strength, the RAF claiming 20 victories for the loss of five Hurricanes and one Spitfire, an aircraft of No. 65 Squadron. The fighters accounted for six Dornier Do 17s of III/KG3, and several more sustained battle damage; at one blow, half of III/KG3's effective strength had been wiped out. III/KG2 fared little better, as its commanding officer, Major Werner Kreipe, reported: "The enemy fighters pounced on our tightly knit formation with the fury of maniacs." According to German records, Fliegerkorps II lost 23 bombers on May 26, with 64 aircrew killed and 7 wounded.

Under the patrol system devised by Fighter Command, the squadrons assigned to cover the evacuation were frequently rotated; those that suffered a high rate of attrition were sent north for a rest and replaced by fresh units drawn from Nos. 12 and 13 Groups, the former assigned to the air defense of the Midlands and the latter to northern Britain. One of the replacement Spitfire squadrons was No. 610,

which went into action on May 27 from a forward base at Gravesend, in Kent. Its War Diary described its first encounter with the enemy:

"On their first sortie the pilots of No. 610 Squadron, flying in their Spitfires at 18,000ft [5,486m], sighted a twin-engined Heinkel He 111 bomber some 3,000ft [914m] below. Anxious, in this first combat, to make certain it was a Hun, Squadron Leader Franks dived down and calmly flew alongside taking a good look: the swastika on the tail, the black crosses on the wings were plain to see. Franks ordered Red Two and Red Three to attack. Flying Officer Smith poured all his ammunition into the Heinkel, only breaking off when the starboard engine was in flames. Sergeant Medway followed him up with a five-second burst, then the three Spitfires of Yellow Section joined in. Blue Section lined up to speed the Heinkel to its doom, but were called off by Franks. Plunging down out of control, the German pilot managed to fire Very flares, which brought 40 Messerschmitt 109s to avenge him. Undismayed by odds of more than three to one, the Spitfire pilots went straight in to attack and sent three Messerschmitts spinning down in flames, with another three probables."

For the Spitfire squadrons, the worst day was June 1, when Fighter Command lost 39 aircraft, 9 of them Spitfires. The Luftwaffe admitted the loss of 19 bombers and ten fighters; the RAF claimed 78, a figure that was later reduced to 43.

During the Dunkirk evacuation, between May 18 and June 3, 1940, the RAF lost 52 Spitfires and 47 Hurricanes. The Germans lost 132 aircraft in the Dunkirk sector. Notably, the same kind of ratio between the losses of RAF Fighter Command and the Luftwaffe was to apply later, during the Battle of Britain.

Spitfires in the Battle of Britain: The first phase

On June 30, 1940, Reichsmarschall Hermann Göring, the Luftwaffe Commander-in-Chief, issued a general directive, setting out the aims of the planned air assault on Britain. The Luftwaffe's primary target was to be the Royal Air Force, with particular focus on its fighter airfields and aircraft factories; as long as Fighter Command remained unbeaten, the Luftwaffe's first priority had to be to attack it by day and night and at every opportunity, in the air and on the ground, until it was destroyed. Early in July, as a first step toward meeting this objective, Göring authorized his bombers to begin attacks on British merchant convoys in the English Channel, the twofold object being to inflict serious losses on British shipping and to bring RAF Fighter Command to combat. So began the first phase of what was to become known as the Battle of Britain.

On July 7, following a night of sporadic air attacks on towns in southern England in which 62 people were killed, No. 11 Group scrambled its fighters to intercept Dornier 17 reconnaissance aircraft (three of which were shot down by Hurricanes) and fighter sweeps over the south coast by Bf 109s. In the morning, the Messerschmitts pounced on "B" Flight of No. 54 Squadron, damaging three Spitfires; the same evening, No. 65 Squadron had a similar unfortunate experience, losing three Spitfires that had taken off to intercept a formation of 45 Dornier 17s attacking a convoy off Folkestone. On July 8, Fighter Command shot down seven enemy aircraft, including four Bf 109s, for the loss of four of its own, two of which were Spitfires. One Spitfire pilot was killed. The next day, four Spitfires were lost, all victims of Bf 109s in skirmishes over the Channel; all four pilots were killed.

On July 10, 26 Dornier Do 17s, heavily escorted by fighters, were dispatched to attack a large convoy off Dover. The attack was intercepted by 30 RAF fighters, which destroyed eight enemy aircraft for the loss of one Hurricane, but three Spitfires had to make forced landings after suffering combat damage. Falmouth was attacked by 63 Junkers Ju 88s, whose bombs damaged railways and ships at anchor and caused 86 casualties. The following day saw heavy fighting over the Channel, during which the RAF shot down 15 enemy aircraft for the loss of six, two of which were Spitfires.

During the next five days it was the Hurricane squadrons that bore the brunt of the fighting over the Channel. Four Spitfires were lost in accidents, although several were damaged in air combat. The only loss of July 17 was K9916 of No. 603 Squadron,

BELOW LEFT A formation of Heinkel He 111 bombers under attack. The aircraft at bottom right receives a burst of machine gun fire; one of its engines is already in flames.

BELOW One of the targets successfully hit by the Luftwaffe in September 1940 was the oil storage tanks at Thameshaven.

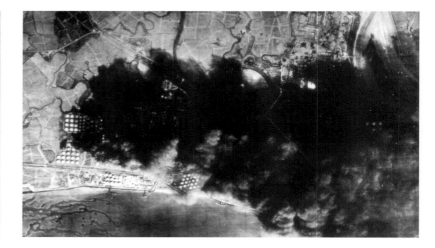

Spitfires, and once again No. 54 Squadron from Rochford suffered badly, losing three aircraft.

Apart from a two-day spell of bad weather, the furious combats over the English Channel continued unabated. One fight was witnessed by BBC radio correspondent, Charles Gardner:

"Well, now, the Germans are dive-bombing a convoy at sea. There are one, two, three, four, five, six, seven German bombers—Junkers 87s—there's one going down on its target now. Bomb—no, there—he's missed the ships . . . He hasn't got a single ship. There's one coming down with a long streak. You can't see these fighters coherently for long. You just see about four twirling machines and you hear little bursts of machine gun fire, and by the time you've picked up the machine they've gone . . .

"There's a dogfight going on up there—there are four, five, six machines, wheeling and turning round. Hark at the machine guns. Hark, one, two, three, four, five, six . . . now there's something coming right down on the tail of another. Here they go—yes, they're being chased home, and how they're being chased home! There are three Spitfires chasing three Messerschmitts now . . . oh boy! Look at them going. And look how the Messerschmitts—oh, this is really grand! And there's a Spitfire just behind the first two—he'll get them! Oh, yes—oh boy! I've never seen anything as good as this . . . the RAF fighter boys have really got these boys taped!"

By the end of July, the RAF had lost 27 Spitfires in the convoy battles, together with a similar number of Hurricanes. And the real air battle was only just beginning.

which took off from Turnhouse on an operational patrol. Neither it nor its pilot, Flying Officer C. D. Peel, was seen again.

Six more Spitfires were lost between then and July 25, when the Luftwaffe adopted a change of tactics, sending out strong fighter sweeps to bring the RAF fighters to battle before launching its bomber attacks. As a result, 60 Ju 87 Stukas were able to bomb a convoy with impunity while the fighters of No. 11 Group were on the ground refueling. Later in the day, the convoy was attacked by 30 Ju 88s, escorted by Bf 109s. The attacks continued until 18:30, and 15 RAF fighter squadrons were engaged, losing nine aircraft. Seven of these were

TOP A vortex of vapour trails shows the course of a fierce air battle over southern England.

ABOVE LEFT A first-aid package for on-the-spot treatment of burns. Fire, dreaded by all pilots, was an ever-present hazard.

LEFT The early single-step pedals from a crashed Mk I Spitfire, complete with the straps to keep the pilot's feet from slipping off.

Spitfires in the Battle of Britain: The climax

The main daylight phase of the Battle of Britain lasted around 17 weeks. It began on July 10, 1940, with the first major attacks on the Channel convoys, and lasted until the end of October, when the Luftwaffe began its night offensive against the British Isles. The German code name for the air offensive was Adler Angriff (Eagle Attack). To put the plan into operation, the Germans mustered some 3,500 fighters and bombers, of which about 2,200 were serviceable at any one time. Against them, on the other side of the English Channel, the RAF had 620 Hurricanes and Spitfires. To fly them, in the beginning, there were about 1,000 pilots, although the number would rise to more than 3,000 before the battle was over. Eighty per cent were British; the rest came from all over the world, from Australia, Canada, New Zealand, India, Poland, Czechoslovakia, Belgium, France, Scandinavia, and the United States, a country not yet at war with Germany. More than 500 would lose their lives in the twisting air battles over the harvest fields of southern England; many others would be maimed, sometimes terribly burned, as they strove to escape from a cockpit that had become an inferno.

When the battle began in earnest in July 1940, 29 squadrons of RAF Fighter Command were equipped with Hawker Hurricanes and 19 with Spitfires, and it was the Hurricane, although often eclipsed in the public eye by the more glamorous Spitfire, that destroyed 80 per cent of the enemy aircraft brought down during the fighting. The reason, apart from the Hawker fighter's numerical advantage in this battle, was one of tactics; as a general policy, the Hurricanes were given the task of intercepting the Luftwaffe bomber formations while the faster, more maneuverable Spitfires took on the enemy fighter escort.

Following attacks on the British coastal radar stations, which inflicted some damage but left most of the stations still functioning, Adler Angriff was launched on August 13.

The attacks were to be repeated day after day, their ferocity mitigated only by spells of bad weather. The heaviest day's fighting was on August 15, with attacks on targets in both northern and southern England. The northern attack was carried out by Luftflotte 5, its aircraft based in Norway and Denmark. Flying from Stavanger in Norway, 63 He 111s of KG 26, escorted by 21 Bf 110s, made landfall on the Northumbrian coast. They were intercepted by five squadrons of Spitfires and Hurricanes, which broke up the attack and shot down eight Heinkels and six Bf 110s for no loss. Forty Junkers 88s, attempting to attack airfields in Yorkshire, also lost six from their group. The day's operations cost the Luftwaffe 71 aircraft, mostly bombers and Bf 110s. The RAF's loss was 30 fighters, of which 12 were Spitfires.

BELOW A wooden box for 20mm cannon rounds. Cannon were experimentally fitted to some Spitfires during the Battle of Britain.

During the next two days the RAF destroyed 104 additional enemy aircraft for the loss of 57 of its own fighters. On the second day, Thursday August 18, a strong force of Junkers Ju 87 Stuka dive-bombers crossed the coast without fighter escort and was massacred by the Hurricanes of No. 43 Squadron and the Spitfires of No. 152, which shot down 18 of them. The Spitfire squadrons escaped with relatively light casualties during the day's fighting, losing 5 aircraft with 13 more damaged; the Hurricane squadrons, on the other hand, took a terrible mauling, losing 29 aircraft, some in attacks on their airfields.

Day after day, the onslaught against the RAF's airfields continued. On September 6, reconnaissance aircraft reported growing numbers of invasion craft assembling in Dutch, Belgian, and French Channel ports, and the British ordered Invasion Alert No. 2; attack was expected within three days. For the first time, a Polish fighter squadron—No. 303, at Northolt—was committed to the battle. Fighter Command was now very close to exhaustion; in the two weeks from August 24 to September 6 the Command had lost 103 pilots and 128 were badly wounded—almost one-quarter of its available trained personnel. For the first time, losses began to exceed replacements.

It was at this point that the Germans made the mistake that would ultimately cost them the battle. On September 4, Adolf

ABOVE LEFT Prime Minister Winston Churchill visits a Fighter Command airfield during the Battle of Britain. His presence inspired pilots and ground crews alike.

ABOVE Ground crew turning round a Spitfire during the Battle of Britain. The highly-trained team could have the aircraft ready for another sortie within minutes.

RIGHT There was money to be made by writing accounts of the Battle of Britain experience. And Kent was in the forefront of the battle.

Hitler declared in public that his intention was to "erase" Britain's cities, and on the following day he gave orders to attack London and other large cities by day and night. For the people of London and elsewhere, a nightmare was beginning—but the Luftwaffe, by switching its attacks away from the airfields, gave the battered Fighter Command the respite it so desperately needed.

" Scramble!

Despite the warning time provided by the Chain Home and Chain Home Low radar systems (p32), success or failure depended on whether the RAF fighters could get off the ground and climb quickly enough to intercept the raiders.

The hectic business of a "scramble" was described in graphic detail by Pilot Officer (later Squadron Leader) D. H. Clarke:

"Jump on the port wing . . . right foot in over the stick, now left . . . ease down to avoid rucking the parachute back straps. Strap on the chute first: body belt . . . left shoulder . . . right shoulder . . . pull up the crutch loop . . . left leg . . . right leg—each metal tag clips into the quick release box with a familiar click. Safety straps: left shoulder . . . right shoulder . . . underpin in your own well-known position . . . right leg . . . left leg . . . right shoulder . . . flick the cord holding the fastening pin and slam it in. Petrol on; I grab my helmet off the control column and pull it on with a practised nod of my head . . . unscrew the Ki-gass [The Ki-gass pump was part of the engine cold start procedure, injecting raw fuel into the system] and prime; one to get pressure, then half a squirt of fuel. Switches on. A nod to the erk [an affectionate term used by aircrew for the term for the airmen who serviced their aircraft that originated in the Navy, and was probably introduced into the RAF by way of the Royal Naval Air Service in 1918] standing by the leading edge of the port wing and I press the starter button. The Koffman cartridge fires and my Spitfire comes to life with her characteristic blare and rumbling vibration.

"I set the throttle—1,000 revs, lock the brake lever on the stick and check pressure by ruddering left and right, make sure the rad is fully open, wave my hand from side to side, and in the few seconds it takes the erks to remove the chocks I slam up the cockpit flap, strap on my helmet, clip on my face mask, and press Button A on the VHF set by the throttle quadrant. To the familiar rush of atmospheric disturbance I release the brakes with a hiss and ease the throttle open, ruddering the long nose of my Spit from side to side.

ABOVE Pilots of No. 19 Squadron pictured relaxing at Fowlmere, a satellite airfield near their main base at Duxford in Cambridgeshire.

BELOW LEFT The head of a Ki-gas pump, which injected raw fuel into the Merlin engine during the start-up procedure.

"Turn into wind . . . trim rudder and elevators . . . check petrol on . . . check pitch in fine; mixture rich . . . a quick look at oil pressure . . . glycol temperature. Spitfires on all sides taking off . . . I open my throttle to plus 2 boost and ease the stick forward—then gently back to prevent the airscrew blades from chopping into the turf. Within seconds the pounding of the undercarriage over the uneven, sun-hardened ground smoothes to an unfelt grumbling, then—airborne. I squeeze the brake lever, then select U/C [undercarriage] up. As the indicator lights wink to red, I reach behind my head and slam the hood shut, mentally praising my ground crew for its smooth operation. Then I close the rad.

"As we climb at around 2,000ft [610m] per minute, we all begin the endless search: left, right, above, below, behind, and into the sun . . . always searching, never relaxing. 2,600 revs; plus 2 boost; turn on the oxygen at 10,000ft [3,048m] (or 15,000 [4,572m] if you want to save some for an emergency; weaken the mixture as much as possible; concentrate on sliding into formation without too much fuel-wasting throttle movements; check glycol temperature; check oil pressure and temperature; and search . . . search . . . above, below, left, right, behind and always into the sun."

Then came the exhilaration of contact with the enemy, an experience described in the laconic terms of a combat report compiled by Polish Spitfire pilot Janusz Zurakowski, later to become a renowned test pilot with Gloster Aircraft and Avro Canada. He gained his first victory with the RAF while flying with No. 234 Squadron on September 5, 1940.

"I was Blue 2. We were flying at 22,000ft [6,706m]. I went down to investigate two machines and then saw an Me 109 flying south at 14,000ft [4,267m]. I approached from astern and as he turned I gave a short burst from 100 yards [91m]. He half rolled and dived and flew low due south. I stayed on his tail firing one short burst at 140 yards [128m] and then the rest of my ammunition from very close. After my first attack he was smoking slightly and later heavily. The enemy pilot opened his hood as he crash-landed on the sea. The pilot got out and two minutes later the machine sank."

Zurakowski's victory had come fairly easily, but for another pilot, caught in a twisting dogfight, things were very different, as Pilot Officer Dennis David explains.

"There was a lot of nonsense at the time about 'perfect deflection shots.' [A deflection shot is where the pilot of an attacking aircraft aims ahead of the target in the hope that his bullets will converge on it.] There was never a time for that in a dogfight. The only way you could shoot down a German fighter was getting very close to its backside and letting it have everything. Then you'd pull the stick right back into your guts for a sharp turn. You were pushed way down into your seat. Your eyeballs were pushed down into your face . . . You couldn't keep it up for long, but you were pulling a lot of 'G' while it was happening. There were a lot of aircraft in the sky. If you could, you made your attack on the bombers. But almost immediately, you were in a dogfight with the fighters which had come down to protect them . . . "

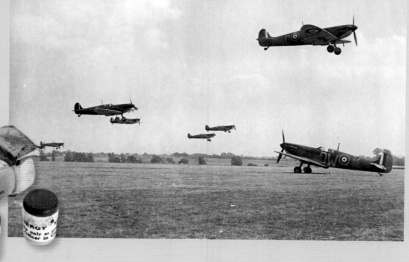

ABOVE RAF fighter pilots were equipped with an Irvin seat-type parachute, developed by the American Leslie Irvin. It was opened by means of a hand-pulled ripcord.

RIGHT Fighter pilots were often prescribed energy tablets to offset the fatigue of combat sorties, which could be as many as three or four a day at the height of the Battle of Britain.

FAR RIGHT Spitfire scramble. Radar usually gave fighter pilots adequate warning of an incoming raid, but not always.

Lifting the nation's spirits

In 1940, Lord Beaverbrook, the Canadian-born Minister of Aircraft Production, launched an appeal titled "To the Women of Britain," in which he exhorted them to "Give us your aluminium . . . we will turn pots and pans into Spitfires and Hurricanes, Blenheims and Wellingtons. I ask therefore that anyone who has pots and pans, coat hangers, shoe trees, bathroom fittings . . . made wholly or in part of aluminium, should hand them over at once to the local headquarters of the Women's Voluntary Services."

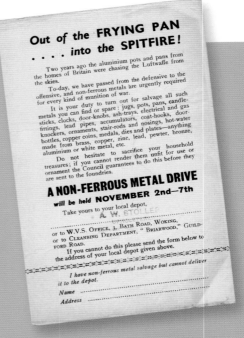

Out of the FRYING PAN . . . . into the SPITFIRE!

Two years ago the aluminium pots and pans from the homes of Britain were chasing the Luftwaffe from the skies.

To-day, we have passed from the defensive to the offensive, and non-ferrous metals are urgently required for every kind of munition of war.

It is your duty to turn out for salvage all such metals you can find or spare : jugs, pots, pans, candlesticks, clocks, door-knobs, ash-trays, electrical and gas fittings, lead pipes, accumulators, coat-hooks, door-knockers, ornaments, stair-rods and nosings, hot-water bottles, copper coins, medals, dies and plates—anything made from brass, copper, zinc, lead, pewter, bronze, aluminium or white metal, etc.

Do not hesitate to sacrifice your household treasures ; if you cannot render them unfit for use or ornament the Council guarantees to do this before they are sent to the foundries.

A NON-FERROUS METAL DRIVE
will be held **NOVEMBER 2nd—7th**

Take yours to your local depot,

A. W. STOLLER

or to W.V.S. OFFICE, 3, BATH ROAD, WOKING, or to CLEANSING DEPARTMENT, "BRIARWOOD," GUILDFORD ROAD.

If you cannot do this please send the form below to the address of your local depot given above.

I have non-ferrous metal salvage but cannot deliver it to the depot.

Name ....

Address ....

"Out of the frying pan . . . into the Spitfire", the headlines trumpeted. In reality, the mountains of saucepans collected by Britain's housewives made little practical contribution to aircraft production, but Beaverbrook's appeal had an enormous effect on civilian morale. Ordinary people, bewildered by the speed of German conquest and conscious of Britain's dire peril, felt that here at last was something they could do. Fighters, fighters, and still more fighters—Britain's survival depended on the Spitfire and Hurricane, and the young men who flew them.

While the housewives of Britain willingly donated their precious utensils, other organizations took pride in setting up "Spitfire funds," (p52) raising money that would cover the cost of a Spitfire, which in the summer of 1940 was about £5,000 ($7,815). Hundreds of Spitfires were presented to the RAF in this way, each bearing a name suggested by the donor. The city of Bradford alone raised enough money for six Spitfires, while eight more came from organizations in Manchester. Others were donated by organizations and individuals from all points of the compass; one, for example, was donated by an Indian prince. Not all the donors were directly connected with Britain; the name Spirit of Uruguay speaks for itself. One of the largest donations came from the Netherlands East Indies; a cheque for £323,377 and 17 shillings

ABOVE A clever exhortation to housewives to part with their aluminum utensils, which would be used in the manufacture of Spitfires.

BELOW LEFT This Spitfire Mk Va P8088, sponsored by the Borough of Lambeth, is seen with the markings of No. 118 Squadron, one of several in which it served.

BELOW North West Frontier IV, a Mk II (P8695), was one of many Spits donated with funds raised in India; it served from June 1941 through to August 1945.

THE HAMPSHIRE SPITFIRE SONG

Words and Music by H. M. KING.

Price: SIXPENCE

The Hampshire Planes are Coming!

Words and Music by H. M. KING.

FOUR FIGHTER FUND

JIGSAW PUZZLE
Over 200 pieces fully interlocking
HENDON FITS THE BIT
IF YOU PAY YOUR PART
FOUR FIGHTER FUND

LEFT The Spitfire also inspired songwriters. Profits from this song sheet went to the Spitfire Fund.

CENTER The Spitfire theme was seen in lots of spin-offs, including jigsaw puzzles.

BELOW Playing cards were another Spitfire spin-off, bearing attractive images of the fighter.

($505,471), presented by Queen Wilhelmina, provided for 40 Spitfires and 18 Lockheed Hudsons, each to be named after locations in the Netherlands East Indies.

Some of the fund-raising schemes were quite novel: one Spitfire was named Dorothy because it resulted from a campaign to which girls named Dorothy all over Britain were invited to contribute. More Spitfires bore presentation details than any other aircraft type in the RAF. These Spitfires were not specially ordered; instead, a current production model was selected to bear the name suggested by the donor.

Another morale-boosting scheme was to put shot-down German aircraft on display. The more riddled they were with bullet holes, the better. All of them, of course, had been shot down by Spitfires according to the general public, although in fact most were the victims of Hurricanes. On a rather more bizarre note, one enterprising farmer invited members of the public to visit his field at sixpence ($0.39) apiece, which was to be donated to the Spitfire fund; he claimed that it was the only field in Kent without a wrecked German aircraft in it!

The Spitfire—graceful and immediately recognizable by its elliptical wings— caught the imagination of the British people. They could identify with it; its name rolled off the tongue, and it seemed to epitomize Britain's spirit of resistance. By the end of the Battle of Britain the country was swept by what amounted to Spitfire fever:

images of Spitfires appeared on playing cards, on matchboxes, on towels and china mugs.

The newsreels, too, promoted the Spitfire and its achievements whenever possible, and in 1942 a film was made about the fighter—*The First of the Few*, starring David Niven and Leslie Howard, the latter playing the part of Reginald Mitchell. It was a box-office hit all over the free world, and Leslie Howard's part in promoting the Spitfire's propaganda image may have been responsible for his death. In June 1943, the Dutch KLM Dakota airliner in which Howard was a passenger was intercepted and shot down by Junkers 88s while en route from Lisbon to London, resulting in the loss of all on board. Whether Howard was the principal target, or whether another passenger had been mistaken for Winston Churchill, will never be known.

Perhaps the charisma of the Spitfire was best summed up by Pierre Clostermann, the celebrated French pilot who flew Spitfires on many operations and who described his experiences in his book *The Big Show*:

"The Spitfire . . . is typically British. Temperate, a perfect compromise for all the qualities required of a fighter, ideally suited to its task of defence. An essentially reasonable piece of machinery, conceived by cool, precise brains and built by conscientious hands. The Spitfire left such an imprint on these who flew it that when they changed to other types they found it very hard to get acclimatised."

Spitfire: Symbol of hope

Partly for commercial reasons, and partly for reasons of national morale, the British public was encouraged to donate money in support of the war effort. Although the funding of aircraft initially involved several types of fighters and bombers it very quickly focused on the nation's favourite—the Spitfire. For a nominal sum of £5,000 the Ministry of Aircraft Production (MAP) would award the donor organization a special plaque, and place the chosen name on the side of the "presentation" aircraft.

The plaque reads:

IN THE HOUR OF PERIL
LONDON PROVISION
EXCHANGE FIGHTER FUND
EARNED THE GRATITUDE
OF THE BRITISH NATIONS
SUSTAINING THE VALOUR OF
THE ROYAL AIR FORCE
AND FORTIFYING THE CAUSE
OF FREEDOM
BY THE GIFT OF
SPITFIRE AIRCRAFT
They shall mount up with wings as eagles
Issued by the Ministry of Aircraft Production
1941

Some major corporations, foreign companies and wealthy individuals provided funds for a single Spitfire, and in some cases donated enough money to equip a whole squadron. For the general public, though, many funds were started by local councils, mayors, schools and factories, and for a modest sum a small token was given to the donor. Such tokens ranged from simple paper flags with a pin, through press-sheet metal badges to the classy enamel and cast badges made by such famous makers as Thomas Fattorini of Birmingham. Some badges would just be generic with the words "Spitfire Fund" inscribed on them, while many would identify the specific fund directly or by an associated connection. Many local funds were supported by sponsored events, dances, cinema programs and endorsements on commercial items.

ABOVE A typical example of the type of plaque awarded by the Ministry of Aircraft Production to an organization providing substantial funding for the purchase of one or more Spitfires.

OPPOSITE PAGE

1. Clifton Cinemas flyer. Captain S.W. Clift of Birmingham. Spitfire Mk VBM240 named *Clifton Cinemas*.
2. Tonbridge Spitfire Fund concert. This fund probably failed to raise the necessary £5,000 ($20,150 in 1941) and no Spitfire was named after Tonbridge. However, the County of Kent Spitfire Fund raised £108,451 ($437,058) having 32 Spitfires named after towns in Kent.
3. Maidenhead and District. The Mayor's fund raised £5,722 ($23,060) for Mk V W3216 named *Maidenhead & District*.
4. The N.I. Spitfire Fund. The Netherlands East Indies, Queen Juliana and Prince Bernhard presented £726,000 ($2,925,780) to fund 322 Squadron RAF, manned by Dutch personnel. Some 149 Spitfires were presented, mostly named after townships in the Netherlands East Indies.
5. General appeal for savings for Propaganda and Spitfire funding. Not associated with a specific Spitfire.
6 & 7. A seed packet identifier supporting the Hampton's Employees Spitfire Fund East Acton Branch. Hampton and Sons Ltd presented Mk IX BS227 named *The Magic Carpet*.
8. Shareholder badge; part of the Motor Industries Fighter fund. Shareholder represented the collective dealerships for Vauxhall Motors and Bedford trucks. Two Spitfire were presented, Mk V BM465 *Wyvern I* and Mk V BL571 *Wyvern II*.
9. The Fellowship of the Bellows fund. South America.
10. The Lord Mayor of Leicester's fund. By November 1940 £20,000 ($80,600) had been raised; this was added to, providing funds for five Spitfires. Mk V P8532 *The Harry Livingstone, Leicester,* Mk.V P8538 *The George Barbury, Leicester,* Mk II P8563 *City of Leicester I*, Mk II P8565 *City of Leicester Flight - City of Leicester II* and Mk II P8657 *City of Leicester Flight - City of Leicester III*.
11. Beverley Spitfire Fund. The Mayor of Beverley, East Riding Yorks, raised initially £5,137 8s 4d ($20,706) for Spitfire Mk V R7271 named *Beverley and District* and further funds for Mk V ER778 *Spirit of Beverley*.
12. Spitfire Club. A generic pin aimed at children.
13. A generic blue pressed tin badge individually numbered; no specific fund associated.
14. A generic red pressed tin badge individually numbered; no specific fund associated.
15. A generic cast enamel badge for no particular fund. This design, in the same blue, is frequently seen with a named fund printed in the upper portion of the scroll.
16. The Barrier District Pastoralists; a farming husbandry group from Australia. There is no direct link with a known presentation Spitfire and the fund may have been amalgamated with others
17. Scots College. This badge almost certainly originated in Australia; however, there are no records of it achieving £5,000 and a named Spitfire.
18. Spitfire fund; a generic badge like 12. However, this one has almost certainly been painted after purchase.

1

REGAL CINEMA. WEDNESFIELD.
ALL STAR CONCERT
Organised by H. J. E. Davis.

In Aid of the Regal (Clifton Cinemas, Ltd.), SPITFIRE FUND.

SUNDAY, 10TH NOVEMBER, 1940.

MAY SOMERFIELD
SOPRANO. Of B.B.C. and London Concert Fame.

Accompanist : FLIGHT LIEUT. R. PARSONS.

DONALD G. CROMBIE — The Magical Gentleman
WALTER S. FARMER — Solo Broadcasting Pianist

THOMAS PHOENIX — Baritone
THE HYLTON BROTHERS — (Bob & Wallie Comedians)

ROBERT & DORA HODGSON — Entertainers

Compere : ROBERT HODGSON.

PROGRAMME.

2

TONBRIDGE
SPITFIRE FUND

RITZ CINEMA
TONBRIDGE

GRAND
CONCERT

★

SOUVENIR
PROGRAMME

SUNDAY,
DEC. 8th

3

THE MAYOR'S
"SPITFIRE" FUND
for Maidenhead & District.

●

SUGGESTIONS have been received from many of our influential inhabitants that it would be a fine gesture and reflect considerable credit on Maidenhead if a Fund were started to present a "Spitfire" plane (costing approximately £5,000) for the use of the Royal Air Force.

In accordance with these suggestions the Mayor has kindly consented to open such a Fund, and to that end a Committee has been formed to work the scheme.

Contributions are invited from every inhabitant in the Borough and surrounding districts. Subscriptions may be paid into Lloyds Bank or sent to the Mayor at the Guildhall, Maidenhead.

Various schemes for raising money have been under consideration such as Whist Drives and Bridge Parties, a Tombola, Jumble Sales, Collection Boxes in Hotels and Public Places, Flag Days, etc., etc.

It is thought that the above scheme will make a strong appeal to the patriotism of the inhabitants and the Mayor confidently relies upon all local citizens to put forward their greatest effort in order that the necessary funds may be collected in the minimum of time.

Amounts large or small will be gratefully received.

Advertiser Printing Works.

4

HELP BUY ONE !

SUPPORT THE N. I.
"SPITFIRE" FUND.

5

SPITFIRE FUND
& EMPIRE PROPAGANDA STAMPS

TELL THE WORLD OUR AIMS

THE BRITISH EMPIRE STANDS FOR WORLD PEACE AND SECURITY — DEFEND IT

MORE & MORE PLANES ESSENTIAL

ALL ASKED TO HELP — HALF SPITFIRES · ·
24 STAMPS 1/- — HALF PROPAGANDA

ISSUING HOUSE
Constitutional Publishing Co. · 42 Maiden Lane · Strand · W.C.2.

6

ZENOBIA
True
Flower
Perfume

WALLFLOWER

7

In aid of
HAMPTON'S EMPLOYEES
SPITFIRE FUND.

East Acton Branch.

8
SHAREHOLDER

9

10
THE LORD MAYOR'S
LEICESTER & COUNTY
SPITFIRE FUND
24886

11
BEVERLEY
SPITFIRE FUND

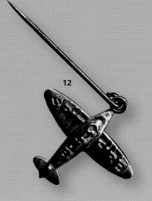

12

13
SPITFIRE FUND
73183

14
SPITFIRE FUND
1323

15
SPITFIRE
FUND

16
THE BARRIER DISTRICT PASTORALISTS'
Pastoralists' Queen
SPITFIRE FUND

17
SCOTS COLLEGE
6d
SPITFIRE FUND

18

CARNEGIE BUILDING
1 LaGrange Street
Newnan, GA 30263

Spitfire and Messerschmitt 109 compared

Of the two German fighter types encountered in the Battle of Britain, the Messerschmitt Bf 109 was by far the most dangerous adversary. Although the performances of the Bf 109 and the Spitfire were generally similar, in some respects the Spitfire pilots found themselves at a disadvantage. During the battles of France and Britain, RAF fighter pilots had discovered a disconcerting habit of the Merlin engine—a tendency to cut out during negative-G maneuvers.

This tendency was not seen in German aero-engines; in Germany, aero-engine development had progressed rapidly during the early 1930s, with four main companies involved: Daimler-Benz, Junkers, BMW, and Siemens-Halske. The first two companies built inverted 12-cylinder liquid-cooled engines, and the other two made air-cooled radials. The Daimler-Benz engine, fitted in the Messerschmitt Bf 109, was also designed to take a 20mm gun, which was installed in the V formed by the cylinder blocks, and fired through the hollow shaft of the propeller reduction gear. This arrangement produced an unexpected result: the supercharger had to be repositioned and it proved impracticable to fit the carburetor in the normal way. The designers tried several variations, but in the end they dispensed with the carburetor altogether and instead used a multipoint fuel injection system spraying directly into the cylinders. The result was that, unlike the Merlin, the Daimler engine continued to perform well during all combat maneuvers.

Until a new carburetor could be designed, the problem was temporarily solved by fitting the Merlin with a small fuel flow restrictor, resembling a plain metal washer, which prevented the carburetor from flooding. It was the brainchild of an engineer at Farnborough, Beatrice "Tilly" Shilling, and was known to Spitfire and Hurricane pilots as "Miss Shilling's Orifice."

RAF pilots who got the chance to fly captured examples of the Messerschmitt Bf 109E, the variant encountered during the Battle of Britain, were generally impressed by the aircraft, although most were critical of the cockpit, which they found to be cramped and with restricted vision to the rear. However, one pilot had the following comment:

"The cockpit enclosure . . . excelled among all other aircraft I had flown . . . in the complete absence of draught from its clear vision opening. Though rain at times made the windscreen opaque, I could see ahead whatever the speed of the Me 109. In Hurricane or Spitfire it would have been necessary to throttle back and open the hood."

Pilots also praised the 109's cockpit layout. "The control column grip came nicely to hand, the single lever, gateless throttle was delightfully straightforward . . . the juxtaposition of wheel controls for flap operation and tailplane was excellent."

Horror stories about the 109's tendency to swing viciously on takeoff and drop the left wing were quickly dispelled.

"Response to the throttle was instantaneous . . . there was no hasty jamming of rudder to counteract the heavy swing often found with single-engined fighters and the tail lifted firmly and cleanly when the stick was held well forward . . . The takeoff was surprisingly short; the aeroplane left the ground sweetly, and slanted up at a rate of climb which would have beaten a competing Spitfire."

BELOW Beatrice "Tilly" Shilling, who produced a temporary solution to the Rolls-Royce Merlin's fuel starvation problem, was also an accomplished racing cyclist.

ABOVE The cockpit of the Messerschmitt Bf 109 was more cramped than the Spitfire's, and featured a canopy that opened sideways.

ABOVE The Spitfire's cockpit was more easily accessible than the Bf 109's, being fitted with a small side door.

The evaluation flights usually involved a mock combat with a Hurricane or Spitfire, as one RAF test pilot describes:

"The Spitfire . . . was alongside with its broad wing tucked between mine and the tail. The pilot grinned and jerked a thumb. I pulled back on the stick, and laughed to see the Spit shoot underneath as the little Messerschmitt stood on its tail and climbed steeply away.

"In an endeavour to retrieve his position the Spitfire pilot climbed steeply, but only resulted in placing himself in a position where I could make a short dive for his tail. I jammed the nose down so hard that a Spitfire or Hurricane doing the same manoeuvre would have choked its engine, but the direct-injection system did not even falter. Gun sights could only be held momentarily on the Spitfire; then he did a flick half roll and was off in a steep dive with a change of direction which the Me 109 could not quickly follow.

"For a few minutes we climbed, twisted and dived after each other. It was an interesting contest. Many times the steep climbing attitude of the German machine would evade the Spitfire, and the abruptness with which its nose could be thrust down had its undoubted advantage. Yet when it came to manoeuvring at speed . . . the heavy weight of the Messerschmitt's controls proved not only exhausting but impossible. Aileron could only be applied slowly, and so the response was slow; the best one could do was to evade the Spitfire by gentle turns at very low speed and then strike him down by cunning. Tighten these turns to 4G and the machine began to drop out of the sky after a preparatory warning flick caused by the opening of the (automatic leading edge) slats. However, the behaviour even then was excellent, for no spin resulted, and normal flight was instantly regained by easing the backward pressure on the stick."

LEFT Later models of the Merlin engine featured a two-stage supercharger for increased efficiency at altitude, a cutaway boost control unit of which is pictured here.

Spitfire v 109: Staying ahead

As soon as the RAF became aware of any changes introduced by the Luftwaffe, either in the form of modifications to the Bf 109 (and later the Fw190) or revised tactics, a requirement was ssued that led to corresponding countermeasures. The result was an ongoing development of the Spitfire's airframe and of its powerplant.

Summing up the Spitfire test program, Jeffrey Quill, who was in charge of Spitfire test flying, wrote:

"Every major modification or change, especially those affecting performance or handling qualities, was exhaustively tested by the firm before submission to the Aircraft and Armament Experimental Establishment (A&AEE) at Boscombe Down for official approval. Establishing the accurate performance of any variant involved a lot of flying and a great deal of full-power bashing of the engine and systems.

"As time went on, Boscombe Down came increasingly to accept the firm's figures, making only spot checks for themselves, in order to save wear and tear on the prototypes. In other words, Boscombe Down provided the official seal of approval, though many of the performance figures quoted in their reports were in fact measured by Supermarine's experimental flight test unit at Worthy Down . . . the A&AEE made their own judgements on the aircraft's handling and other qualities.

"The Air Fighting Development Unit represented Fighter Command, and thus the main users of the Spitfire. They did a most useful job in relating the various British fighters to those of the enemy and in developing tactics on behalf of the command. They were fully entitled to express their opinions about the handling of the aircraft and they certainly did so. But the people at Boscombe Down were the final arbiters of what was fit for service use and what was not, and whether or not the aircraft met its specifications and contractual conditions."

ABOVE Jeffrey Quill with a group of fellow test pilots during the early days of the Spitfire; the aircraft are Mk Is with two-bladed propellers.

LEFT A Merlin engine being lowered into place in a Spitfire. The Merlin was the subject of constant development by Rolls-Royce throughout its career.

Some modifications to the Spitfire, such as the little device invented by "Tilly" Shilling [see p54] as a temporary solution to the aircraft's carburetor problems, took time to implement, and in the meantime the problems continued to be a source of both danger and annoyance to the RAF fighter pilots, as Flying Officer (later Wing Commander) Bob Doe found out during one combat in 1941, when he engaged some Bf 109s over the English Channel:

"I opened fire at about 300 yards [274m] and seemed to hit the one I was aiming at because he pulled up sharply. At that moment I must have been down to about a hundred yards [91m]. I hit his slipstream and my engine cut—stone dead!

"At that time the spitfire was equipped with a normal carburettor that did not function under negative gravity conditions. Later we were given one that did. But at that moment in time my engine had cut out due to the violent movement induced by the enemy's slipstream, and I had some fifty 109s who were getting interested in me, due, no doubt to a call from the one I had shot at.

"So I reverted to my dive and waited for my engine to restart, all the time keeping an eye on the one that I had shot at, who seemed to be pulling away on his own and turning toward France. Having restarted my engine and seeing that I was clear of danger, I turned on the one that I had obviously hit.

"As I crept up to him from behind, it was apparent that he had not seen me. I was able to get very close and concentrated on hitting him properly. The aeroplane seemed to stop in mid-air, the wheels came down and parts of the plane fell off . . . "

The Germans experienced more serious problems in their ongoing development of the Messerschmitt 109. The best of all Bf 109 variants, the Bf 109F, began to reach Luftwaffe units in France in May 1941 and was superior in most respects to the principal RAF fighter of the time, the Spitfire Mk V, but before that it had been plagued by serious troubles. In February 1941 three pilots, in separate incidents, made frantic radio calls reporting that the fighter was vibrating violently, and before they could bail out the 109s went out of control and dived into the ground. A few weeks later a 109F-1 lost its entire tail assembly, and engineers examining the wreckage discovered the cause of the vibration, which built up in the rear fuselage and caused the tail unit to fail. The tail was strengthened, and the problem solved.

The Bf 109F was succeeded by the Bf 109G, which appeared late in 1942. The "Gustav", much heavier than the earlier 109 variants, soon earned itself a reputation as a killer among its pilots, but in experienced hands it was an excellent fighting machine.

ABOVE Pilot Officer (later Wing Commander) Bob Doe was the joint-third most successful fighter pilot of the Battle of Britain, with 14 victories. He survived the war and died in 2010, aged 89.

RIGHT The Messerschmitt Bf 109F was the best of the 109 variants, once its tail problems had been rectified. This example is seen on an airfield in Italy.

Spitfire aces of the Battle of Britain

The term "ace," as applied to fighter pilots, originated in France during World War I. It was later qualified by the Americans to include any pilot who had destroyed five or more enemy aircraft in air combat.

During World War II, the "ace factor" was eagerly seized upon by the German, American, and Soviet propaganda machines. Neither the British nor the Japanese would have anything to do with it. As far as the RAF was concerned, air combat was a matter of

teamwork, and it consistently refused to publicize the achievements of individual pilots. However, in the summer of 1940 the Air Ministry saw fit to release regular bulletins in which the exploits of certain RAF fighter pilots were mentioned, albeit without revealing their names. Even then, officer pilots got the lion's share of the publicity, despite the fact that the top-scoring fighter pilots during the Battle of Britain were mostly non-commissioned officers (NCOs).

The leading scorer was Sergeant Josef Frantisek, a Czech pilot who had already destroyed 11 enemy aircraft while flying with the Polish and French Air Forces. He added 17 more victories to his tally before his death in a flying accident on October 8, 1940. No other Czech fighter pilot was to surpass his total of 28 victories, and he remained the top scorer in the Battle of Britain.

Frantisek flew Hurricanes with No. 303 (Polish) Squadron, but close behind him, with 16 confirmed victories, was a Spitfire pilot, Flying Officer Eric Lock of No. 41 Squadron, which was based at Catterick in North Yorkshire at the start of the battle of Britain. He destroyed his first enemy aircraft off the northeast coast on August 15, 1940. Lock got into the thick of the fighting in the first week of September, when No. 41 Squadron moved to RAF Hornchurch in Essex. On September 5, he destroyed two Heinkel 111s and a Messerschmitt 109, and the next day he shot down a Ju 88, which fell into the Channel. Three days later he destroyed two Bf 109s over Kent, and on September 11 he shot down a Ju 88 and a Bf 110. This brought his total kills so far to nine, all of them confirmed; he had destroyed eight of the enemy aircraft in one week, a feat that brought him the award of a DFC. He went on to destroy 7 more aircraft before the end of October and shared in the destruction of another, bringing his tally to 16. On November 17, by which time he had scored 6 more kills, Lock was badly wounded in a

LEFT Exhibitions of shot-down German aircraft attracted huge crowds, as did propaganda talks by the leading "aces" of the day.

ABOVE Wing Commander Robert Stanford Tuck flew both Spitfires and Hurricanes during the Battle of Britain. He went on to become a wing leader, and destroyed 30 enemy aircraft before he was shot down and captured in 1942.

RIGHT "Sailor" Malan beside the famous blackboard, bearing the signatures of Battle of Britain fighter pilots, which was a prized possession of the White Hart Inn near Biggin Hill for many years. It is now in the RAF Museum.

ABOVE Colin Gray, fourth top-scoring ace of the Battle of Britain, seen with his Spitfire. He was New Zealand's most decorated pilot.

LEFT James Brendan "Paddy" Finucane, seen here on the right, shot down his first aircraft during the Battle of Britain and went on to destroy 31 more before he was lost in the English Channel in July 1942.

battle over the Thames Estuary. He brought his Spitfire down to a crash landing at Martlesham Heath and was hospitalized until May 1941.

Three pilots vied for third place in the Battle of Britain, each shooting down 15 aircraft. They were Sergeant J. H. "Ginger" Lacey of No. 501 Squadron, Flying Officer Brian Carberry of No. 603, and Pilot Officer Bob Doe of No. 234; Lacey and Doe were both Hurricane pilots.

In fourth place was Flying Officer Colin Gray, a New Zealander who flew Spitfires in No. 54 Squadron alongside another New Zealander, Flying Officer Alan Deere. Although Deere, who was later to lead the famous Biggin Hill Wing on fighter sweeps and escort missions over France in 1943, was much publicized, Gray's achievements went largely unrecorded until long after the war.

Colin Gray's first taste of action came over Dunkirk in May 1940, when he shared in the destruction of a Bf 109 (not counted in his score). His next victory came on July 24, during the

preliminary phase of the Battle of Britain, when he shot down a Bf 109 over Margate. When the main battle began on August 12, Gray destroyed two Bf 109s, repeating this success three days later. On August 18 he attacked a Bf 110 and sent it down on fire, and later that day he crippled a Bf 109, which crashed in the middle of Clacton. On August 24 he chased a Bf 110 almost all the way across the Channel and shot it down off the French coast, and two days later he added a Bf 109 to his score. In the four days from August 31 to September 3 he destroyed five more enemy aircraft and had a number of lucky escapes, one when a cannon shell exploded behind his cockpit without injuring him. On his last day of action No, 54 Squadron was sent north to RAF Catterick for a rest, which probably saved his life. However, one Spitfire pilot achieved fame by destroying five enemy aircraft, claiming one probably destroyed, and damaging two more, all in a single day. He was Flight Lieutenant H. M. Stephen.

" Aces' stories

Flight Lieutenant Harbourne Mackay Stephen, simply known as "Steve" by his fellow pilots, was a Scot flying with No. 74 Squadron. His "day of days" was August 11, 1940, when, at 06:45, 74 Squadron encountered 30 Bf 109s as they patrolled the Channel.
"I had a quick bang at one of the enemy, then at another [Stephen reported]. Then I happened to turn up sun and joined two aircraft that were climbing, when I discovered that I was following two Messerschmitt 109 fighters at only a few yards' distance; in fact, I was formating [flying in formation] on them. By the time I'd realised my mistake they had turned away from the sun, and I opened fire on the leader. I came up behind him and gave him a burst, and he dropped down into the Channel. When I gave the second one a burst he just exploded in mid-air."

A couple of hours later 74 Squadron was airborne again, patrolling over a convoy in the Thames Estuary. Stephen's combat report describes a subsequent engagement with Messerschmitt 110s, which he describes as Messerschmitt Jaguar fighter-bombers. This is of note, because there was indeed a Messerschmitt Jaguar, the Bf 161, but only three prototypes were built; German propaganda gave the impression that it was in widespread service. It was the same story with another aircraft, the "Heinkel 113." Its true designation was Heinkel He 100 and only 12 were built, but the Germans issued photographs showing the 12 in different unit markings, and for weeks RAF pilots mistakenly reported engagements with it over southern England.
"The German aircraft were going round in steep turns [Stephen said]. Imagine them—40 light bombers, very manoeuvrable and fast, the famous Messerschmitt 110 Jaguar fighter-bombers. We were chasing them, and they were chasing us in and out of the clouds. In a few minutes they started to form one of their well-known defensive circles. By this time several Germans were lying smashed up in the water, with their crews swimming around. The Spitfires were now diving in and out of the circle and never letting them complete it. I got my sights on one aircraft and gave him a long burst, and one of my tracer bullets must have hit his petrol tank, as in a few seconds he went down flaming into the sea. I climbed into clouds just as another bomber darted at me, and we passed each other so closely that I do not know how we avoided a smash. Turning on his tail, I silenced his rear-gunner with a burst, and as I closed the range the Messerschmitt rolled over and fell upside down into the sea."

The twin-engined Messerschmitt 110 showed its vulnerability that morning. Ten were shot down, and half a dozen others staggered back to France badly damaged.

ABOVE Battle of Britain ace Flight Lieutenant H.M. Stephen, in the cockpit of his Spitfire, swaps experiences with a fellow pilot.

Stephen was in action again that afternoon, attacking a formation of Junkers Ju 87 dive-bombers.
One of them "dived and I followed him down, giving him another burst just before the pilots jumped out. He was so low that his parachute did not open, and his aircraft crashed and burst into flames on the beach."

Spitfire ace Eric Lock's combat report described the first of his 26 victories. He had taken off with other pilots of No. 41 Squadron from RAF Catterick, in North Yorkshire, to intercept the German attack from Norway and Denmark on August 15, 1940.
"I was flying in formation with 41 Squadron when we were ordered to patrol north of base at 20,000ft [6,096m]. After flying for a while we saw a formation of Junkers 88s and Messerschmitt 110s. The squadron then went into line astern and we made an attack. During our second attack, I fired two short bursts into the starboard engine of a Messerschmitt 110. I followed it down to 10,000ft [3,048m], firing at the fuselage. The machine gunner stopped firing. Continuing my dive

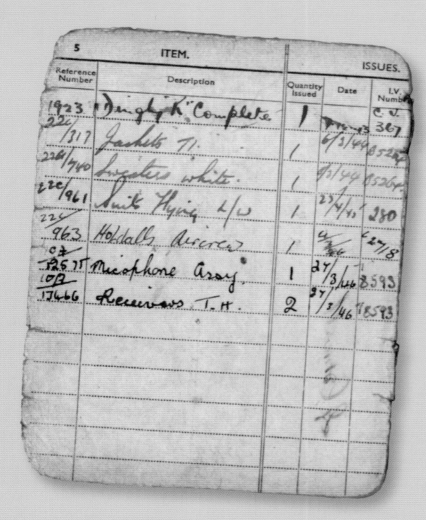

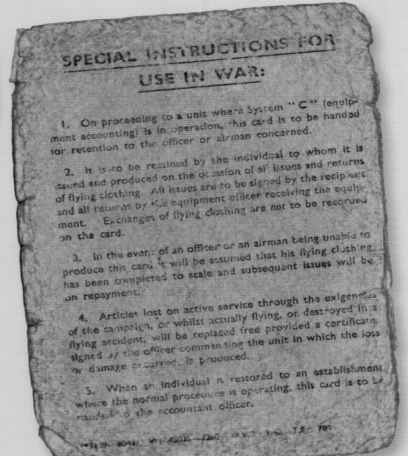

ABOVE Another RAF form on which details were meticulously entered—in this case, the scale of personal equipment issued to a fighter pilot and instructions.

BELOW Six shots from a gun camera sequence showing a Messerschmitt Bf 109 going down in flames, the victim of a Spitfire.

I fired at the port engine, which caught fire. I left it at 5,000ft [1,524m], still in a vertical dive, with both engines on fire."

The Messerschmitt plunged into Seaham Harbour, on the coast of County Durham.

Some aces were very lucky to survive the battle. One was Pilot Officer George Bennions, who on October 1, 1940, had just gained his 12th victory when a cannon shell exploded near the left side of his face.

"I cleared my other eye with my glove and found that I was able to see vaguely [he said later]. I could see that the hood and cockpit were shattered, so I decided to bail out . . . I felt a terrific jerk as my parachute opened, then I lost consciousness. The next thing I remember is lying on the ground telling my name and squadron to someone attending me."

George Bennions's left eye was destroyed, and there was a hole in his skull through which his brain was exposed. He recovered after months of hospitalization, and he underwent plastic surgery at the hands of the celebrated surgeon Archibald McIndoe. He died in 2004, at age 91.

3 On the offensive

Spitfire "circus" over France

Early in 1941, with the Luftwaffe still attacking Britain's cities under cover of darkness, RAF Fighter Command—now under the leadership of Air Marshal William Sholto Douglas—decided to take the war to the enemy by sending its fighters across the Channel to draw the Luftwaffe into battle. These operations, which involved Spitfire and Hurricane squadrons penetrating enemy territory in wing strength, were known as "Rodeos". Bomber escort missions, involving one or more fighter wings escorting a fairly small number of bombers, were called "Circuses"; smaller incursions, usually by fighters operating in pairs at low level, were known as "Rhubarbs."

A fighter command wing was composed of 3 squadrons, each with 12 aircraft; the Spitfire wings were concentrated on Biggin Hill in Kent, Hornchurch in Essex and Tangmere in Sussex.

The Tangmere wing was commanded by the famous Douglas Bader, who flew with artificial legs as the result of a pre-war flying accident, and who had commanded a Hurricane squadron, No. 242, in the Battle of Britain. Bader formed a wonderful partnership with Tangmere's station commander and fighter controller, Group Captain Woodhall, as Tangmere wing pilot J. E. "Johnnie" Johnson, who later became the RAF's official top-scoring fighter ace, explains.

"Over the radio, Woodhall's deep resonant voice seemed to fill our earphones with confidence and assurance. When we were far out over France and he spoke into his microphone, it was as if the man was in the air with you, not issuing orders but giving encouragement and advice and always watching the precious minutes, and the headwind which would delay our withdrawal, and the low cloud creeping up from the west which might cover Tangmere when we returned, tired and short of petrol. Then he

ABOVE Air Chief Marshal Sholto Douglas succeeded Sir Hugh Dowding as Air Officer Commanding-in-Chief, RAF Fighter Command, in November 1940, and saw it go over to the offensive.

was always on the ground to meet us after the big shows, to compare notes with Bader and the other leaders. Always he had time for a cheerful word with the novices . . ."

The Biggin Hill Wing was led by "Sailor" Malan, who was by now a wing commander with 18 confirmed victories to his credit, a DSO (Distinguished Service Order), and two DFCs (Distinguished Flying Cross). Malan's manner was forthright; once, when asked by a reporter how he went about shooting down a German bomber, he replied as follows.

"I try not to, now [was his surprising reply]. I think it's a bad thing. If you shoot them down they don't get back, and no one over there knows what's happening. So I think the right thing to do is to let them get back. With a dead rear gunner, a dead navigator, and the pilot coughing up his lungs as he lands. If you do that, it has a better effect on their morale. Of course, if you just mean to shoot them down—well, what I generally do is knock out both engines."

From May 1941, RAF pilots operating over France began to encounter a new variant of the Messerschmitt Bf 109, the 109F, which was more than a match for the Hurricane and Spitfire Mk II (p57). Fortunately, the RAF fighter squadrons had begun to reequip with the Spitfire Mk V, which was basically a strengthened Mk I airframe with a new Merlin 45 engine, and this new variant was able to fight the Bf 109F on equal terms.

Circus and Rodeo operations in the first half of 1941 produced results that were far from encouraging. They involved, from January to June, a total of 190 bomber and 2,700 fighter sorties, in the course of which Fighter Command lost 51 aircraft and claimed 44 enemy aircraft in return. Later analysis showed even this to be an exaggeration; the Luftwaffe in fact lost just over 20 aircraft. It was only the German invasion of the Soviet Union in June 1941, with its attendant pressures for more intense British action in the west, that brought Circus and Rodeo operations a reprieve, and within a matter of weeks Circus operations were greatly expanded, with as many as 18 squadrons of Spitfires covering a small force of bombers.

Timing was a critical factor in making rendezvous with the bombers, which usually took place over RAF Manston in Kent. A Spitfire's tanks held 85 gallons (386 liters) of fuel, and every minute spent waiting for the bombers (normally twin-engined Bristol Blenheims) to turn up reduced a pilot's chances of getting home after combat over France.

Then, in September 1941, things took a turn for the worse. RAF pilots reported that they were being attacked by a mysterious and highly agile radial-engined enemy fighter, which was superior in most respects to the Spitfire V. The Focke-Wulf Fw 190, soon to be dubbed the "Butcher Bird" because of its combat prowess, had arrived in France.

ABOVE By 1941 Spitfires were armed with both cannon and machine guns; the pilot's hand grip featured a switch enabling him to control both by means of a rocker that replaced the circular button previously used (p41).

LEFT Group Captain Douglas Bader (center) with Air Chief Marshal Sir Hugh Dowding at the Battle of Britain commemorative flypast over London, September 1945. Bader was shot down and taken prisoner in August 1941 while leading the Tangmere Wing.

"A fighter sweep

The pilots of the Biggin Hill Wing were proud to belong to what they believed to be an elite organization. One of them was Sergeant Jim Rosser of No. 72 Squadron, which was commanded by Squadron Leader Desmond Sheen, of Australia. Rosser flew his first sweeps in the spring of 1941.

"In general terms [said Rosser], when the squadron was attacked it tended to split up into pairs, but in practice a lot of people ended up on their own. On my third or fourth sweep—it was somewhere well up into Holland—we ran into a lot of trouble, and I ended up all by myself with about five 109s around me. There were no clouds to escape into, and the position was very dicey. I collected a few holes and got off a few shots, but the situation would have been really serious if some other Spitfires had not appeared and seen off the Huns. Nevertheless, quite a scrap developed, and one of the Huns got off a deflection shot which put my propeller out of gear. Fortunately we were at about 20,000ft [6,096m], and out to sea off the Dutch coast, and I was able to glide home, scraping into Martlesham Heath by the skin of my teeth.

"Dogfights never really lasted very long, consisting of very fast passes, quick 'squirts' and so on. I remember being involved in only one 'classical' dogfight with a 109; I was alone and the scrap took place at about 8,000ft [2,438m], 20 miles [32km] or so into France. He came down on to me out of the sun; fortunately I spotted him in time and pulled hard round to meet him, seeing his tracer go past me as he opened fire. He was turning fast, but I knew that the Spitfire would out-turn him so I hauled back on the stick to get behind him, momentarily blacking out with the 'G.' When my vision cleared I saw that he was in position for me to take a deflection shot at him, so I let him have it with my cannon and machine guns. I hit him round the cockpit area as he went down; I think I probably killed the pilot.

"I always found it very difficult to see enemy aircraft. The second time I was technically shot down, the squadron was split up into four flights after being attacked. I was Yellow Two, and we got into a gaggle of about 18 109s. The scrap only lasted a couple of seconds and I got in a burst at a 109, but whether I hit him or not I don't know. But while I was engaged with this Hun, another had a go at me and hit me in the skew gear on top of the engine, which put the whole thing out of action. There I was, engineless, so I just stuffed the nose down. Fortunately I was not followed, and I was well out to sea, so I flattened out and headed for home. Once again I just managed to scrape in, making a forced landing literally on top of the cliffs."

LEFT Spitfire pilots of No 72 Squadron, RAF Biggin Hill. Pilot Officer Jim Rosser is on the left of the group.

OPPOSITE LEFT All operational RAF stations kept a record of casualties sustained. This book belonged to RAF Manston in Kent, always in the thick of the fighting.

OPPOSITE RIGHT The most famous Belgian Spitfire ace was Jean "Pyker" Offenberg of No 609 Squadron. He was killed in a mid-air collision with another Spitfire on January 22, 1942.

DATE	SQUADRON	TIME UP	TIME DOWN	NAME OF OPERATION	PLACE OF COMBAT OR OBJECTIVE	OWN CAS- PILO NAME		CASUALTIES TS AIRCRAFT			DAMAGE TO SHIPS			DAMAGE TO OTHER OBJECTIVES	ENEMY A/C CASUALTIES			
							NATURE	No	TYPE	CAT	No	TYPE	CAT		TYPE	DEST	PROB	DAM
JULY 10	222²	1230	1325	Circus 42	Bethune	—								—				
16	222²	1350	1445	Jim Crow	E. of Deal	—			1	SPITFIRE 2B	3				—			
18	222²	1100	1220	Roadstead	Gravelines	SGT JENKINS	M	1	SPITFIRE 2B	3				—	Do17z	—	—	1
19	222²	1820	1550	Circus 51	Lille	—		1	SPITFIRE 2B	2				—	Me109E	1	1	1
14	242²	1951	2035	Roadstead	Ostend	—								—	Me109E	—	—	1
20	242²	1215	1300	Roadstead	Dunkirk	—					1	FLAKSHIP	3	—	—			
20	242²	1525	1625	Roadstead	Conche Estuary	—					1	FLAKSHIP	3	—	—			
											1	TANKER	3					
											1	M/V	3	—	—			
21	242²	0820	0915	Roadstead	Off Staples	—					2	FLAKSHIPS	3	—	—			
21	242²	1255	145	Roadstead	Gravelines	—					1	FLAKSHIP	2	—	—			
27	242²	1415	1565	Offensive Patrol	Calais	SGT PROSSER	M	1	HURRICANE 2B	3	1	R-BOAT	3	—	Me109	1	3	—
																2		

One experienced fighter pilot who took part in the sweeps over France was Battle of Britain ace Eric Lock, pronounced fit again in June 1941 after his lengthy spell in the hospital (p59). Now posted as a flight commander to No. 611 Squadron, flying Spitfires from Hornchurch, Lock added four more enemy aircraft to his score during the next few weeks. He had 26 victories to date. On August 3, 1941, he failed to return from an operation over northern France and was posted missing, presumed killed. No one ever found out what had happened to him.

Between June 14 and September 3, 1941, Air Vice-Marshal Trafford Leigh-Mallory, who had commanded No. 12 Group in the Battle of Britain and who was now Air Officer Commanding (AOC) No. 11 Group, claimed that his pilots had destroyed 437 enemy fighters, with another 182 probably destroyed. Because the Luftwaffe never had more than 260 single-engine fighters in France and the Low Countries at any one time during this period, the claim was clearly exaggerated. The Germans, in fact, lost 128 aircraft, with a further 76 damaged, while Fighter Command lost 194 pilots. The Blenheim bomber squadrons of No. 2 Group, too, suffered appalling casualties, particularly during attacks on the Channel ports.

Fighter Command could not support such a rate of attrition, which became even more marked with the deployment of the Focke-Wulf 190. Within weeks, it had established air superiority for the Germans. In the end, on the orders of Britain's prime minister, Winston Churchill, large-scale sweeps over the Continent were discontinued in November 1941, to enable Fighter Command to gather its strength for a renewed offensive the following spring.

The Eagle squadrons

On October 8, 1940, while the Battle of Britain still raged, the British Secretary of State for Air, Sir Archibald Sinclair, declared that American volunteers serving with the Royal Air Force would be incorporated into a single fighting unit, an Eagle Squadron. In fact, this unit—No. 71 Squadron—had already formed on September 19, at RAF Church Fenton in Yorkshire. The squadron had a history dating back to 1917, when it had been manned by Australian personnel.

Ten American pilots fought in the Battle of Britain, and one of them, Pilot Officer William M.L. Fiske of No. 601 Squadron, lost his life. "Billy" Fiske died of his wounds while hospitalized on August 17, 1940 after bringing his damaged Hurricane back to his base at Tangmere.

Under a special arrangement with the United Kingdom, the American volunteers serving with the RAF were not required to relinquish their US citizenship. Most arrived in Britain by way of the Royal Canadian Air Force, which took them in with no questions asked; however, Pilot Officers Vernon C. Keough, Andrew Mamedoff, and Eugene Q. Tobin of No. 609 Squadron were three notable exceptions, who had traveled to France with the intention of joining the French Air Force in the tradition of the Lafayette Escadrille volunteers of World War I. But France fell before they could play an active part, and they found their way to England.

These three pilots were assigned to No. 71 Eagle Squadron, and they arrived at Church Fenton on October 19, 1940, to find that so far they were the only three, and that the squadron's equipment consisted of a single Miles Magister trainer aircraft. Ten days later, a squadron commander also arrived, Squadron Leader W. M. Churchill, DSO, DFC, from No. 605 Squadron. Some combat aircraft also arrived—not Spitfires, as the pilots had hoped, but Brewster Buffaloes, which were used for training until they were replaced by Hawker Hurricanes in November. The squadron flew Hurricanes until August 1941, when it rearmed with Spitfire Mk IIAs; these were replaced in turn with Mk VAs soon afterward.

ABOVE The "boxing chicken," based on a Walt Disney cartoon character, was adopted as the unofficial insignia of the Eagle Squadrons.

LEFT: This attractive shoulder flash was worn by all pilots of the eagle squadrons.

BELOW A leading American Eagle pilot, Don Gentile is pictured here later in the war, with his P-51B Mustang "Shangri-La."

Meanwhile, by May 1941, a second Eagle Squadron, No. 121, had formed at Kirton-in-Lindsay, Lincolnshire, and a third, No. 133, formed at Coltishall in Norfolk in August. Both were equipped with Hurricanes, much to the pilots' disappointment, but these were exchanged for Spitfire Vs by the end of the year.

The Eagle Squadrons, operating from various bases, were initially assigned to defense duties, patrolling the English coastline or covering convoys, but early in 1942, having received Spitfires, they began taking part in fighter sweeps over the Continent.

On August 19, 1942, the three Eagle Squadrons operated as a wing for the first time, joining other squadrons of Fighter Command in covering Operation Jubilee, the disastrous and costly landing by mainly Canadian forces at Dieppe. Nos. 71 and 133 Squadrons flew four missions over the landing area, and No. 121 Squadron flew three. Between them, they claimed 9 enemy aircraft destroyed, 4 probably destroyed, and 14 damaged for the loss of two Spitfires, both from No. 121 Squadron.

Some 250 American pilots served with the Eagle Squadrons. Of these, 78 were killed and 16 became prisoners of war. Of the latter, seven were captured as the result of an unfortunate incident on September 4, 1942, when No. 133 Squadron, flying 12 brand-new Spitfire IXs and escorting Boeing B-17s in an attack on Morlaix, became lost in bad weather. Only one pilot made it home; 11 ran out of fuel over the Brest Peninsula, 4 of whom were killed and the remainder taken prisoner.

It was a sad end to the Eagle Squadrons' association with the RAF. Three weeks later, at a ceremonial parade at Debden in Essex, where the three squadrons were now based, they were transferred to VIII Fighter Command of the United States Army Air Force, becoming the 334th, 335th, and 336th Fighter Squadrons of the 4th Fighter Group.

The Group continued to fly Spitfires until early in 1943, when it rearmed with the Republic P-47 Thunderbolt.

Some of the former Eagle Squadron pilots went on to become household names. Foremost among them was Don Gentile, who gained the first of his 27 victories, a Junkers Ju 88 and a Focke-Wulf Fw 190, over Dieppe while flying with No. 133 Squadron. For this, he was awarded the Distinguished Flying Cross. Gentile survived the war, only to be killed in a Lockheed T-33 jet trainer accident in 1951.

And there was Don Blakeslee, who also scored two "kills" while flying with No. 133 Squadron. In April 1943 he became the first Thunderbolt pilot to destroy an enemy aircraft, an Fw 190, and in January 1944 he assumed command of the 4th Fighter Group, known as the "Debden Eagles." He ended the war with a score of 15.5 enemy aircraft destroyed and later commanded the 27th Fighter Escort Wing, whose Republic F-84 Thunderjets participated in the Korean War. He died in 2008, aged 89.

LEFT Don Blakeslee gained two victories with No 133 Squadron, and went on to command the USAAF's 4th Fighter Group, flying P-47 Thunderbolts.

BELOW Pilots of the 334th Fighter Squadron, 4th Fighter Group, Debden, 1942. Lt Col Chesley Peterson is in the Spitfire's cockpit. All the pilots here flew with No 71 Squadron RAF.

" Eagles in action

By the summer of 1942, large formations of Spitfires had been crossing the Channel with the twofold objective of engaging the Luftwaffe and attacking enemy shipping. Often, this meant squadrons flying from their respective bases to make rendezvous at an airfield closer to the target area. On May 31, 1943, for example, No. 121 Eagle Squadron deployed from North Weald in Essex to Martlesham Heath, near Ipswich in Suffolk, to take part in a cross-Channel sweep with three other Spitfire squadrons.

At 15:05 hours on May 31, the Wing—47 Spitfire VBs in total, led by Wing Commander Scott-Malden—left Martlesham and set course for Walcheren at sea level. No. 222 Squadron was in front, 121 Squadron second, and 331 Squadron followed with 403 Squadron in the rear. The Wing Intelligence summary describes the operation.

"North of Blankenberghe the Wing split up, 403 Squadron scouting the coast between Ostend and Blankenberghe but seeing no shipping to attack. 222 Squadron and 121 Squadron continued North East to Walcheren where they found two diesel-engined minesweepers close in shore near West Kapelle. All pilots attacked in turn and both vessels turned for shore, severely damaged. P/O Beaumont, 222 Squadron, was

hit by M/G fire from one minesweeper and force-landed down wind in a field on Walcheren Island. He is believed safe.

"121 Squadron continued to a point North East of Walcheren Island and in the Scheldt Estuary an armed trawler was attacked by all pilots. Following S/L Kennard's attack, explosions were seen. 331 Squadron had also attacked and the vessel was later seen to sink after blazing fiercely. In making his attack F/Lt Allen (USA) is believed to have hit the sea. He climbed to 1,000ft [305m] and then crashed 4 miles [6km] off shore, the A/C sinking immediately. He was not seen to get out.

"As they turned from the Walcheren coast, 331 Squadron were followed out by two Me 109Fs. The whole squadron turned and one E/A pulled up to port, the other breaking away downwards. Red 2 Lt. Gran (Norwegian), 331 Squadron, fired at the former from 250 yards [229m] range from astern and below, seeing strikes behind the cockpit, and the E/A dived smoking black. Yellow 1, Lt. Berg (Norwegian), 331 Squadron, followed him down firing two short bursts from dead astern at 500 yards [457m] range. This E/A is claimed as damaged by the two pilots concerned. The second E/A had been about to attack Red 4 Sgt. Fearnley (Norwegian), 331 Squadron, who turned and dived firing from

OPPOSITE TOP In 1942, with the United States in the war, the Eagle squadrons began to receive much publicity. This issue of Collier's Weekly (August 22, 1942) features a photo spread by the famed photographer Robert Capa.

OPPOSITE BOTTOM Many sorties were flown against German installations on Walcheren Island, which was to be the scene of bitter fighting later in the war.

RIGHT A Dornier Do 217, the principal German bomber type encountered over France and the Low Countries from 1942.

BELOW Chesley "Pete" Peterson flew 130 sorties with the Eagle Squadrons before transferring to the 4th Fighter Group. He became the 4th FG's commanding officer in April 1943.

A few weeks later, on August 19, 1942, all the Eagle squadrons were operating over Dieppe, covering the "Reconnaissance in Force," as the ill-fated landing was later termed. In his combat report, Pilot Officer R. N. Beaty of No. 133 Squadron described his experience:

"I was flying Blue 3. I was at 5,000ft [1,524m] flying south towards Dieppe when I saw one Fw 190 about 3,000ft [914m] below me. I went down, losing Blue 4 on the break, but pulled violently up to the right when two Fw 190s opened fire behind me. I made a turn and a half and came out below and behind the Fw 190s as they pulled out of their dive. This was just over a thin cloud layer. I gave the second Fw 190 a long burst of cannon and M/G at about 350 yards [320m], but was unable to close as we were both in full stall position. I observed strikes behind the cockpit and on the hood. He fell off the stall towards the clouds, seemingly under control. I stalled down through cloud and recovered about 2,000ft [610m] above water. As I recovered, a Fw 190 fell through the clouds about 100 yards [91m] from me in a spin and crashed in the water. There was no sign of the pilot. I saw no other Spitfires in this area throughout the engagement . . . I am sure that the Fw 190 I saw crash is the same one I fired at.

"A few minutes later, I was at 5,000ft flying west about 5 miles [8km] north of the convoy, when two Do 217s passed under me, headed east. The rear one was already engaged by a number of Spitfires as were the two Fw 190 escorts. I half-rolled and dove after the leading Do 217, who jettisoned his bombs and pulled up into a steep left-hand climbing turn. I gave a two-second burst, mostly machine guns . . . and saw parts of the rear turret fly off. The range was 200 yards [183m] closing to 75 yards [69m]. The rear gunner stopped firing at me at the same time las I saw the hits on his turret. I claim this aircraft as damaged."

astern at 180 yards [165m] and seeing strikes. The E/A was engaged at the same time by Red 3 Lt. Som (Norwegian), 331 Squadron who, diving gave a short burst at 500 yards closing in to 150 yards [137m] astern. Tracer strikes were seen on the E/A's tail followed by an explosion behind the cockpit. The E/A then crashed into the sea and is claimed as destroyed, shared by Red 3 and Red 4. Three Fw 190s were encountered by 222 Squadron on the way home off the Belgian coast. They were attacked but no claims were made."

They kept the spits flying: The ground crews

It took a lot of people to keep a Spitfire flying. Each Spitfire had a two-man ground crew routinely assigned to it; one of the pair, the most highly qualified, was a corporal. Other tradesmen—armorers, wireless mechanics, electricians, and instrument technicians—also played their part in maintaining the aircraft as required. Exercising general supervision over the ground crews was a sergeant, qualified in each trade, who was directly responsible to a flight sergeant, who in turn acted as technical adviser should any difficulties arise. The flight sergeant, known as "Chief" to his officers and men alike, was himself answerable to the Station Engineering Officer.

When the ground crews reported to the squadron hangar (or dispersal) each morning, they were assigned their duties, which generally began with a complete daily inspection (D/I) of each aircraft. The engine fitters examined the engine, checking pipe lines for security; inspecting magnetos; looking for leaks in any of the components; and going over fuel, oil, and coolant tanks. Oil pressures and the oil and coolant temperatures were checked, together with the boost pressure. The variable pitch propeller was also examined and tested for its full range of movement once the engine was running.

During this time the riggers examined the airframe, checking the freedom of movement of the controls and correcting any slackness. The hydraulic system of the undercarriage was checked, as were tire pressures and oil levels in the air compressors, and the whole metal surface of the Spitfire meticulously examined for tears and signs of corrosion. Also, the aircraft—particularly the cockpit interior—had to be cleared of oil and dust. Meanwhile, an electrician, assigned to the aircraft from the squadron's 'pool' of technicians, tested the Spitfire's transmitting and receiving equipment and checked the batteries, coils, and wiring system. Climbing into the cockpit, an instrument fitter checked the settings of the aircraft's altimeter, air speed indicator, directional gyro, artificial horizon, rpm indicator, turn and bank indicator, and compass, as well as the all-important reflector sight.

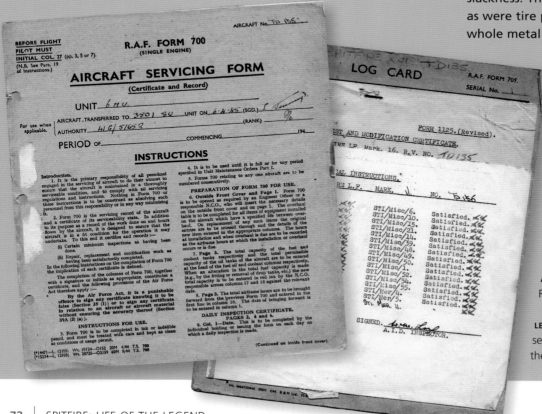

ABOVE Dated 1940, this object is an oil can of the type issued to RAF engine and airframe fitters working on Spitfires.

LEFT Each aircraft had a technical log, a Form 700, on which its servicing record was meticulously entered. It had to be signed by the pilot when the aircraft was handed over to him.

Ground crews would work around the clock if necessary to keep the Spitfires airworthy, sometimes in the most appalling conditions, including rain, mud, and snow. As a result, the rapport forged between the pilots and their ground crews was excellent. Aircrew referred to the airmen who serviced their aircraft as "Erks," but it was a term of affection and was in no sense derogatory.

As the war progressed, airmen in the technical trades found themselves working alongside women. The Women's Auxiliary Air Force (WAAF) had been established in June 1939. At the outbreak of war there were only five trades in which women could enlist, but, as airwomen continued to do their work efficiently and well, the Air Ministry realized that there was enormous potential in expanding their activities, so that 26 trades were open to them by 1941, ranging from administrative assistant to wireless telegraph operator. WAAF personnel did not participate in active combat, although they experienced the same dangers as their male counterparts when the RAF's airfields were under attack. One of their most vital tasks during the Battle of Britain was to act as plotters in Fighter Command's operations rooms.

While all this was going on the armorers arrived with the ammunition boxes, each containing 300 rounds in a belt. These were fitted into their slots inside the wing structure, one on either side of the battery of four 0.303-inch machine guns, and the belt fed into the breech mechanisms. The armorers also checked the harmonization of the eight machine guns, whose fire was set to converge at 250 yards (229m) in front of the fighter's nose. A three-second burst of fire would send 10lb (4.5kg) of lead into a relatively small area of the target aircraft, enough to cause significant damage.

Finally, the aircraft would be refueled and the Merlin engine tested. It was now ready to be handed over to the pilot. Of course, when the squadron was under the pressure of combat—at the height of the Battle of Britain, for example—the whole procedure would be carried out very quickly. A Spitfire could be checked over, refueled, and rearmed in less than ten minutes between sorties.

The Air Transport Auxiliary, established in 1939, was another important organization, its task being to ferry aircraft from the maintenance units and manufacturers to the operational squadrons. All of its personnel were civilian, and many were women. The jaws of fighter pilots on many a Fighter Command airfield dropped wide open when a replacement Spitfire taxied in and a woman stepped down from the cockpit.

ABOVE LEFT Ground crew working on a Spitfire of No 332 (Norwegian) Squadron, which formed at RAF Catterick in Yorkshire in 1942.

LEFT The battery charger for the trolley-accumulator, the battery that was plugged into the Spitfire engine during the engine start-up process; see photograph above.

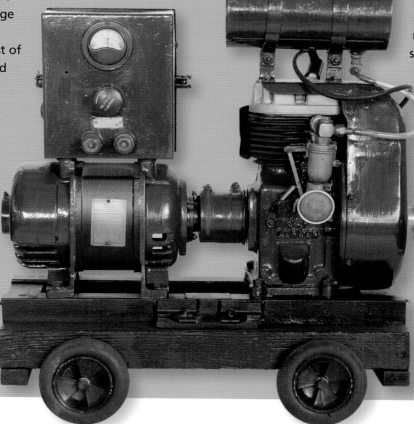

The new danger: The Focke-Wulf Fw 190

RAF Fighter Command entered 1942 with 60 squadrons of Spitfires; a threefold expansion achieved over little more than 18 months. More squadrons would be formed in the course of the year, as the demands of the Middle East and Far East, where a new theater of hostilities had just opened up against Japan, made inroads into these home-based assets. Despite this, it seemed that the Command, in 1942, was strong enough not only to fulfill its primary task of defending Britain from air attack but also to renew its offensive against the enemy.

However, the rapier thrust of disillusionment was quick to come, and it was delivered by the Focke-Wulf 190. From the moment the Fw 190 first clashed with the Spitfire V, it was clear that the latter was outclassed in every aspect of combat except turning radius.

On February 12, 1942, news came that the German battle cruisers *Scharnhorst* and *Gneisenau* and the heavy cruiser *Prinz Eugen* had left their harbors on the French Atlantic coast and were proceeding at speed through the English Channel, making for the North German ports; this news was broken by a Spitfire

ABOVE A neat formation of Spitfires of No 611 Squadron, one of the first units to re-arm with the Mk IX version. This photograph was taken early in 1943.

BELOW The Channel Dash, February 12, 1942. Germany put up every available fighter to cover the escape of the *Scharnhorst*, *Gneisenau* and *Prinz Eugen*.

pilot who had located the warships off Le Touquet. What followed, as far as the British were concerned, was a complete fiasco. During the hours that followed, RAF Bomber Command launched a total of 242 sorties, but, although most aircraft reached the target area, only one in six managed to attack the warships. Most failed to sight the enemy vessels at all; others were unable to bomb, because of the low cloud base. Worse, 15 bombers were shot down, in addition to three Bristol Beaufort torpedo-bombers.

Also among the victims were six Fairey Swordfish biplane torpedo-bombers of No. 825 Squadron, Fleet Air Arm. Led by Lieutenant-Commander Eugene Esmonde, an Irishman from Tipperary, the Swordfish circled over Manston, waiting for their fighter escort of three Spitfire squadrons. Only No. 72 Squadron turned up, to find that the Swordfish had already gone. In the words of one of the Spitfire pilots:

"It was an absolutely foul day. We were told to take off and rendezvous with a strike of Fleet Air Arm Swordfish torpedo-bombers which were to attack the warships from Manston. We arrived overhead exactly on the time we had been given according to our Ops Room clock. You couldn't see from one side of the airfield to the other, conditions were so bad, but we flew one circuit around Manston and were then told over the R/T that

the Navy aircraft had gone, so we set course for the action at very low level.

"We eventually sighted the warships just as the Swordfish were going in, and we were too late; they were mown down. Our whole squadron made a rather abortive attack on the warships, strafing their superstructures, and it was remarkable that no one was shot down. It was a very tragic affair, and it was tragic to see the Swordfish going into the water, but there was nothing we could do, because it was the flak that was getting them."

All six Swordfish were destroyed, with the loss of all but a handful of their aircrew. Lieutenant-Commander Esmonde was later awarded a posthumous Victoria Cross.

The other two squadrons assigned to escort the Swordfish, Nos. 121 (Eagle) and 401 (RCAF), had cut straight out over the Kent coast in an attempt to locate the torpedo-bombers en route. Failing to find them, they flew back to Manston and headed out to sea again, reaching the combat area a few minutes after the Swordfish had made their attack. The Spitfire pilots soon found themselves engaged in savage air combats with enemy fighters, as did other Spitfire squadrons sent out to cover attacking bombers.

The Germans had assembled a formidable array of fighters to cover the naval force: 102 Bf 109Fs, covering the sector Le Havre-Cherbourg; 90 Focke-Wulf Fw 190s, covering the Channel narrows from Abbeville to Calais; and 60 more Bf 109s, covering the final sector from the river Scheldt to Wilhelmshaven, the warships' destination. The air battles that raged over the Channel cost the RAF and Fleet Air Arm dearly; 31 aircraft failed to return, mostly bombers. The Luftwaffe lost seven aircraft. All three German warships reached their bases in Germany, although *Scharnhorst* and *Gneisenau* were damaged by mines.

During the next few weeks, Spitfire losses climbed steeply as the Fw 190s and Bf 109Fs continued to show their superiority over the Spitfire V. For example, 11 Spitfires were lost on April 4, 1942, 15 on April 12, and 12 on April 25. Spitfire losses for the whole of the month were 59 aircraft. The situation for Fighter Command was fast becoming critical.

ABOVE A pilot's life preserver, known as the "Mae West" after the American film star for a reason that became obvious once it was inflated.

LEFT A captured Focke-Wulf Fw 190A-3 being examined by Air Ministry specialists. Its pilot, Oberleutnant Arnim Faber of JG2, landed in error at RAF Pembrey, near Swansea, Wales on June 23, 1942.

Flying the Spitfire Mk V in combat

One instance of hectic combat with Fw 190s was described by Flying Officer Colin Hodgkinson, a remarkable man who, like Douglas Bader, had lost both legs in a flying accident and who now flew with artificial ones. Hodgkinson's first action took place in August 1943, when he was flying with No. 611 Squadron, part of the Tangmere Wing led by Wing Commander "Johnnie" Johnson. The squadron was still equipped with Spitfire LF.VBs, armed with four Browning machine guns and two 20mm Hispano cannon.

"The wing was taking a box of Mitchells (North American B-25s) briefed to bomb Poix Aerodrome, near Amiens. Things were quiet on the way over. I was feeling confident, glued to my No. 1 with engine singing sweetly and all the wing reassuringly visible in the clear air. Looking ahead, I could even see the bombers, beautifully compact like a double-six domino. We crossed the coast, flew on in silence, and then, as the Mitchells queued up for their run, the controller's voice came in: 'Forty plus bandits climbing to meet you from the south-west.'

"South-west. I peered out alertly in that direction. I saw Poix Aerodrome, flashes around it and black-grey smoke lifting lazily. I saw Spitfires nosing over the smoke in a gentle starboard turn. But I saw no enemy; it was eerie, no one appeared to be disturbed. Then I saw a bomber go down, cartwheeling slowly with one wing gone, brick-coloured flame oozing from the belly. A parachute opened like a white bubble and at that moment everyone started talking.

'Two bastards at three o'clock.'

'Three plus twelve o'clock above.'

Johnnie's voice, impossible to mistake: 'Going down. Going down.'

"I turned on my back to follow the squadron, but I was far too late. I looked round wildly, seeing nothing but an empty sky and the earth coming nearer, scribbled with smoke. I had lost my No. 1, lost the squadron, lost myself. I was electrified, amazed. This is what they had warned me about, this happened to all tyros [novices]. Never get isolated. Never leave your No. 1. But if you're alone in a dogfight, turn, turn, turn.

"I pulled up abruptly and turned tight, tighter, too tightly—'greying out' for a moment. As the blood returned and I rose back in my seat I saw them: four Fw 190s to port and above. They flipped over and came straight down past me, wings winking tracer in white cords which fizzed

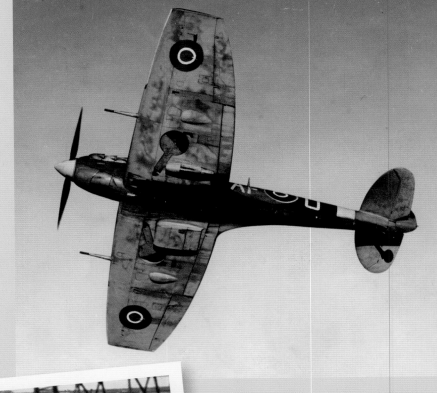

ABOVE A Spitfire VB shows off its clipped wings, which increased its rate of roll and enhanced its performance at medium and low altitudes.

LEFT Colin Hodgkinson (center) putting his best foot forward. This photograph was taken when he was in the Royal Auxiliary Air Force, post-war.

OPPOSITE TOP A fighter pilot's accoutrements—flying helmet, oxygen mask, goggles and microphone lead; the opening for the right earpiece is visible in the lining.

OPPOSITE BOTTOM The powerful Hawker Typhoon was not a success as a pure fighter, but went on to make its mark as a fighter-bomber in north-west Europe.

past my tail. Missed! And the first moment of panic had gone. I glanced in my mirror, saw nothing there, and went down vertically myself with no clear intention but to find a Spit and stick close with it. I saw one in a shallow dive ahead, but as I closed it went on fire, turning gracefully on its back to vanish spinning in a wake of smoke. I felt immediately alone again, though clearly in the middle of the battle.

"The headphones were a babble of exclamations, oaths, warnings. Some pilots knew what they were doing, were fighting together, helping each other. No one was helping me. I pulled the stick to my stomach and started my idiot turning.

"I don't remember for how long I turned. I remember seeing a 190 sheering in towards me, apparently in a half roll, taking a hopeless shot as he plummeted away on his back, and watching the tracer stream alarmingly near a Spitfire which screamed past in pursuit.

"Finally, bemused and becoming dizzy, I saw two Spits formating and climbed up to join them. To my astonishment, we were crossing the coast. I looked below: more Spitfires, and above still more. How long had the action lasted, three, seven, ten minutes? I had no idea, though my petrol gauge told me I couldn't have stayed over the target more than a few minutes longer . . .

"What a damned fool I must have looked, going round and round in the middle of a battle like a cat chasing its tail. But I had at least seen the enemy, had been fired on and fired, and was at least in one piece. And I had absorbed, I hoped, some useful lessons."

When the Fw 190 had entered service in the summer of 1941, the only RAF fighter with the potential of matching it was the Hawker Typhoon, which was then being delivered to No. 56 Squadron at Duxford. But the Typhoon was beset by all sort of problems to do with its airframe and Napier Sabre engine; although it was fast and handled well at medium and low altitudes, its performance at high altitude was inferior to that of both the Fw 190 and the Bf 109F, and its rate of climb was poor. The Typhoon would eventually find its true vocation as a formidable fighter-bomber. It was the Spitfire that would continue to hold the line against the Focke-Wulf 190.

Spitfire Mk V

Developed from the Mk II airframe, the Mk V was to be the major Spitfire production version, with 6,479 examples completed. The debut of the Spitfire V came just in time, for in May 1941 the Luftwaffe fighter units began to receive the improved Messerschmitt Bf 109F. The Mk VB and VC were armed with cannon and machine guns, requiring a dual gun rocker button (p65) to fire one or both.

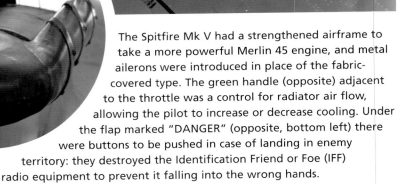

The Spitfire Mk V had a strengthened airframe to take a more powerful Merlin 45 engine, and metal ailerons were introduced in place of the fabric-covered type. The green handle (opposite) adjacent to the throttle was a control for radiator air flow, allowing the pilot to increase or decrease cooling. Under the flap marked "DANGER" (opposite, bottom left) there were buttons to be pushed in case of landing in enemy territory: they destroyed the Identification Friend or Foe (IFF) radio equipment to prevent it falling into the wrong hands.

Opposite is the cockpit of Spitfire VC JG891, which also bore the civil registration G-LFVC. The illustration above shows detail from Mk VB ab910 in the colors of No. 303 (Polish) Squadron; the club-wielding Donald Duck is the personal insignia of the squadron commander, Squadron Leader Jan Zumbach. To the right is the cockpit; just visible top left is an additional instrument that logs the G forces the aircraft experiences, effectively reporting on any pilots who put the structure under too much stress; it is reset by crew before each flight.

Defending the bombers: Spitfire escort missions

Late in 1941 the squadrons of No. 2 Group, RAF—which had been equipped with the Bristol Blenheim Mk IV and whose task had been to carry out daylight attacks on enemy shipping and targets in western Europe— began to rearm with new types of twin-engined medium bomber. Two of these were of American design; the first was the "Douglas Boston," the RAF's name for the DB-7 attack bomber.

The Bostons had formed part of a French consignment of 100 aircraft having been taken over by the RAF after France was overrun in 1940. Designated "Boston I" and "Boston II," these aircraft were respectively used for crew conversion and intruder operations. The RAF also received 781 improved DB-7As, named "Boston III," and 202 Boston IIIAs. The Boston entered service with No. 88 Squadron in October 1941, and a few weeks later it joined a second Boston-equipped unit, No. 226 Squadron, at Swanton Morley in Norfolk. The two squadrons made their first operational sorties with Bostons on February 12, 1942, during the "Channel Dash" by the *Scharnhorst*, *Gneisenau*, and *Prinz Eugen* (p74). Ten Bostons set out, but only one found a target and attacked. The Bostons did not go into action against land targets until March 8 1942, when aircraft of Nos. 88 and 226 Squadrons bombed the Matford works at Poissy, France, while others, under strong Spitfire escort,

ABOVE Death of a blockade runner: the German freighter Münsterland in flames in the English Channel. After repeated air attacks, she was destroyed by shore batteries on January 20, 1944.

LEFT Attacks on enemy shipping in the English Channel were never a "piece of cake"—the title of this booklet explaining RAF jargon to the uninitiated.

took part in a diversionary attack against a power station at Comines, in Belgium.

The second American type was the Lockheed Ventura, which was basically a military version of the Lodestar transport and which was originally developed to meet an RAF requirement for a successor to the Lockheed Hudson maritime patrol aircraft. It entered service with No. 2 Group of Bomber Command in October 1942, equipping No. 21 Squadron at Methwold, in Norfolk.

The original belief was that the Boston and the Ventura were fast enough to make low-level daylight attacks without having to rely on a strong fighter escort. In fact, only the third new type to enter service with No. 2 Group was capable of doing so; this was the de Havilland Mosquito. The vulnerability of the other two was soon demonstrated.

In 1943, the Spitfire squadrons of Fighter Command devoted much of their effort to escorting the medium bombers of No. 2 Group in attacks on fringe targets in France and the Low Countries. On occasion, they were also tasked with escorting the Westland Whirlwind fighter-bombers of No. 263 Squadron in attacks on enemy shipping, a job the Spitfire pilots did not relish, as the intelligence summary of No. 118 Squadron for November 15, 1941, relates:

"The Middle Wallop Wing rendezvoused with the Whirlwinds of 263 Squadron over Warmwell and carried out a sweep of the Channel Islands area. The whole sortie seems to have been one long muddle. The Whirlwinds led the Spits much too far south and then returned right over the flak area. 501 Squadron were sent out to deal with a few Huns that put in an appearance when we were on the way back. 118 went back to help, but 501 were not located. The net result was at least three planes damaged by flak and

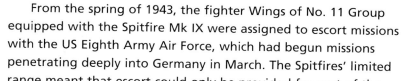

RIGHT Pierre Clostermann pictured after the war, bearing many British and French decorations. He flew both Spitfires and Hawker Tempests.

BELOW A formation of B-17 flying fortresses on a bombing mission over Germany. The American bombers suffered appalling losses until they received adequate fighter escort.

enemy aircraft, and one shot down, and all we could claim was one enemy aircraft damaged."

From the spring of 1943, the fighter Wings of No. 11 Group equipped with the Spitfire Mk IX were assigned to escort missions with the US Eighth Army Air Force, which had begun missions penetrating deeply into Germany in March. The Spitfires' limited range meant that escort could only be provided for part of the way, leaving the bombers to continue unescorted into Germany.

The USAAF fitted P-47 Thunderbolts with long-range fuel tanks, enabling the fighters to penetrate as far as the German border, but it was not long before the German fighter leaders developed new combat tactics meant to eliminate the Americans' advantage. The Focke-Wulfs and Messerschmitts would attack the Thunderbolts as they crossed the Dutch coast, forcing the P-47s to jettison their auxiliary tanks to increase maneuverability. As a consequence, the American bombers suffered appalling casualties in 1943, particularly on two major raids, the first against Regensburg on August 17 and the second against Schweinfurt on October 14. On the latter day the Luftwaffe flew 500 sorties and destroyed 60 of the 280 bombers taking part—more than 20 percent.

On each mission, the Spitfire squadrons went out to escort the Flying Fortress and Liberators home.

"Here and there in the Fortress formation there were gaps [wrote French pilot Pierre Clostermann, flying with No. 602 Squadron]. From close to you could see machines with one, sometimes two stationary engines and feathered propellers. Others had lacerated tail-planes, gaping holes in the fuselages, wings tarnished by fire or glistening with black oil oozing from gutted engines . . . You could imagine the blood pouring over the heaps of empty cartridges, the pilot nursing his remaining engines and anxiously eyeing the long white trail of petrol escaping from his riddled tanks . . . "

Escort missions: The Spitfire pilots' view

"It was a clear afternoon, and we first saw their contrails many miles away, as well as the thinner daring contrails of the enemy fighters above and on either flank. As we closed the gap we could see that they had taken a terrible mauling, for there were gaping holes in their precise formations. Some Fortresses were gradually losing height, and a few stragglers, lagging well behind, were struggling to get home on three engines.

"We swept well behind the stragglers and drove off a few 109s and 110s, but the great air battle was over, and what a fight it must have been, because more than half the bombers we nursed across the North Sea were shot up. One or two ditched in the sea, and many others, carrying dead or badly injured crew members, had to make crash landings. How we longed for more drop tanks, so that some of the many hundreds of Spitfires based in Britain could play their part in the great battles over Germany."

So wrote Wing Commander "Johnnie" Johnson, now commanding the all-Canadian Spitfire Wing at Kenley, in Surrey, as his Spitfires made rendezvous with the B-17s returning from Schweinfurt on that terrible October day in 1944. The problem was not that the Spitfire was not equipped to carry drop tanks—in fact, both the Mk V and Mk IX Spitfire had provision for auxiliary blister-type drop tanks of 45, 90, or 170 gallons, or a cigar-shaped "slipper" tank of 50 gallons (227 liters). Instead the problem was that the drop tanks were in short supply.

While the squadrons of No. 11 Group witnessed the martyrdom of the American bomber crews at close quarters, their counterparts in No. 12 Group continued to escort the RAF's medium bombers. Two of the squadrons involved were No. 118, operating from Coltishall in Norfolk, and No. 167, based at Ludham a few miles away and nearer the coast. No. 118 Squadron's Intelligence Officer, Flight Lieutenant Le Mesurier (called "Misery" by the pilots) describes an operation on February 13, 1943 when the two squadrons made two sweeps to IJmuiden, Holland, in support of Ventura bombers.

"The first sweep was carried out without opposition. No results of bombing were observed and it is thought that the Venturas may not have dropped their bombs, so a second sweep was laid on after lunch.

"This time, Focke-Wulf 190s attempted to frustrate the bombing. As the coast was crossed by the bombers and their escort 10 miles [16km] south of IJmuiden, the enemy put up eight aircraft who made a head-on attack on the bombers from extreme range as they made their sweep towards the target. 118 positioned themselves in the sun and

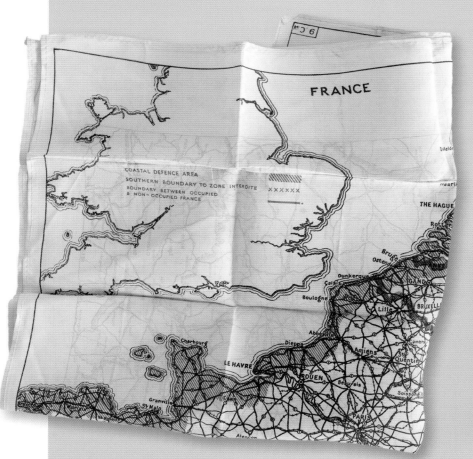

LEFT A map issued to Allied aircrews showing the extent of the German defenses along the coast of France and the Low Countries.

BELOW "Johnnie" Johnson in the cockpit of his Spitfire, which bears the legend "Bader's Bus Co - still running," painted on the nose to keep up morale after Bader was shot down over France in August 1941.

approached IJmuiden parallel to the coast at 12,000ft [3,658m], the bombers and escort being at 9,000ft [2,743m]. After making their run, the bombers and escort dived down to sea level. Further attacks were made by the 190s and we sent down Red and Yellow Sections, Blue Section remaining above as top cover.

"Four enemy aircraft were seen climbing to attack the bombers on their port side; they were engaged by our aircraft and three dived rapidly for the coast, but the fourth pressed home its attack with explosive ammunition. It was later pursued by Red Section and climbed away very steeply, but not before Shepherd, Smith and Watson had got in short bursts from quarter astern as they climbed after it. The 190 got away in cloud at full throttle with black smoke coming from it, but no claim was made. The 190 completely outclimbed our poor Spit Vs.

"This time the bombing looked very successful and the bombs fell in the docks area, a direct hit being made on an 8,000-ton MV, the rearmost of three ships moored along the southern quay."

However, few attacks were as successful as this one: in an earlier raid, on December 6, 1942, 36 Bostons, 47 Venturas, and 10 Mosquitoes had set out to make an unescorted low-level attack on the Philips radio and valve factory at Eindhoven, Holland. The factory was badly damaged, but 9 Venturas, 5 Bostons and a Mosquito failed to return, and another 37 Venturas, 13 Bostons and 3 Mosquitoes were damaged.

The result did not encourage future operations of this kind, and the unsuitability of the Ventura as a day bomber was further tragically underlined on May 3, 1943, when 10 out of 11 Venturas of No. 487 Squadron, RNZAF (Royal New Zealand Airforce) were shot down during an attack on a power station in Amsterdam.

4 Spitfires Overseas

Spitfires overseas

By the late 1930s the two new British monoplane fighters, the Hurricane and Spitfire, had represented such a major advance in fighter technology that they were attracting the attention of foreign air forces. Between 1936 and 1939 the governments of 13 foreign nations, starting with France, approached the Air Ministry for quotes. (The others were Belgium, Estonia, Turkey, Romania, Portugal, Switzerland, Yugoslavia, Holland, Greece, Bulgaria, Iran, and Lithuania.)

Hurricanes were supplied to Yugoslavia and Romania before the outbreak of World War II, but it was the Spitfire that most air forces wanted. The French, who were pursuing enquiries in the United States with a view to purchasing 100 Curtiss Hawk 75A fighters, were the biggest potential customers, and they asked whether Supermarine could deliver 100 Spitfires by the middle of 1939; they were also interested in acquiring a manufacturing license, as were Switzerland, Yugoslavia, Belgium, and Holland.

In September 1938 two Armée de l'Air pilots came to England to fly the Spitfire, and one aircraft, a Spitfire Mk I—the 251st production machine—was flown to France on July 18, 1939, for

evaluation; it was last seen at Orléans in a very dilapidated state some time after the German occupation.

It was not the first Spitfire to leave British soil. The French were also interested in acquiring a military version of the "High Speed Spitfire," which was a one-off digression from the main stream of Spitfire production. It was intended to present a direct challenge to Germany's Messerschmitt Bf 109 in a bid to capture the world air speed record. Supermarine took an aircraft off the Mk I production line and set about modifying it for the attempt; the wing was shortened and given a new tip, and the cockpit area was streamlined. A Rolls-Royce team, meanwhile, developed a racing

ABOVE Strange bedfellows—a Spitfire VC in formation with a Focke-Wulf Fw 190, both types having been supplied to the Turkish Air Force.

LEFT The French Air Force showed an interest in acquiring a military version of the High Speed Spitfire, but the plan came to nothing.

OPPOSITE TOP The High Speed Spitfire—also known simply as the "Speed Spitfire"—incorporated a number of aerodynamic refinements, including a streamlined cockpit canopy.

OPPOSITE BOTTOM Supermarine produced a comprehensive sales brochure for the Spitfire, and the fighter would undoubtedly have become a best-seller overseas had it not been for the onset of war.

version of the Merlin II engine, capable of producing 1995hp to give a level speed of 375mph (603km/h), and fitted with a de Havilland four-blade metal propeller. The aircraft was duly adapted and flown, and in July 1938 it was exhibited at the Brussels Air Show. However, by this time serious doubts were being expressed about its performance, and the project was abandoned. The Germans went on to establish their domination of the speed record arena on April 26, 1939, when a Messerschmitt Me 209V-1, specially designed for the purpose, set up a new absolute speed record of 466.92mph (755.138km/h). They cheated a little and called the aircraft the "Me 109R," to give the world the impression that it was merely a souped-up version of the standard fighter.

The onset of World War II thwarted any prospect of the Spitfire being exported, since every available aircraft was needed for the RAF. In fact, only two of the potential prewar customers received deliveries while the conflict was in progress. The major recipient was Turkey, which took delivery of 56 Mk VBs and 185 Mk IXs from 1943 onward. The aircraft were sold to Turkey at nominal prices, the British government realizing the need to keep that country in a state of neutrality following the failure of attempts to persuade her to join the Allied cause. Not to be outdone, the Germans also supplied the Turkish Air Force with a number of Focke-Wulf Fw 190A-5s, the two types operating side by side until they were replaced by P-47D Thunderbolts in the late 1940s.

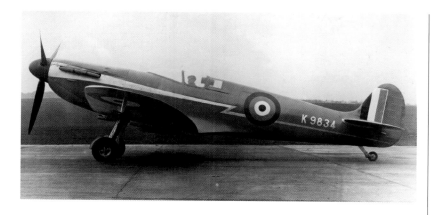

The other customer was Portugal, which received 15 Mk 1As in August 1943, together with some Hawker Hurricanes and Westland Lysanders. This initial purchase was followed by an order for 50 Spitfire VBs, most of which were delivered in 1943. The Spitfire Vs remained in first-line service until 1952, when they too were replaced by Republic P-47 Thunderbolts.

The RAF's first overseas Spitfire deployment occurred on November 1, 1939, when a single Spitfire—N3071, a Mk I modified for photographic reconnaissance—was sent to Seclin, near Lille. From this base, on November 18, Flying Officer Maurice Longbottom set out to photograph Aachen. The sortie proved abortive because of bad weather, but it demonstrated that the Spitfire was more than adequate for the all-important task of PR.

As the war progressed, the Spitfire and its naval variant, the Seafire, would see service in every theater of war, from the snows of north Russia to the coral islands of the Pacific. They would fly and fight over the desert sands of North Africa and the mountain ranges of Italy, over the mangrove swamps of northern Australia and the jungles of Burma. But, in 1942, the biggest deployment of Spitfires was made to the one place on Earth outside the United Kingdom that desperately needed them—the besieged island of Malta.

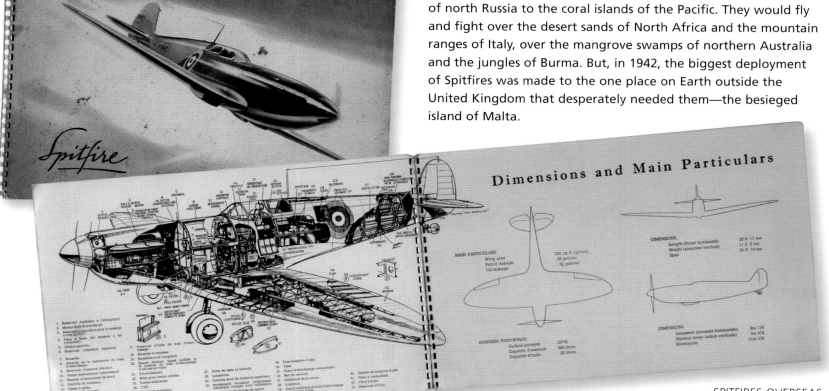

Spitfires over Malta

Malta's ordeal began on June 11, 1940, the day after Italy declared war on the Allies, when 35 Savoia-Marchetti SM.79 bombers of the *Regia Aeronautica*, escorted by Macchi MC.200 fighters, attacked Hal Far airfield and the seaplane depot of Kalafrana. One SM.79 was slightly damaged by one of four Gloster Sea Gladiator fighters that formed the island's only fighter defense. By the end of the day, Malta had been attacked seven times, and no Italian aircraft had been shot down.

Hawker Hurricanes were rushed to the island—the reinforcements being flown from aircraft carriers. Throughout 1941 these aircraft defended Malta against constant air attacks by Italian and German bombers, the later based on Sicily only 70 miles (112km) away. Early in 1942 the Luftwaffe began an all-out onslaught on the island. The threefold aim was to (1) destroy the RAF's fighter defenses on Malta by means of heavy and repeated air attacks on the airfields, (2) neutralize the bomber and torpedo-bomber bases on the island, and (3) attack the docks and harbor installations. When these objectives were achieved, Malta would be open to invasion.

Major-General Conrad, commanding the German air transport forces, was allocated 500 Junkers Ju 52 transport aircraft for the task of landing 70,000 German and Italian troops on the island. He wrote:

"I suggested that all B-2 aircraft (single-engined training machines) should be assembled to tow the DFS-230 gliders. As soon as the last bomb fell the latter should make pinpoint landings beside flak positions, known command posts and the mysterious caves [containing repair shops and so on]. Immediately afterwards six transport *Gruppen* would drop their paratroops over their allotted targets, and the four carrying airborne troops would land them on the first airfield to be captured."

LEFT A map of Malta and Gozo issued to the defending fighter pilots, giving the locations of radio beacons and frequencies.

BELOW LEFT Rescuers dig for survivors in Valletta after a heavy air raid. The people of Malta endured terrible hardships with great fortitude.

BELOW The American aircraft carrier USS *Wasp* was deployed to the Mediterranean to fly off desperately needed Spitfires for Malta.

ABOVE George Beurling, leading air ace of the siege of Malta, painting a "kill" marking on his Spitfire. Although generally called "Screwball Beurling" by the popular press, he was known as "Buzz" to his friends.

With the air defenses down to their last few Hurricanes and Malta starved of supplies, the situation was desperate. Air Vice-Marshal Hugh Lloyd, the RAF commander, stated:

"Our diet was a slice and a half of very poor bread with jam for breakfast, bully beef for lunch with one slice of bread, and the same fare for dinner . . . even the drinking water, lighting and heating were rationed. All the things which had been taken for granted closed down . . . Malta was faced with the unpleasant fact of being starved and forced into surrender from lack of equipment."

What Malta needed were supplies, and Spitfires to beat off the air attacks that would try to destroy the supply ships. The first 15 Spitfires reached Malta on March 7, 1942, flown in at enormous risk from the carrier HMS *Eagle*. With the surviving Hurricanes they held the line until April 20, when the American carrier USS *Wasp* flew off 54 Spitfires for Malta, of which 47 reached the island. By the end of the next day, under repeated air attack, only 18 remained airworthy, but on May 9 the USS *Wasp* and HMS *Eagle* sent off 64 more Spitfires, 60 reaching the island safely.

In the summer of 1942, supply convoys, battling their way though savage air attacks, at last began to reach the island, suffering terrible losses en route. On Malta itself, pilots and ground crews alike operated in terrible conditions, as one account tells:

"Tinned corned beef, dried peas, hard biscuits and olives formed the main diet with a sulphur pill taken after meals to ward off the raging diarrhoea. Pilots lived under the most trying conditions but were more fortunate than the over-worked ground crews who serviced and repaired aircraft with the same never-flagging devotion as their Battle of Britain comrades, despite the dust, the flies, the shortages of food and water, the bombings and strafings, and the lack of proper hangars in which to work, not to mention the acute shortage of spares . . . "

Overhead, the air battles raged. One of the Spitfire pilots was Squadron Leader Mike Stephens of No. 249 Squadron, based on Takali, who had a lucky escape:

"We had been scrambled soon after first light to intercept an incoming raid, and had become tangled with a bunch of 109s. In the ensuing dogfight I shot down two 109s and as so often happened found myself alone. I saw a single Spitfire in the distance and headed towards it with the object of joining up and making a pair, when I was surprised by a single 109 which I saw just too late. He scored a hit on my engine, which started smoking and eventually came to a grinding halt. In the meantime the 109 had headed for home, as soon as I turned into his attack. After my engine cut I had plenty of time to transmit for a fix before bailing out. I spent a long time in the water . . . "

The defense of Malta—which was awarded the George Cross for the tenacity of its people—produced several legends before the air attacks faded away after November 1942. Foremost among them was a Canadian Spitfire pilot, Pilot Officer George Beurling, also of No. 249 Squadron. When he arrived on Malta in June 1942 he had 2 victories to his credit; by the time he left, in November, his score had risen to 28.

BELOW Ground crew manhandling a Spitfire into its blast pen. Malta's airfields were situated close together and were dangerously vulnerable to air attack.

Spitfires over Africa

Throughout 1940 and 1941, the RAF's fighter resources in North Africa comprised, first, the Gloster Gladiator biplane, followed by the Hawker Hurricane and the Curtiss P-40 Kittyhawk. The first Spitfire squadron in North Africa, No. 145, was not established until April 1942, at Heliopolis. In the following month it received its first Spitfire VBs, fitted with tropical filters, and moved up to Gambut, from where it flew its first operational mission—as an escort for Hurricane fighter-bombers—on June 1.

During the next few weeks No. 145 was joined by two more Spitfire squadrons deployed from the United Kingdom, Nos. 92 and 601, which formed No. 244 Wing of No. 211 Group, together with the Hurricanes of No. 73 Squadron. The Wing operated a mixture of Spitfire VBs and VCs. Some of the latter—aircraft in storage at the Aboukir Aircraft Depot—were stripped down and used to intercept Junkers Ju 86P reconnaissance aircraft, which had been making regular overflights of the Suez Canal Zone at altitudes of 42,000ft (12,800m) from a base on the island of Crete. After three Ju 86Ps were shot down, the overflights ceased.

Although the Spitfires of No. 244 Wing made an important contribution to operations by the Desert Air Force, the main effort throughout the summer of 1942 was sustained by the Hurricane and Kittyhawk squadrons, joined later in the year by three squadrons of the 57th Fighter Group, USAAF, which was also equipped with P-40s.

It was not until after the Allied landings in the Vichy French colonies of Algeria and Morocco in November 1942 (Operation Torch) that the Spitfire began to make its mark on the North African campaign. Among the first to arrive after the landings were the Spitfires of the USAAF's 31st Fighter Group, which flew into Tafaroui, Algeria on November 8; the Spitfires of Nos. 81 and 242 Squadrons were also early arrivals, deploying to the Algerian airfield of Maison Blanche on November 9; No. 154 Squadron flew into Djidjelli on November 12, and No. 152 flew into Maison Blanche; and No. 111 arrived at Bone from Gibraltar on November 14.

As the Allies began their advance into Tunisia, the lack of suitable forward airfields became a serious problem. Existing airfields became overcrowded, and their ever-increasing distance from the front line meant that the fighters could spend only ten minutes, or even less, in the combat area. In an attempt to remedy the situation, the Spitfires of No. 93 Squadron were deployed forward to a muddy airstrip at Medjez el Bab early in December, but they had barely arrived when they were shot up on the ground by Bf 109s, from Germany.

RIGHT The Luftwaffe's massive Messerschmitt Me 323 transports suffered terrible losses in frantic attempts to resupply the Afrika Korps. One is pictured here moments before being shot down.

FAR RIGHT The desert was an inhospitable place. Eventually, the RAF produced booklets to provide aircrew with useful tips on how to survive.

DESERT SURVIVAL

AIR MINISTRY PAMPHLET 225

In February 1943, sufficient Spitfire Mk IXs had arrived in North Africa to permit the reequipment of No. 72 Squadron, just in time for the Allied offensive that would end, on April 7, with the link-up of the American II Corps and the British Eighth Army, the essential preliminary to the final Allied drive northward into Tunisia. During the final stages of the campaign, RAF Spitfires joined USAAF and South African Air Force P-40s in wreaking havoc among the German formations of transport aircraft that were attempting to ferry men and supplies into Tunisia; for example, on April 18, 1943, 12 Spitfires of No. 92 Squadron and 47 P-40s destroyed 77 Junkers Ju 52s, more enemy aircraft than had been shot down in a single day during the Battle of Britain.

Back on November 8, 1942, as the Allied forces were going ashore in Operation Torch, many of the troops had looked up to see what appeared to be formations of Spitfires bearing American markings, patrolling overhead. They were in fact Supermarine Seafires, the Royal Navy's version of the Spitfire, making their combat debut.

A new challenge to Allied air superiority in North Africa had now arrived in North Africa in the shape of the Focke-Wulf 190, which operated mainly in the fighter-bomber role under the control of Fliegerführer Tunis. The deployment of the Fw 190s posed a serious threat to the Allied airfields, crowded as they were; for example, in mid-December five Spitfire squadrons—Nos. 72, 81, 93, 111, and 152—were crammed into Souk el Arba, 60 miles (96km) behind the front line.

To counter the Focke-Wulfs, some Spitfire Mk IXs were shipped to the theater late in December 1942 and attached to No. 145 Squadron. They were flown by a highly experienced group of Polish fighter pilots led by Squadron Leader Stanislaw Skalski and collectively known as the Polish Fighting Team, or more popularly as "Skalski's Circus." In eight weeks of operations, they shot down more enemy aircraft than any other Polish unit that whole year, and the pilots were subsequently offered appointments as commanding officers of other RAF fighter squadrons. Skalski, who shot down two Bf 109s and a Junkers 88 over Tunisia, became the first Pole to command an RAF fighter squadron, No. 601.

ABOVE LEFT Air Vice-Marshal Arthur Coningham, commanding the Desert Air Force, confers with General Bernard Montgomery (right), commander of the British Eighth Army.

LEFT The rigors of desert warfare did not deter personnel from celebrating the festive season, as this Christmas card reveals.

BELOW Squadron Leader Stanislaw Skalski, a very experienced fighter pilot, commanded the Polish Fighting Team in North Africa. He is seen here in the cockpit of a Hurricane.

Seafires over the beaches

New Zealander H. E. Guthie, a sublieutenant in the RNZNVR flying with the Royal Navy, recalls his experiences in a Seafire of No. 801 Squadron in the Mediterranean in late 1942.

"After converting to Spitfires at RNAS Stretton, in Cheshire, the squadron was equipped with Seafire 1Bs, my allocated aircraft being MB359, and embarked on HMS *Furious* in the Clyde on October 19, 1942, its task being to provide cover for the North African landings at Oran.

"Just prior to the Oran landing, *Furious* did a so-called 'Club Run,' flying off Spitfires a hundred miles [160km] or so off Malta. It was customary on these runs for a couple of sections of naval aircraft to be at the front of the range of 20 or so Spitfires and to take off first. This was partly to provide top cover while the main fly-off took place and partly to reassure the RAF pilots, on board a carrier for the first time, that take-off was possible from what must have appeared to them as a frighteningly short distance.

"I have recorded that on October 29, 1942, I flew two sorties of over an hour each listed as 'patrol over fleet,' and I believe that this was the first time that the Seafire was used operationally.

"In the early Seafires, the flap control was a tap-like device with only two positions, up and down. It was found that there was a need for partial flap in take-off in various adverse conditions, for example when *Furious* was down to half speed due to mechanical

trouble—a not unusual occurrence—and when operating with overload petrol tanks. The highly technical solution to this problem was for four mechanics to hold wooden wedges between the trailing edge and the flaps while the latter were being raised. This provided about 20 degrees of flap, and the procedure was that once the aircraft got clear of the flight deck the pilot would flick the flap tap down and up quickly so that the wedges dropped out and the aircraft reverted to smooth flight, losing only a few feet of height in the process. It was not always quite as simple as it sounds, though. As it turned out, a Seafire could show some quite remarkable flying characteristics 20ft [6m] above the sea with one wedge left in!

"The Oran landings were to be undertaken by American forces, and to avoid any possible confusion between the British roundels and those carried by Vichy French aircraft all our

TOP A Seafire being manhandled into position on the deck of an escort carrier. These vessels played a hugely important part in naval operations from late 1942.

ABOVE A 60-round ammunition magazine of the type used in the Seafire Mk IB. The magazines were later replaced by belt-fed ammunition.

LEFT The aircraft carrier HMS *Furious*, whose Seafires helped to provide air cover for the Allied landings in North Africa.

aircraft had their insignia overpainted with American stars. I have read more than one account which states that American Spitfires provided the air cover over the initial landings, which is incorrect. The landings were covered by our Seafires of 801 and 807 Squadrons, the American Spitfires later giving support to the advance inland. I have always thought it a pity that we had to fly in false colours, so to speak!

"In the first attack, No. 807 Squadron provided top cover for the Fairey Albacores of No. 822 Squadron. Due to the fact that the morning was completely windless and there was not enough wind speed over the decks of the slow 'Woolworth carriers' *Biter* and *Dasher* for them to operate their Hurricanes, which were to have provided ground support, this task was assigned at short notice to No. 801 Squadron, which consequently did not take off until the first Albacore strike had returned and was ready to land on. The windless conditions caused a mist to develop over the sea, which worsened considerably as the morning wore on.

"The Seafire 1B carried two 20mm cannon, each fed by a magazine of 60 rounds. To accommodate this magazine it was necessary for the upper surfaces of the wing to have a bulge. In the aircraft of 807 Squadron the magazines were replaced by belt-feed mechanisms which permitted a load of 120 rounds per

gun and a smooth surface on the mainplane. The armament was one of our main concerns, as 60 rounds went very quickly.

"A normal type of deck landing—i.e. nose up, hanging on the prop just above stalling speed at about half engine speed then cutting the engine to drop into the wires without floating—was not possible in a Seafire. In the correct landing position the deck and the batsman disappeared completely beneath the nose. To have any view at all it was necessary to land off the turn. At a knot or two above stalling speed this needed to be a finely judged manoeuvre, and although there were a few undercarriage collapses due to landings with sideslip still on, there were surprisingly few landing accidents during those early days of Seafire operation."

ABOVE A Seafire IIc cruises past the carrier HMS *Indomitable*. An Illustrious-class Fleet Carrier, she saw war service in the Atlantic, Mediterranean, Indian Ocean and Pacific.

LEFT Pilots had to judge their approach very accurately with the help of the deck landing officer. Here, a Sea Hurricane is about to touch down on the escort carrier HMS *Ravager* in 1942.

Spitfires in the Italian campaign

With the enemy eliminated from North Africa, the stage was now set for the next phase of the Allies' plans: the invasion of Sicily. In the early summer of 1943, the bomb-battered island of Malta underwent a complete transformation. It was now that the gallant resistance of the island's people and garrison bore fruit, for in June 1943 Malta swarmed with aircraft and personnel, all standing ready for the coming operation.

The whole of the Desert Air Force flew in, together with much of the First Tactical Air Force from Tunisia; to accommodate the influx, a new airstrip was bulldozed on Malta's sister island, Gozo, and the overspill went to airfields on the newly captured Italian islands of Pantelleria and Lampedusa. Following airborne landings during the night of July 9, 1943, the seaborne landings that began on Sicily at dawn were covered by a massive fighter umbrella of Spitfires and P-40s. The landings were also covered by the two British fleet carriers HMS *Formidable* and HMS *Indomitable*, with Seafires of Nos. 807, 880, 885, and 899 Squadrons flying combat air patrols over the invasion fleet. Small numbers of Ju 88 dive-bombers succeeded in sinking 12 ships in the course of the day, but opposition to the landings themselves was mostly left to Italy's Regia Aeronautica, whose 165 aircraft already on the island were rapidly reinforced. The Italians suffered appalling losses, both on the ground and to Allied fighters and antiaircraft fire, and by July 27 the last Italian air units had been withdrawn to the mainland.

The first Spitfire to land on Sicily, on the morning of July 11, was an aircraft of No. 72 Squadron piloted by Flying Officer D. N. Keith. Running out of fuel after shooting down two enemy

ABOVE RIGHT Aircraft carriers, with Seafires embarked, en route for Sicily. Although the Seafire was a far from ideal carrier aircraft, the air cover it provided was indispensable.

RIGHT A Seafire over HMS *Indomitable*, one of the Royal Navy's new fast Fleet Carriers. She was later to play an important part in the Pacific war.

aircraft, Keith spotted the airfield at Pachino, which had been captured in a ploughed-up state and which was being prepared for occupation by engineers. Keith went down to land on the furrowed runway; his Spitfire was refueled, rearmed, and dragged to a nearby road, from which he took off. By July 13 the airfield was serviceable and the Spitfire squadrons of No. 244 Wing arrived from Malta. Six more Spitfire squadrons, together with six USAAF fighter units, flew to the island on July 16, and were established at Comiso, Licata, and Ponte Olivo, respectively.

"Thereafter [says the official history], the transference of Tactical Air Force squadrons to Sicily in accordance with the Air Plan occurred at regular intervals, and full air support to our advancing land forces was continued without a break."

On September 3, British forces landed at Reggio in Calabria, on the Italian mainland, and on September 9—the day after the Italian government surrendered unconditionally, a move that resulted in the Germans seizing control of all defensive measures—a second Allied landing was made at Salerno, with the object of capturing the port of Naples and cutting off the German forces retreating before the British advance from Reggio. Because of the distance of Salerno from the airfields on Sicily, air cover was mostly provided by Seafires of the Royal Navy and by USAAF P-38 Lightnings and P-51 Mustangs, which had a longer range than the Sicily-based Spitfires and P-40s. The Germans resisted the landings fiercely, and for a time it seemed that the Anglo-American forces might be pushed back into the sea, but by September 12 the Allies were able to use newly captured airfields in Italy itself, and air superiority was assured.

The crisis of battle came on September 14, a day that saw 700 sorties flown by the fighters and fighter-bombers of the First Tactical Air Force, the Desert Air Force being employed mainly in strafing German transport. By September 16 the Salerno beachhead was secure, and on October 1 the British 7th Armoured Division—the "Desert Rats"—entered Naples. The Fifth and Eighth Armies now began a steady advance; by October 6 the former was on the line of the Volturno River and the Eighth was

ABOVE Italian peasants help to clear a landing strip for RAF Spitfires near Naples. In general, the Italians were glad to see the end of the fascist regime.

LEFT Italian lire feature among this sheaf of occupation currency issued by the Allies, who were keen to see a viable form of economy retained.

facing Termoli, thus completing the second phase of the campaign.

Yet for the Allied armies in Italy there would be no easy victory. Salerno had given them a taste of what was to come.

A second landing, this time at Anzio—a move designed to outflank formidable German defenses at Monte Cassino—was contained by savage German counterattacks in January 1944. During this critical period there was some reshuffling of the Spitfire Wings operating in Italy. For example, No. 7 Wing, South African Air Force, whose four squadrons—Nos. 1, 2, 4, and 7—were now all equipped with Spitfires, crossed the Apennines to support the US Fifth Army. On January 30, 1944, its Spitfires escorted 215 B-17 Fortresses and B-24 Liberators, which dropped 29,000 fragmentation bombs on four enemy airfields, causing much damage among enemy fighters assembling there to reinforce the Luftwaffe.

In 1944, with an absence of enemy air opposition, the Spitfire squadrons in Italy turned increasingly to ground attack. It was a role that had never been envisaged for the Spitfire, but it was one to which the Supermarine fighter proved surprisingly adaptable.

The intelligence gatherers

The Allied victory in the Mediterranean was attributable to a constant flow of accurate and up-to-date intelligence, a success made possible chiefly, but not entirely, by the activities of the code breakers at Bletchley Park, the Government Code and Cypher School (GC&CS) in Buckinghamshire. Their task was to crack the enemy's high-grade cyphers, and in particular to decrypt the general-purpose German Enigma code.

That they succeeded in doing so, from May 1940 until the end of the war, was due in no small measure to the Polish, who provided the British with an intact Enigma code machine in 1939 and also supplied a great deal of associated information. The copious intelligence, assembled on the composition, designation, location, strength, serviceability, casualties, wastage, and reserves of every German unit in every theater of war, was known as "Ultra", and its details remained a closely guarded secret for 30 years after the end of hostilities. Bletchley Park also provided the Royal Navy with intelligence on the movements of the powerful Italian fleet, enabling Swordfish torpedo-bombers to inflict a crippling blow to it in its harbor at Taranto in November 1940. Later, the RAF took an enormous toll on merchant ships bringing supplies from Italy and Greece to ports in North Africa; the consequent shortages, especially of oil, handicapped the Axis forces throughout their campaign and contributed decisively to their defeat. In the case of almost every ship the British sank, details of its route, timing, escort, and cargo had been sent in advance from Bletchley Park to the British commanders in the Mediterranean. It was Ultra, too, that eventually brought the Allies victory in the Battle of the Atlantic, by establishing the movements of U-boat "wolfpacks," and making it possible to reroute convoys accordingly.

However, Ultra was by no means the only source of intelligence. It also came from photographic reconnaissance (PR)—the next in importance to Ultra —prisoners of war, captured documents and equipment, and the RAF's "Y" Service, which

ABOVE An Enigma code machine. The possession of this vital piece of equipment by the Allies provided them with an intelligence advantage that they never lost.

LEFT German signals specialists using an Enigma machine in the field. One of its advantages was that it was easily transportable.

eavesdropped on all low-grade enemy signals. For example, on March 25, 1943, accurate intelligence enabled British commanders to precede a planned frontal assault on enemy positions covering a certain feature of the Mareth Line in Tunisia, which was very heavily defended, with a massive air strike against enemy gun positions, defense posts, and landline communications. The strike the following day involved every tactical aircraft in the theater; its

immense effectiveness led to an armored breakthrough. The thorough and precise target intelligence given to the pilots, which had come mainly from PR and the "Y" Service, was compiled and distributed only a few hours before takeoff.

The US Army's Signals Intelligence Service (SIS), headquartered in 1942 at Arlington Hall Station in Virginia, was responsible for the interception of enemy radio message traffic and code breaking for the Army and Army Air Forces. Before the Pearl Harbor attack in December 1941, the SIS had achieved outstanding success with breaking the high-grade cyphers of the Japanese diplomatic message traffic, produced by a sophisticated cypher machine that the Americans dubbed "Purple". The Americans called the signals intelligence emerging from their cryptanalysis Magic and gave a Purple device to the GC&CS at Bletchley.

In the spring of 1942, British Intelligence representatives traveled to the United States and secured an agreement with the SIS for the coordination of radio intercept programs and the development of equipment and techniques, the exchange of intercepted material, and the establishment of an Allied "Y Committee" to oversee signals intelligence. In June 1942 the SIS established a subordinate organization in the European Theater, headquartered in London, first at Grosvenor Square and then on Weymouth Street. The cooperative effort was neatly summed up

ABOVE The Government Code and Cypher School at Bletchley Park in Buckinghamshire, where the enemy's secret codes were analyzed, collated and disseminated in the form of Ultra.

LEFT American cypher clerks at work on Magic, breaking the high-grade cyphers of Japanese diplomatic and military traffic.

by Brigadier-General George C. McDonald, the US Strategic Air Forces' Assistant Chief of Staff, Intelligence:

"When America entered the war against Germany, we found that the British had in existence a large and efficient Air Intelligence organization. It was decided to integrate our own Air Intelligence with that of the British on the basis of full and frank co-operation, and not to duplicate facilities or compete in the exploitation of basic intelligence sources. The British contribution remained predominant throughout the war, although American participation gradually expanded both in extent and significance."

The British and American interception of enemy voice traffic was undertaken by both ground and airborne stations. The Americans first tried airborne interception in the Mediterranean theater in the autumn of 1943, and from May 1944 six airborne intercept operators regularly flew missions with the Eighth Air Force's heavy bombardment divisions. In September 1944 nearly 100 operators were in either training or flying missions; much of the training was provided by experienced RAF operators.

Photo-reconnaissance Spitfires

Not long before the outbreak of World War II, Generaloberst Freiherr Werner von Fritsch, an officer of the old school and a former cavalryman, who was Commander-in-Chief of the German Army during the early years of the Nazi regime in Germany, let fall a prophetic remark: "The next war [he said] will be won by the military organization with the most effective photographic reconnaissance."

Clandestine PR flights over Germany were carried out in 1939 by a remarkable man called Sidney Cotton, who had been approached by Wing Commander F. W. Winterbotham, Chief of Air Intelligence in the Secret Intelligence Service. The flights were made from Heston in Middlesex, using a commercial Lockheed 12A fitted with cameras. From September 1939 the PR organization at Heston was placed on an official footing,

receiving three Bristol Blenheims and two Spitfires, one of the latter being deployed to Seclin, near Lille, in November.

It was clear that, without its service load of guns and other equipment, a Spitfire adapted for the PR role could carry a large amount of extra fuel, oil, and oxygen, in addition to the cameras. What was needed was an extension of its combat radius, and that meant extra fuel tankage. A further 29 gallons [132 liters] took the fuel to 114 gallons [518 liters], and with this modification—the tank being fitted behind the pilot's seat—the aircraft was known as the Spitfire PR.1B.

On February 10, 1940, the PR Spitfire detachment in France, known as the Special Survey Flight, was established as No. 212 (PR) Squadron. This squadron consisted of three flights and a mixture of Blenheims and Spitfires. The parent unit at Heston was named the Photographic Development Unit. By the spring of 1940 the Spitfires had photographed practically the whole of the Ruhr, and they had also shared with the Blenheims the task of locating major units of the German fleet, which for the most part were still in home

ABOVE The principal threat to high-flying reconnaissance Spitfires was the Messerschmitt 109G, with its supercharged engine. Seen here is an aircraft of JG 54 "Greenhearts."

LEFT RAF reconnaissance pilots receive a briefing on their targets. They usually flew complex routes to confuse the enemy radar defenses.

waters making ready for the coming invasion of Norway. In the first three months of operations the Squadron flew 57 sorties, about equally divided between Seclin and Heston. The Squadron's first sortie, in fact, was flown on its first day, February 10, 1940, when Longbottom—now a Flight Lieutenant—made a four-hour round trip to Wilhelmshaven and Emden.

Flying a PR Spitfire was not a comfortable task, as Flight Lieutenant (later Air Chief Marshal Sir) Neil Wheeler, who flew some of 212 Squadron's early missions, relates:

"Most of our early problems came from the altitude at which we were flying. Most of our Spitfire sorties took place between 25,000 and 35,000ft [7,620 and 10,668m] where temperatures were around minus 50°C. I found the extreme cold most uncomfortable. On my feet I wore a pair of ladies' silk stockings, a pair of football stockings, a pair of oiled Scandinavian ski socks and RAF fur-lined boots. On my hands I wore two pairs of RAF silk gloves and some special fur-backed and lined gauntlets which I had to buy for myself. It was essential to retain some fingertip control, especially for the camera control box. Otherwise, I wore normal uniform with a thick vest, roll-neck sweater and a thing called a Tropal lining, which was stuffed with a form of Kapok."

One of greatest dangers on a PR mission was the Spitfire's condensation trail, betraying its presence to the enemy, as Wheeler explains:

"I have to admit that I had never heard of a condensation trail . . . From Heston we carried out a great deal of research into the formation of condensation trails, aided by Oxford University, before we established that it was the exhaust and not the propeller that produced the tell-tale trail. Normally one endeavoured to keep just below condensation height, but on rare occasions one could pass through the layer and fly above with the advantage that one could see the enemy fighters climbing up."

On one occasion, at 28,000ft [8,534m] over Germany, the moisture collecting in Wheeler's oxygen mask froze solid, cutting off the supply, and he passed out. He regained consciousness at 1,500ft [457m] over Kiel harbor, "just in time [he said with characteristic understatement] to extricate myself from quite a tricky situation."

In November 1940 the PR unit at Heston was designated No. 1 Photographic Reconnaissance Unit (PRU). In 1941 it was expanded to four Spitfire flights, each with six aircraft: two flights at RAF Benson in Oxfordshire, another at Wick in northern Scotland covering Norway, and a fourth at St. Eval in Cornwall covering Brest and western France down to and including the full length of the Franco-Spanish frontier. By the end of 1943, ten specialist PR squadrons had been formed at home and overseas within the framework of No. 1 PRU and other PRUs. The USAAF also used Spitfires in the PR role, the 7th Photographic Reconnaissance Group operating from Mount Farm in Oxfordshire and later from Chalgrove. Various marks of Spitfire were adapted to the PR role, ending with the Griffon-engine PR.XIX of 1944.

The task of the PR Spitfire pilots was lonely, dangerous, and sometimes excruciatingly painful. They fulfilled it without complaint, and the contribution they made to the Allied victory was measureless.

ABOVE The control box for a Type 35 camera. This was mounted on the cockpit wall, within easy reach of the pilot.

BELOW The German battleship *Tirpitz* photographed from low level by a Spitfire as she sheltered in a Norwegian fjord. She was eventually sunk by RAF Lancasters in 1944.

Spits in the stratosphere: A PR pilot's tale

Flight Lieutenant Alfred Ball (later Air Marshal Sir Alfred Ball), a pilot with No. 1 Photographic Reconnaissance Unit in the UK, who went on to command No. 4 PRU in North Africa, described the dangers involved in photo-reconnaissance work.

"It took only a few minutes to cross the Channel, and immediately one started searching the sky for enemy aircraft. The coastal belt was always dangerous for it contained many Luftwaffe bases and one expected to see fighters; however, provided one saw them in good time, one could evade them. The same situation obtained on the return flight and one could not afford to relax when crossing out of enemy territory (we lost some of our best pilots due to this temptation); it was particularly risky coming out of NW Germany with the fighter bases in the Friesian Islands.

"The interception threat, of course, continued all through a sortie, but there were high-risk areas, such as the coastal belt and over key industrial cities, particularly if they had just been bombed. Furthermore, having to concentrate on map-reading and navigation en route made keeping a continuous and effective look-out difficult, but it was essential. One always had to remember that for a sortie to be successful, one had to bring back interpretable photographs of one's targets, not merely to get back in one piece having successfully evaded enemy fighters, although that had its points! It was, for example, inadvisable to fly in a long straight track to a major target area, such as Hamburg, Stettin or Frankfurt. Irregular feints and doglegs were much more sensible and pragmatic. Although they complicated navigation and used a little extra fuel, they made interceptions much more difficult for the enemy (it was extraordinary how, if one did so, one often saw nothing en route even when, from listening to his radar or from seeing his marker flak, you knew that he was attempting to intercept you). Unplanned doglegs definitely paid off.

"Over major targets, such as the Ruhr and Brest, one was almost invariably shot at, sometimes with remarkable accuracy (one of my chaps was hit at 37,000ft [11,278m] over Hamburg, and another shot down at 30,000ft [9,144m] over Brest), but on many occasions it tended to be some distance away and low. A PR pilot was particularly

RIGHT A vertically-mounted F-52 reconnaissance camera. Such equipment produced very high-resolution photos that were invaluable in planning raids and assessing post-attack damage.

vulnerable during long photographic runs when he was concentrating on accuracy and did not see a fighter or flak until too late.

"However, there were ways of overcoming this problem. When the *Scharnhorst*, *Gneisenau* and *Prinz Eugen* were in Brest, a standing patrol of Me 109s, circling up sun over Ushant, used to wait for us coming into Brest every day (only a German mind could plan like that!). The Navy wanted photographs of the ships and port area every day at the same times, first and last light (only a Naval mind could plan like that!). We usually saw the fighters in time and raced and raced in to Brest flat out. We had to get the job done very quickly and so, to avoid having to do two or three photo-runs, we turned the camera time interval down to its minimum and rocked the wings (about a two-second cycle) as we crossed the port, thus covering the whole port area in one run. Then we were off home, still flat out, with the 109s, hopefully, not yet in range—I was caught only once in 25 sorties, but got back to St. Eval with the necessary photographs and some rather unnecessary holes.

"I have touched on interception risks but not on the capabilities of PR Spitfires and enemy fighters, the Me 109Es and Fs until mid-1942, then increasingly Me 109Gs and FW 190s. Until the end of 1942 we were still flying the old Mk Vs (Mk IVs overseas) with RR Merlin 45 engines. We could match the 109Es in speed and cope with the Fs too, provided we saw them in time for we could out-turn them, but we could not afford to lose much height as they could always out-dive us.

"It was another story with the 109G and 190s. They were both faster, but the 190's best height was around 24,000ft [7,315m] and provided we could stay at 30,000ft we had a chance at full throttle, but it depended on an early sighting of the enemy fighters, and preferably well before they saw you. The 109G had a better ceiling than the 190 but we could out-turn them both, so an experienced pilot could get away with it so long as he got his time to turn just right, but it was touch and go until we received the Spitfire Mk XI in early 1943."

ABOVE PR Spitfires were fitted with both vertical and oblique F-24 cameras (above). To use the oblique camera, the pilot had to roll the aircraft on to its side.

LEFT This photograph shows Halifax bombers attacking the German battlecruisers *Scharnhorst* and *Gneisenau* in Brest harbour. The warships (top right) are sheltered by the beginnings of a smokescreen.

Spitfire Mk IX

Because of delays in producing the Mk VIII Spitfire, the Mk V Spitfire airframe was combined with a Merlin 61 engine as an interim measure. The resulting combination was the Spitfire Mk IX, which for a stop-gap aircraft turned out to be a resounding success. Deliveries to the RAF began in June 1942, and 5,665 were built, more than any other mark except the Mk V. More importantly, the Mk IX enabled us to fight the Focke Wulf 190 on equal terms.

Numerous variants of the Mk IX were produced, with innovations that included a modified wing, increased rudder area, an additional fuselage fuel tank, and a rear-view hood. As with all marks of Spitfire, the close proximity of the radiator to the undercarriage caused overheating problems when the gear was down (see inset). Post-war, a two-seat conversion was produced by Vickers, called the Mk IX Trainer. The aircraft opposite is a privately converted Mk IX Trainer that first flew in 2006 in Bartow, Florida. The wing is configured as a IXE; the original would not have had cannon fitted.

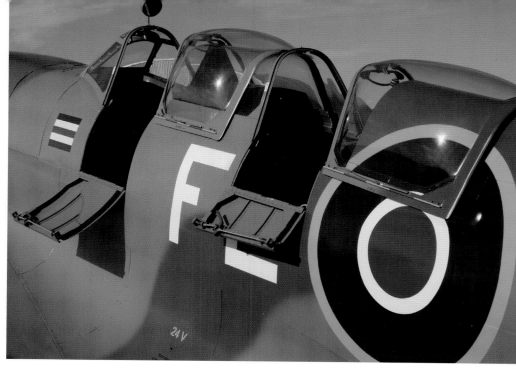

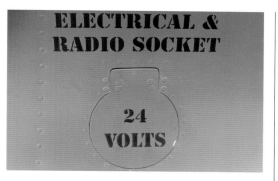

ELECTRICAL &
RADIO SOCKET

24
VOLTS

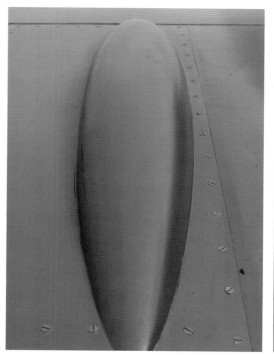

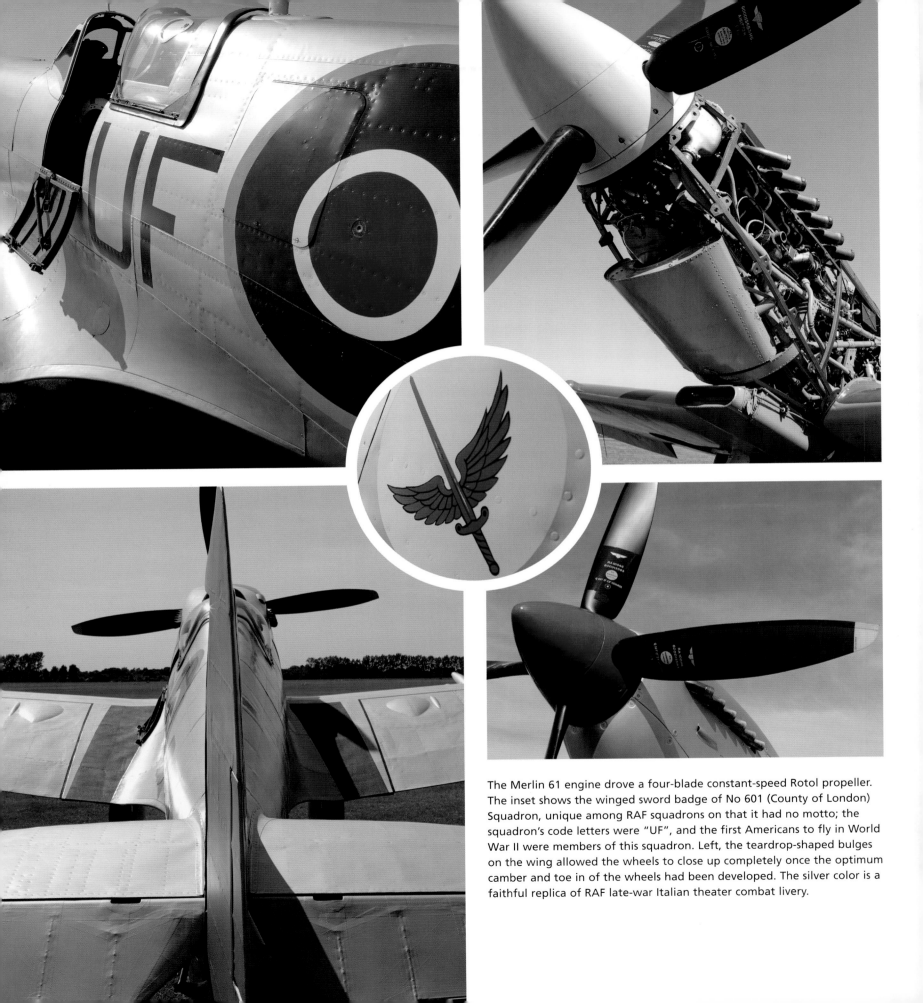

The Merlin 61 engine drove a four-blade constant-speed Rotol propeller. The inset shows the winged sword badge of No 601 (County of London) Squadron, unique among RAF squadrons on that it had no motto; the squadron's code letters were "UF", and the first Americans to fly in World War II were members of this squadron. Left, the teardrop-shaped bulges on the wing allowed the wheels to close up completely once the optimum camber and toe in of the wheels had been developed. The silver color is a faithful replica of RAF late-war Italian theater combat livery.

Australia's Spitfires

During 1942, following their initial landings in eastern New Guinea, the Japanese put most of their efforts toward attempting to capture the vital harbor of Port Moresby, stepping stone for an invasion of Australia. The air defense of this objective was the responsibility of No. 75 Squadron RAAF, with P-40E Kittyhawks. The USAAF's 49th Fighter Group (FG), also with P-40s, undertook the air defense of northern Australia and in particular Darwin, which had been subjected to Japanese air attacks.

Although the 49th FG performed its task valiantly, the P-40 was no match for the Mitsubishi A6M Zero fighter (also known as "Zeke" by the Allies) that escorted the enemy bombers. What the Australian government wanted was the Spitfire, and in January 1943, following urgent requests to the UK government, No. 1 Fighter Wing, comprising No. 54 Squadron RAF and Nos. 452 and 457 Squadrons RAAF, was established for the air defense of Darwin, the 49th FG being redeployed to New Guinea. No. 1 Fighter Wing— all armed with the "tropicalized" Spitfire VC—was commanded by Squadron Leader Clive Caldwell, an experienced fighter pilot who had already gained 20 victories in the Middle East.

BELOW This photograph shows the first Mk V Spitfire to be fitted with a Vokes tropical filter for operations in hot and dusty climates.

In February 1943 the Japanese renewed their bombing offensive against Northern Australia, and on the sixth day of that month Flight Lieutenant R. W. Foster opened the Spitfire's scoreboard in the theater by shooting down a Mitsubishi Ki.46 Dinah reconnaissance aircraft 35 miles [56km] off Cape van Diemen. On March 2, Caldwell, now a wing commander, destroyed a Zero and a Nakajima B5N Kate torpedo-bomber, while Squadron Leader Raymond Thorold-Smith, commanding No. 452 Squadron, also shot down a Zero. The latter pilot was killed on March 15, when the Wing intercepted 14 Japanese aircraft over Darwin and claimed 7 of the enemy for the loss of four Spitfires.

The first major battle occurred on May 2, when the Japanese sent in a force of 18 bombers and 27 Zeros from Timor. The Japanese were detected by radar when they were still a long way out to sea—49 minutes' flying time from the coast, in fact. In response, the Wing's 33 Spitfires were all airborne within 15 minutes, climbing hard to meet the raiders. However, when the Spitfires reached 26,000ft [7,925m], Caldwell saw that the Japanese formation was still about 4,000ft [1,219m] higher up. To attack it on the climb would have been foolhardy, for the nimble Zeros would have held all the advantages, so Caldwell delayed while his Spitfires got into position above the enemy, with the glare of the sun behind them. This meant that the Japanese were able to bomb Darwin without meeting any fighter opposition, a fact that later caused a big outcry in the popular press; however, Caldwell was quite right in his decision.

Caldwell's Spitfires, unseen against the sun, shadowed the Japanese until they were out over the Timor Sea, then he ordered No. 54 Squadron to attack the Zeros while the other two squadrons engaged the bombers. The Spitfires went into the attack almost vertically and a furious air battle developed as the Zero pilots, recovering from their surprise, turned to meet the

BELOW RAAF Spitfire VIIIs cruising on patrol high above the cloud-shrouded mountains of New Guinea.

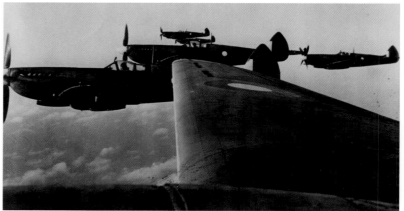

attackers. When the battle was over five Zeros had been destroyed, but five Spitfires had also been shot down, two of the pilots had been killed, and five more had been compelled to make forced ladings after running out of fuel.

In the weeks that followed, Caldwell continued to develop the Wing's tactics, ignoring the growing storm of criticism about the celebrated Spitfire's lack of success, and on July 26, 1943, his efforts paid dividends. On that day, No. 54 Squadron was scrambled to intercept a raid on Darwin by 47 bombers and their fighter escorts. Only seven Spitfires reached the attackers, but they shot down 7 bombers and two Zeros for no loss. Then, on August 20, three Japanese reconnaissance aircraft appeared over Darwin, heralding another raid; the Spitfires shot down all three of them. The Japanese sent another; it was shot down by Clive Caldwell, his 28th and last victory. The Japanese sent yet another, this time

under strong fighter escort; No. 54 Squadron was scrambled to intercept, and the Zeros fell on the Spitfires as they climbed, shooting down three of them. The Spitfires in turn destroyed one Zero and damaged two more so badly that it is almost certain they came down somewhere in the Timor Sea.

In November 1943 the Japanese daylight raids on Darwin ceased and the enemy switched to sporadic night attacks that would continue, with little effect, until early in 1944. Caldwell's Spitfires had achieved their objective.

LEFT This type of ticket was issued to Allied service and civilian personnel required to travel as a passenger in transport aircraft in the south-west Pacific area.

BELOW Spitfire pilots of No 453 Squadron RAAF. This unit, then flying Brewster Buffalo fighters, fought in Malaya and was evacuated to Australia, but instead of being used in the defense of its homeland it was re-formed in the UK as part of Fighter Command in June 1942.

" Fighting the Zero

One of the finest aircraft of all time, the Mitsubishi A6M Reisen (Zero fighter) soon showed itself to be clearly superior to any fighter the Allies could put into the air in the early stages of the Pacific war. Armed with two 20mm cannon and two 7.7mm machine guns, it was highly maneuverable and structurally very strong, despite being lightweight. Instead of being built in several separate sections, it was constructed in two pieces.

The engine, cockpit, and forward fuselage combined with the wings to form one rigid unit; the second unit comprised the rear fuselage and the tail. The two units were joined together by a ring of 80 bolts. Its main drawback was that it had no armor plating for the pilot and no self-sealing fuel tanks, which meant that it could not absorb as much battle damage as Allied fighters could.

Clive Caldwell's combat report of the air battle of May 2, 1943, over Darwin and the Timor Sea tells what it was like to engage such a formidable opponent.

"I . . . flew my formation directly under the No. 3 E/A section and some 3,000ft [914m] below, where any attack from them must be preceded by such maneuvers as to give us sufficient warning to meet it. That is, the Zekes directly above must either turn on their backs and attack vertically downwards (a difficult shot and easily avoided), loop fully as they are credited with doing so freely, thus going behind us, or lose height to turn on to our tails, in either case giving us sufficient warning. When abreast of No. 1 section E/A, I dived to attack at a steep angle from full beam breaking to the rear in a wide climbing turn to port and was followed into the attack by the rest of my formation. No. 3 section of the enemy, the top cover, appeared slow to appreciate the significance of the move and failed to get position behind us in time to be dangerous.

"No. 1 E/A section moved herein to intercept us directly, but were not successful in doing so, and the break to the rear gave us enough clear air momentarily to sustain the altered position, and at the end of the zoom I found I was well up in height in relation to the Zekes, which had lost height after us. A diving head-on attack was refused by a Zeke who broke downward before coming to range. This was repeated in the case of another Zeke a few minutes later. I observed several Zekes firing on me and took momentary action, others not seen may have fired, but the shooting was bad despite liberal use of tracer, and the attempts at correcting aim were poor. Engaging in turns with a Zeke at about 180mph [290km/h] IAS [indicated air speed] and pulling my aircraft as tight as possible, the Zeke did not dangerously close, until the speed began to drop, about the

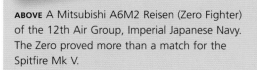

ABOVE A Mitsubishi A6M2 Reisen (Zero Fighter) of the 12th Air Group, Imperial Japanese Navy. The Zero proved more than a match for the Spitfire Mk V.

RIGHT By the end of the Pacific war, Spitfire and Seafire pilots were encountering formidable new Japanese fighters such as the Nakajima K-84 Hayate (Gale), known to the Allies as "Frank."

ABOVE The Spitfire Mk VIII, which replaced the Mk V in RAAF service, was superior in most respects to the Mitsubishi Zero.

LEFT A standard Irvin seat-type parachute, as used by RAAF Spitfire pilots, manufactured by the Dominion Parachute Company of Australia.

completion of the second turn. Breaking severely downward to the inside of the turn I experienced no difficulty in losing the Zeke. My engine cut momentarily in this manoeuvre. I observed Zekes to loop, to half roll and fire while on their backs, which, though interesting as a spectacle, seemed profitless in dogfighting.

"During the engagement I saw a Spitfire diving away with a Zeke on its tail. The Spitfire appeared to be gaining distance. When leaving the combat area, I dived steeply away and was followed down in a dive by a Zeke. At a speed in excess of 400mph [644km/h] IAS the Zeke did not close the distance and gave up quickly, though supported by several of his kind. The Zekes appeared to be armed with MG [machine guns] and 30mm cannon. To summarise, in view of the whole circumstances surrounding the brief engagement, and despite the fact that both height and numbers favored the Zekes, I regard the Spitfire as a superior aircraft generally, though less manoeuvrable at low speeds. In straight and level flight and in dives the Spitfire appears faster. Though the angle of climb of the Zeke is steeper, the actual gaining of height seems much the same, the Spitfire going up at a lesser angle but at greater forward speed—an advantage. No difficulty was experienced in keeping height with the Zekes during combat. I believe that at altitudes above 20,000ft [6,096m] the Spitfire, in relation to the Zekes[,] will prove an even more superior aircraft in general performance.

"It must be remembered however, that the Japanese pilots had been airborne for a very long period and their efficiency must necessarily be impaired by consideration of fuel conservation and fatigue . . . "

5 From Normandy to the Rhine

Operation Overlord: Spitfires over Normandy

From the beginning of 1944, the squadrons of the 2nd Tactical Air Force (TAF)—formed to support the forthcoming invasion of France—were giving increasingly frequent demonstrations of their capabilities against targets on the Continent. While the medium bombers of No. 2 Group, escorted by Spitfires and Mustangs, continued to attack the enemy's power industry and communications, the tactical fighter-bombers of Nos. 83 and 84 groups—Spitfires, Typhoons, Mustangs, and Mosquitoes—stepped up their operations against the transport system in France and the Low Countries, carrying out attacks on rolling stock and other targets of opportunity. These RAF tactical units, together with the United States Ninth Army Air Force, formed the Allied Expeditionary Air Force. Its total strength in May 1944 was 5,667 aircraft, of which 3,011 were fighters, medium bombers, light bombers, and fighter-bombers.

The 2nd TAF operations record for May 1944 describes a fairly typical operation during this period.

"May 28. In conjunction with attacks by Bostons and Mitchells of No. 2 Group, between 15:15 and 18:55 hours, 62 Spitfires carried out sweeps over northern France, attacking and destroying

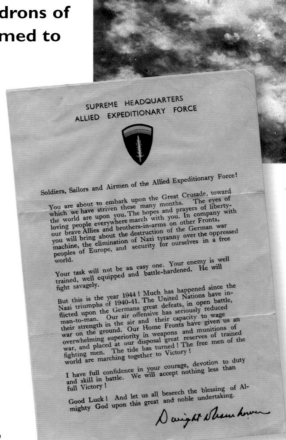

ABOVE A Handley Page Halifax bomber over Normandy, June 1944. Much of RAF Bomber Command's effort was devoted to the support of Allied ground forces during this period.

LEFT A leaflet signed by General Dwight D. Eisenhower, Supreme Allied Commander, exhorting Allied troops to do their utmost during the Normandy landings.

a lorry and damaging two goods trains, a large streamlined locomotive, a lorry, three large and two small cars and five railway wagons in a siding. At the same time, nine Tempests patrolled over Cormeille, during which period two Junkers Ju 88s/188s were destroyed and two Ju 88s/188s damaged, all on the ground."

Before dawn on D–Day, June 6, 1944, Allied bombers dropped 5,000 tons of bombs on the defenses of the "Atlantic Wall," and as the troops went ashore and fought their way toward their initial objectives in the dawn of D-Day, waves of tactical bombers and fighter-bombers continued to batter the German defenses ahead of them. Meanwhile, overhead, squadrons of Spitfires, Thunderbolts, and Mustangs dealt effectively with the small number of Luftwaffe formations that tried to interfere with the landings. In all, the Allied air forces flew 14,674 sorties during the

24 hours of D-Day, for the loss of 113 aircraft—some of which were shot down by friendly naval forces.

Until artillery could be established ashore, the invasion forces had to rely on naval gunfire for support, and an Air Spotting Pool was established at Lee-on-Solent in Hampshire for the purpose of directing this operation. This comprised Nos. 26 and 63 squadrons RAF and US Navy Squadron VCS-7 with Spitfire Vs, and Nos. 808, 885, 886, and 897 Squadrons of the Fleet Air Arm with Seafire IIIs, as part of No. 34 Reconnaissance Wing, 2nd Tactical Air Force. As D-Day approached, three squadrons of RAF Mustang tactical reconnaissance aircraft (Nos. 2, 268, and 264) were added to the strength of the wing, which already stood at 101 Spitfires and Seafires.

No. 34 Wing was brought to readiness on June 3, 1944, and the first pair of Seafires took off at 04:30 on D-Day, June 6, to seek likely naval gunnery targets, one pilot acting as spotter and the other acting as escort. The usual altitude for spotting missions was 6,000ft (1,829m), but poor weather often forced the spotter to operate between 1,500ft (457m) and 2,000ft (610m). With the three Mustang squadrons contributing 96 sorties, the mission total for the day came to 435; losses were three Seafires, three Spitfires, and a Mustang.

With the Allied forces safely ashore, the priority was to construct forward airstrips in Normandy, mainly for the use of the Allied fighter-bombers that would be supporting the breakout from the beachheads. In the meantime, operating from the UK, 18 squadrons of Hawker Typhoons of Nos. 83 and 84 groups, supported by a number of Mustang units, carried out nonstop tactical armed reconnaissance operations. In the early morning of June 7 they delivered a savage attack on the Panzer Lehr Division that was hurrying to the battle area from Alencon. With rockets and cannon fire, the Typhoons and Mustangs destroyed 90 trucks,

40 fuel trucks, and 84 half-tracks. For the Germans, it was a bitter taste of what was to come.

By the morning of June 8, a temporary airstrip had been set up at Ste. Croix-sur-Mer, the construction crews working under constant shellfire. Eventually, 31 similar strips were set up in the Anglo-Canadian zone and 50 in the American zone, enabling the fighter-bombers to take off and attack targets on demand.

Among the first Spitfire units to operate from French soil was No. 144 Wing, Royal Canadian Air Force, comprising Nos. 441, 442, and 443 squadrons, which was in action from June 10. The buildup of Spitfire squadrons in Normandy continued steadily, although some did not arrive until several weeks after the invasion. Among these were the three squadrons of No. 145 Wing, whose pilots and ground crews had been eagerly awaiting their chance to move to France. It was understandable, for they were Free French Forces, and they were coming home.

LEFT A Mk IID gunsight in use from 1944. The pilot could switch from guns to rocket projectiles (RP). The "shade" is non-standard.

BELOW A Royal Air Force Servicing Commando Team preparing a Spitfire for a sortie from a forward airstrip in Normandy.

A French Spitfire squadron in action

One of the squadrons of No. 145 Wing was No. 329, which also bore the famous title Groupe de Chasse GC 1/2 Cigognes. The other two squadrons were Nos. 340 "Ile-de-France" and 341 "Alsace." No. 329 Squadron's War Diary describes its activities over the Normandy beaches:

"Bad weather . . . prevailed on June 4 and 5, but on the evening of the fifth we put up one section to patrol the Isle of Wight. Everywhere, our pilots could see ships of all shapes and sizes assembling, particularly landing craft, all ready to set course southwards. At 21:30 the pilots were assembled in the briefing room and told that D-Day was to be at dawn. Detailed charts showed how the operation was to unfold. The mission of the Spitfire

RIGHT This German propaganda leaflet, dropped over Normandy, was aimed specifically at American soldiers—especially the homesick ones.

BELOW The Cross of Lorraine on the nose of this Spitfire denotes that it belongs to a Free French fighter squadron.

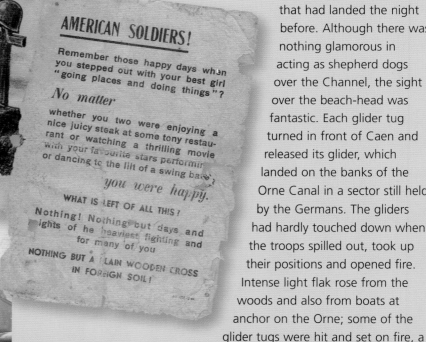

squadrons of No. 145 Wing was to cover the beach-head and destroy any enemy aircraft they encountered.

"This sensational news, although anticipated for some time, provoked great emotions among the pilots. For them, the hope they had nurtured for four long years was about to be realised: the hope that they would be reunited with their families, and stand once more on the soil of France."

At 09:40 on 6 June, after a long wait, the squadron at last took off with No. 145 Wing to cover the beaches in the British sector. Intense flak was encountered to the north of Caen, but the sky was empty of enemy aircraft, which enabled the pilots to observe the massive unfolding of the naval and land operations all along the front, from the Orne to the east coast of the Cotentin Peninsula. All aircraft returned to base by 01:10.

"The second mission began at 14:40. Again, the absence of the Luftwaffe enabled the pilots to turn their attention to events on the ground, this time more closely. One of the sections shot up some Germany armour near Lisieux; Capitaine Ozanne destroyed a motor-cycle with a sidecar. On the third sortie, in the evening, some fuel bowsers [tankers] were destroyed near Caen.

"No. 145 Wing flew its fourth and last sortie of the day at 20:00, escorting a glider train on a re-supply mission to the airborne forces that had landed the night before. Although there was nothing glamorous in acting as shepherd dogs over the Channel, the sight over the beach-head was fantastic. Each glider tug turned in front of Caen and released its glider, which landed on the banks of the Orne Canal in a sector still held by the Germans. The gliders had hardly touched down when the troops spilled out, took up their positions and opened fire. Intense light flak rose from the woods and also from boats at anchor on the Orne; some of the glider tugs were hit and set on fire, a glider fell in flames, others crashed on landing, but every 10 or 20 seconds one came in to reinforce our men on the ground. One of the canal boats proved particularly offensive so Wing Commander Compton, the Wing Leader, went down with Red and Blue Sections and dealt with it. We spent 20 minutes on patrol, then returned to base.

"The Wing flew three low cover missions over the beach-head on June 7 and on the first one, five Ju 88s were encountered north of Caen; one was shot down by Wing Commander Compton. Already, we could see that much destruction had been caused in Caen, with fires visible a long way off. Three sorties were also flown on the eighth [of June] despite poor weather which again prevailed on the tenth, when four missions were flown. We sighted a Focke-Wulf 190 among the clouds, but it was lost to sight almost at once."

On July 25, 1944, for the first time, the Cigognes were patrolling the beachhead area when they received orders to land and refuel in Normandy. The majority of the Spitfires set down at St.-Aubin-sur-Mer. The event was recorded in the squadron's *Livre d'Or* (Golden Book), a day-to-day account of the unit's activities.
"We were in France at last, our feet on French earth, the dust of France in our nostrils (and God knows, there was plenty of it!). The most moving thing was the welcome we received from the local people, overjoyed at being liberated after four years of German oppression and to discover that Frenchmen were among their liberators. We were overwhelmed, with tears in our eyes. They wanted to pin little souvenirs on our battledress—Crosses of Lorraine, French flags, all kinds of things.

"An old man came up to Colonel Fleurquin, with a little girl in his arms. '*Mon Colonel*,' he said, 'would you be kind enough to kiss my little grand-daughter?'

"That simple sentence said it all. We were home, and they were free at last."

ABOVE Wing Commander Compton, who led No. 145 Wing during the perod of the Normandy landings.

ABOVE RIGHT A Spitfire Mk IX of No 340 "Ile-de-France" Squadron, which helped provide fighter cover for the Normandy landings.

RIGHT Another propaganda leaflet dropped by the Germans over Normandy—this time portraying President Roosevelt as a bloated plutocrat.

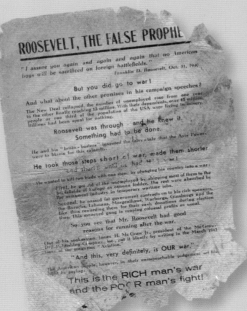

ROOSEVELT, THE FALSE PROPHET

Rich Man's War! *Poor Man's Fight!*

The Griffon Spitfires

Early in 1942, Rolls-Royce at Hucknall carried out extensive trials with a Hawker Henley aircraft fitted with a Griffon engine. A development of the Rolls-Royce "R" engine, which had powered the Supermarine S.6 racing seaplane series (p16), the Griffon produced 1,735hp and weighed 1,980lb (898kg). Although it had a larger frontal area than the Merlin, fitting it to a Spitfire airframe was a logical next step, and it was tested in the Spitfire Mk IV prototype, DP845 (not to be confused with the PR IV). Trials proved satisfactory, and an order for 750 Mk IVs was placed, but this was later canceled; it was not until 1942 that 100 Spitfires, designated Mk XIIs, were converted to Griffon engines.

The first squadron to equip fully with the Spitfire XII, in February 1943, was No. 41, which was soon in action against German fighter-bombers—mostly Focke-Wulf Fw 190s—carrying out hit-and-run attacks on targets along the south coast of England. Once the fighter-bombers had made their attack, Merlin-engined Spitfires stood little chance of catching them on the homeward run, and it was a matter of pure luck if a patrol intercepted them on the way in. The situation had become even worse from June 1942, when the fighter-bomber Geschwader on the Channel coast began to rearm with the Focke-Wulf Fw 190A-3, which could carry a bomb weighing 1,100lb (499kg).

No. 41 Squadron shot down its first FW 190 on April 27, while operating from Hawkinge. The second unit to reequip with the Mk XII, No. 91, destroyed five enemy fighter-bombers in a running battle over the Channel on May 25, 1943. In June the same year, following a marked decline in enemy fighter-bomber activity, and with the low-level air defense of the south coast area being progressively taken over by the Hawker Typhoon, which had hitherto experienced numerous teething troubles, the two Spitfire XII-equipped squadrons moved to Westhampnett to form a bomber support wing. Nos. 41 and 91 Squadrons were the only operational units to be armed with the Spitfire XII.

The most important of the Griffon-engined Spitfires was the Mk XIV, which was based on the airframe of the Mk VIII. The latter was basically a variant of the PR.VII photo-reconnaissance aircraft (which was not a production aircraft, but a service modification of the Mk V). Because the Mk VIII was intended for the low-altitude air-superiority role, it was unpressurized. Necessary modifications, including a general strengthening of the airframe, delayed its service debut, which is why the Spitfire Mk IX preceded it. Only 1,658 Mk VIIIs were built, seeing service predominantly in Italy, the Far East, and Australia.

The advantage of the Mk XIV was that it could be put into production quickly, as the latest version of the Griffon engine was available for installation in an airframe that was already proven. Three prototypes were taken for conversion from the Mk VIII production line—the first of these, JF317, being the first to fly. One of the prototypes was lost during handling trials at Boscombe Down when the engine failed at 30,000ft (9,144m). The pilot—a Norwegian, Lieutenant N. K. Norsted—glided down with the intention of making a forced landing, but the engine caught fire at 1,000ft (305m) and Norsted bailed out, the aircraft crashing in a cemetery at Amesbury, Wiltshire.

Distinguished from the earlier Merlin-engine Spitfire by its longer nose, cut-down rear fuselage, and clear-view bubble canopy, the Mk XIV was produced in two sub-variants with

BELOW Spitfire Mk XIVs undergoing routine maintenance. The powerful Griffon-engined fighter brought a new dimension to the Spitfire saga.

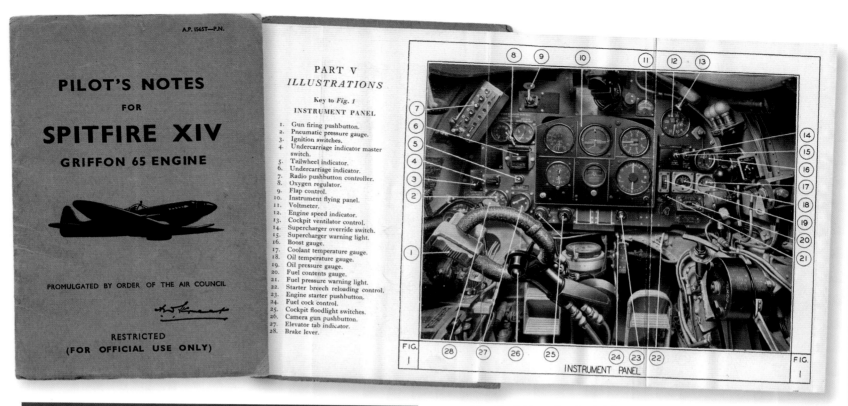

PILOT'S NOTES

FOR

SPITFIRE XIV

GRIFFON 65 ENGINE

PROMULGATED BY ORDER OF THE AIR COUNCIL

RESTRICTED
(FOR OFFICIAL USE ONLY)

A.P. 1565T—P.N.

PART V
ILLUSTRATIONS

Key to *Fig. 1*
INSTRUMENT PANEL

1. Gun firing pushbutton.
2. Pneumatic pressure gauge.
3. Ignition switches.
4. Undercarriage indicator master switch.
5. Tailwheel indicator.
6. Undercarriage indicator.
7. Radio pushbutton controller.
8. Oxygen regulator.
9. Flap control.
10. Instrument flying panel.
11. Voltmeter.
12. Engine speed indicator.
13. Cockpit ventilator control.
14. Supercharger override switch.
15. Supercharger warning light.
16. Boost gauge.
17. Coolant temperature gauge.
18. Oil temperature gauge.
19. Oil pressure gauge.
20. Fuel contents gauge.
21. Fuel pressure warning light.
22. Starter breech reloading control.
23. Engine starter pushbutton.
24. Fuel cock control.
25. Cockpit floodlight switches.
26. Camera gun pushbutton.
27. Elevator tab indicator.
28. Brake lever.

FIG. 1

INSTRUMENT PANEL

FIG. 1

ABOVE The Pilot's Notes for the Spitfire Mk XIV, with a fold-out showing cockpit details. These booklets were simple to understand, but comprehensive.

LEFT The Spitfire Mk XIV was based on the airframe of the elegant Mk VIII, seen here. The first three Mk XIV prototypes were taken from the Mk VIII production line.

differing armament fits. The 527 Mk XIV fighters were complemented by 430 examples of a fighter-reconnaissance version, the FR.XIV, equipped with a fuselage-mounted camera. The Mk XIV, in both versions, went on to equip 25 RAF squadrons.

Another Griffon-engine fighter-reconnaissance version of the Spitfire was the F/FR Mk XVIII, which was the last Griffon-engine development of the original elliptical-wing Spitfire airframe. One hundred were completed as fighters, and a further 200 for the fighter-reconnaissance role. The F/FR XVIII was widely used in the Middle and Far East in the early postwar years.

The only photo-reconnaissance Spitfire with the Griffon engine was the PR.XIX, the last in the line of PR Spitfire conversions. It was basically a late production Mk XIV airframe with an Mk VC bowser wing (a wing adapted for fuel tank stowage) and a universal camera installation based on that of the PR.IV/XI. It was developed early in 1944 to counter German air defenses, which were becoming increasingly sophisticated.

The three last variations of the Spitfire, the Mks 21, 22, and 24, also used the Griffon engine, but they bore little resemblance to the original Spitfire concept.

Flying the Griffon Spitfire

Prior to the Spitfire Mk XIV entering full production, one of the six aircraft originally converted from Mk VIII airframes was sent to the Air Fighting Development Unit (AFDU) at Wittering, near Peterborough for evaluation. The trials were held from July 27 to 29, 1943 and took the form of a direct comparison between the Mk XIV and its Mk VIII predecessor. The AFDU pilots produced this assessment:

"The larger engine involves a much longer engine cowling and the extra weight forward has been balanced by ballast in the tail. The fin has been increased in area to help directional stability and a large rudder is fitted. This aircraft had the normal wings of a Mk VIII with small span ailerons, but the extended wing tips had been replaced by the standard tips as on Mk IX. The engine is not representative of production as the FS gear is higher and the MS lower. A five blade propeller is fitted. The aircraft has a Bendix injection carburettor and boost for combat is limited to plus 15lbs [7kg]. The Mk VIII weighed 7,760lbs [3,520kg], the XIV, 8,376lbs [3,799kg].

"Performance: speeds near the ground are identical; at 10,000ft [3,048m] and 15,000ft [4,572m] the VIII is faster; at 20/25,000ft [6,096/7,620m] similar; at 30,000ft [9,144m] and over the XIV was faster and is the superior aircraft. Climbs: zero to 30,000 feet the VIII is the better aircraft; at 30,000ft and over the XIV is by far the better.

"The elevator control of the XIV was found to be much heavier than that of the VIII, unpleasantly so, and the other controls felt to be slightly heavier than on previous Spitfire Mks. In spite of heavy controls the XIV is more manoeuvrable than the VIII in turns at all heights. Spins were carried out in the XIV at 25,000ft. The aircraft did not spin voluntarily but had to be put into and held in the spin. On releasing the controls the aircraft automatically came out of the spin. Instead of spinning in the normal nose down attitude, the nose of the aircraft oscillated from an almost vertical position downwards to a position with the nose well above the horizon, so that the aircraft was tail down. It spent most of its time in this flat position from which, after four turns, recovery was fast by the normal method or slower if the controls were released. It never appears to become uncontrollable.

"Pilot's view is superior on the XIV due to the lower engine cowling. Both aircraft carry the same amount of fuel (96 gallons [436 liters] in the main tank and 27 gallons [123 liters] in two wing tanks). Refuelling checks made to compare consumption showed that when the two aircraft stayed together throughout the trials, the Griffon engine was using approximately 10–15 gallons [45–68 liters] more fuel per hour than the Merlin.

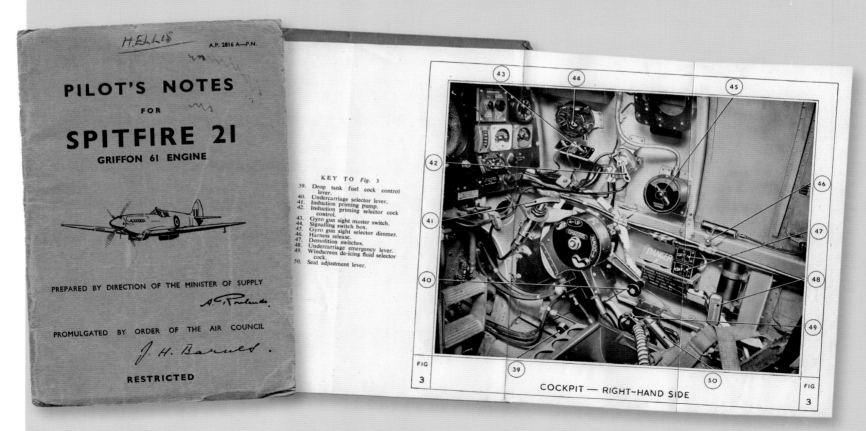

ABOVE Allies cross the Rhine at Wesel, March 1945. Here, gliders and parachutes litter the landing zone while C-47s drop more paratroops from low level.

OPPOSITE The Spitfire F.21 was the first of the re-designed Griffon-engined Spitfires. Although the first of 120 production aircraft was delivered in September 1944, it was a year before the variant went into first-line service.

BELOW The town of Wesel was reduced to rubble by Allied bombing before the Rhine crossing. The air operation was code-named "Varsity."

BELOW RIGHT Spitfire HF.Mk IX MK850 was the trials aircraft for the Packard Merlin 266 engine, and was converted to Mk XVI standard.

"Conclusions: of the two aircraft the Mk VIII is preferable at all heights up to about 25,000ft except for its turning capabilities. It is much lighter on the elevators and easier for the average pilot to fly. Its performance and fuel consumption are better. The Mk XIV is superior above 25,000ft and with its better turning characteristics is more than a match for the VIII . . ."

Although the Mk XIV was clearly suitable for high-altitude work, it was clear that there was a requirement for a new tactical version of the Spitfire optimized for combat at lower altitudes. This emerged as the Spitfire LF.XVI, which was basically an Mk IX with an American Packard-built Merlin 266 in place of a British Rolls-Royce Merlin 66. Packard's involvement with the Merlin dated back to April 1942, when it was suggested that it would be a better engine for the North American Mustang fighter than the existing Allison engine, which did not perform well at high altitudes. The Mustang was duly fitted with the Packard-built Merlin 65, and the combination proved an exceptional one.

Externally, the Mk XVI was identical in appearance to the late-production Spitfire Mk IX. It entered service in the autumn of 1944, in time to play an important part in two major offensives—Veritable and Grenade—launched by Field Marshal Bernard Montgomery's 21st Army Group in January 1945. Air cover over the battlefield was provided by No. 84 Group, with the cooperation of the US XXIX Tactical Air Command, while No. 83 Group maintained an interdiction program beyond the Rhine. Although often frustrated by bad weather, No. 83 Group's Spitfires, Mustangs, Typhoons, and Tempests penetrated deeply into Germany, seeking out railway traffic north of the Ruhr and road transport. On February 22, all available fighter-bomber squadrons took part in Operation Clarion, in which 9,000 aircraft attacked the transportation system over a quarter of a million square miles (648sq km) of Germany. For the "Thousand-Year" Reich, the end was fast approaching.

A Spitfire squadron crew room

For a new pilot fresh from a Spitfire Operational Training Unit, venturing for the first time into a crew room on an operational squadron was an unforgettable experience, as Jim Rosser recalled when he reported to No. 72 Squadron at Coltishall in October 1940:

"I was one of nine or ten replacement pilots. Having reported to Station HQ I was directed to 'A' Flight crew room, or the 'Dispersal Hut' as they were then called. It was a long, single-storey building about 36ft by 10ft [11m by 3m]; there was an office at one end for the flight commander, and down the centre of the room there ran a long, linoleum-covered table which I think had once been used for parachute packing. Against the walls were the now familiar wooden-armed easy chairs; I little realised at the time how many hours I would spend sitting in such chairs at readiness. The table was covered with parachutes, leather flying jackets, 'Mae West' lifejackets, maps and all sorts of assorted junk. At one end was a well preserved shove-ha'penny board, and woe betide anyone who left so much as a finger mark on it.

"The room was crowded with pilots, some in chairs in their flying kit, others standing around. In one corner was a crowd who were clearly new boys, like myself; they were distinguished by the fact that they were wearing ties, for most of the others wore silk scarves of varying hues [This was not an affectation; a collar and tie were too restrictive when a pilot was airborne, since he had to turn his head constantly—Author]. I was suddenly grabbed by someone I recognised, who had been a fellow member of the RAFVR . . . He had joined very much earlier than I had and was therefore a good deal further ahead in flying. He had been in the Battle of Britain . . .

"He introduced me to my new flight commander, Flight Lieutenant Desmond Sheen, who was an Australian and still wore the dark blue uniform of the RAAF with gold rank braid instead of the blue RAF braid. Because of his uniform, I learned that he was often mistaken for a member of the Air Transport Auxiliary, and when that happened his sense of humour completely deserted him. I was to find him a very pleasant, undemonstrative man. He was later to command the Squadron,

TOP A Sector Operations Room wall clock of the mid-war period, with colored triangles pointing outwards. Such items could also be found in squadron crew rooms.

ABOVE Pilots relaxing in a crew room. Every effort was made to provide a degree of comfort.

LEFT Some examples of RAF crockery—a beer tankard and tea mug.

and subsequently the Biggin Hill Wing [Desmond Sheen remained in the RAF after the war and eventually reached the rank of Group Captain, retiring in 1971. He died in 2001, at age 83—Author].

"I was introduced to the other members of the Flight and stood around with the other new boys. To the best of my memory there was only one officer amongst us and that was Pilot Officer Fordham, who was a Canadian [All Canadian aircrew were commissioned—Author]. All the rest were sergeant pilots. Within a year all the rest were to be killed except myself and one other, Bill Lamberton."

Life was not always happy for sergeant pilots, as Rosser discovered when the squadron moved to Leuchars in Scotland at the end of November 1940. Among regular RAF NCOs who had taken years to reach the rank of sergeant, there was considerable resentment over the sudden appearance of young men, barely out of their teens, with three stripes on their arm.

"We found that the Sergeants' Mess, with the support of the Station Commander, refused to accommodate sergeant pilots, and arrangements had been made for us to eat and sleep in rather poor spare accommodation. The other squadrons, one of which was a Dutch unit, went along with this, but our CO, Squadron Leader Grey, did not. After a clash with the Station Commander, and several calls to Group HQ, the Station Commander was ordered to admit us to the Sergeants' Mess, as was our undeniable right. This of course generated quite a bit of bad feeling, so we took only breakfast and lunch in the mess and spent our evenings

in Dundee. Fortunately it was only a few miles away and there was a rail halt on the edge of the airfield. We would catch the most convenient train after we came off readiness at dusk, and return in time for readiness in the morning!

"We were not long at Leuchars, and soon moved to Acklington in Northumberland. This was to be our home for the rest of the winter. The Squadron was well-known in the district, having been in action against the big German attack on August 15, 1940, and we were royally welcomed in pubs from Morpeth to Alnmouth. The days were spent in training of various sorts: simulated dogfights, air-to-air firing, and of course there was always a flight of three or four aircraft at constant readiness, from half an hour before first light until dusk."

ABOVE Chess was a favorite pastime among pilots on readiness, especially those from Poland and Czechoslovakia. Here, a sergeant pilot makes his move.

LEFT Pilots were often to be found filling in their log books in the crew room. This one records some training sorties flown by the pilot at No 53 Operational Training Unit, Heston.

The V-1 menace

In 1943, British Intelligence identified a new threat to Britain's security: the Fieseler F1 103 pilotless bomb, better know as the V-1. By the end of the year the Allies knew all about this weapon, which carried a one-ton warhead and was powered by a pulse-jet engine, timed to cut out after a predetermined distance so that the V-1 dived on its target. It was not precise and was essentially an area attack weapon, but London was a large city and the threat was clear enough.

The closing weeks of 1943 saw the Spitfire squadrons in southeast England taking part in "Noball" operations, as attacks on the V-1 launching sites that were under construction in the Pas de Calais were called. These attacks were made initially by rocket-armed Hurricane IVs of Nos. 164 and 184 squadrons, escorted by Spitfires, and their losses were dreadful. Squadron Leader (later Wing Commander) Jack Rose, No. 184 Squadron's CO, had this to say about the task:

"The Hurricane IV's low speed in comparison with contemporary fighter aircraft, and its poor armament after the rockets had been released (one .303 Browning in each wing) meant that operations could only be carried out in selected circumstances: Spitfire fighter cover, when this could be arranged, good low cloud cover or the use of semi-darkness. Spitfire escorts were unpopular with the Spitfire pilots as all our operations were at low level, and to maintain effective contact with us this meant flying lower, slower and longer than they would have liked."

In December 1943, much to the relief of the pilots, No. 184 Squadron reequipped with Typhoons, and No. 164 Squadron followed suit shortly afterward. By this time the V-1 sites were the target of a major bombing offensive, and it was during these

ABOVE A V-1 streaks low over the Kent countryside, en route to London. The "buzz bombs" presented a very serious threat.

LEFT Wing Commander Jack Rose, DFC, who commanded No 184 Squadron—one of the units tasked with making rocket attacks on the V-1 sites.

operations that two Spitfire squadrons, Nos. 132 and 602, pioneered precision bombing techniques with the aircraft, a task that was not greeted enthusiastically by the pilots. On April 12, 1944, the Spitfires of these two squadrons, each armed with a 500lb (227kg) bomb, attacked the V-1 launching site at Bouillancourt, 12 miles (19km) south of Le Tréport; they were the first bombs to be dropped by Spitfires in northwest Europe.

Despite the tonnage of bombs that fell on the V-1 launch sites, the first missiles were launched against England on the night of June 12/13, 1944. Eleven squadrons of the Air Defence of Great Britain (as RAF Fighter Command was now known, albeit for a short period) were assigned to deal with the threat. No. 11 Group instituted so-called "Diver" patrols, with fighters patrolling along three clearly defined lines: (1) between Beachy Head and Dover, (2) over the coast between Newhaven and Dover, and (3) between Haywards Heath and Ashford. At the same time, nearly 400 antiaircraft guns and 480 barrage balloons were deployed on the V-1 approach route to London.

The only fighter with a real chance of catching the V-1s in a straight speed chase was the Hawker Tempest Mk V (in fact, this aircraft destroyed 638 V-1s out of the RAF's total of 1,771).

However, much effort was put into increasing the Spitfire's speed: its armor was taken out, unnecessary equipment was removed, including some guns, and on many aircraft the paint was stripped and the surfaces polished in order to give a few extra miles per hour. Although the Mk IX Spitfires were hard put to catch the V-1, the Griffon-engine Mks XII and XIV performed well against it; in No. 91 Squadron, 14 pilots flying the Mk XII destroyed five or more flying bombs; five of these pilots destroyed more than ten. Both 41 and 91 Squadrons exchanged their Mk XIIs for LF XIVEs before the V-1 offensive was over, operating the mark alongside Nos. 130, 322 (Netherlands), 350 (Belgian), 402 (RCAF), and 601 Squadrons.

Shooting at the V-1s and causing them to explode in mid-air could be a dangerous business, and from the end of June, pilots began experimenting with a new technique for destroying the flying bombs: they would slide their aircraft's wingtip under that of the V-1 until the airflow caused the bomb to tip over, toppling its gyro so that it dived to the ground and exploded short of its target.

The real answer to the threat, of course, was to eliminate the V-1 launching sites, as mentioned earlier, and Spitfire dive-bombers again joined other types in an offensive that saw 60,000 tons of bombs dropped on them between mid-June and the end of September, when the sites were overrun by the Allied advance. Even then, the flying bomb assault was not over; for some time after that the missiles were air-launched from Heinkel He 111s operating from Holland, but it was the RAF's Mosquito night fighters that were the principal counterforce against this type of operation.

In July 1944, at the height of the V-1 offensive, one of the Spitfire squadrons—No. 616—reequipped with a new fighter type, the Gloster Meteor F.1. The RAF had entered the jet age.

FAR LEFT A Hawker Tempest of No. 501 Squadron closing in on a V-1, just visible at the top right of the photograph.

LEFT Two small V-1 "kill" markings are just visible above the crest of No. 222 Squadron on this honors board, manufactured from a section of a shot-down German aircraft.

Genesis of the jet: The Me 262

The Messerschmitt Me 262 jet fighter presented a serious threat to Allied air superiority during the closing months of World War II. It was faster than the fastest Allied fighter then in service, the Hawker Tempest. However, it had one main drawback: the unreliability of its turbojet engines, which had a life of only about 25 hours before they needed to be changed. It also suffered from the whims of Adolf Hitler, whose obsession with using the aircraft as a bomber rather than a fighter meant that it was six years between the 262 taking shape on Messerschmitt's drawing board and its entry into Luftwaffe service.

The Me 262 has often been described as the world's first operational jet fighter, but that distinction rightfully fell to Britain's Gloster Meteor F.Mk 1—No. 616 Squadron was fully established with the type by August 15, 1944. It was not until September 1944 that a German Me 262 fighter-bomber unit, KG 51, became operational. In addition, a fighter trials unit known as the Kommando Nowotny did not reach operational status until the end of October, being deployed to the airfields of Achmer and Hesepe near Osnabruck, astride the main American daylight bomber approach route.

Because of a shortage of adequately trained pilots and technical problems, the Kommando Nowotny was usually able to fly only three or four sorties a day against the enemy formations, yet in November 1944 the 262s destroyed 22 aircraft. Apart from the problems with its engines, the Me 262 was a superb aircraft, and if it had reached full operational status in the early months of

ABOVE The Gloster Meteor F.Mk 1 was the world's first fully operational jet fighter, beating the Me 262 into squadron service by several weeks.

LEFT An aerodynamically beautiful design, the Me 262 suffered from unreliable engines which had a life of only 25 hours.

ABOVE A 250lb [68kg] bomb with carrier and release mechanism as fitted to 2nd TAF's Spitfire XVIs in 1945. Two were carried. Spitfires based in Italy were also often used for tactical bombing.

BELOW The Arado Ar 234 Blitz (Lightning) was produced both as a bomber and reconnaissance aircraft. In April 1945, flying from Norway, it flew the Luftwaffe's last sortie over Britain.

1944 it might have robbed the Allies of the air superiority they needed for the invasion of Europe.

One of the first encounters between the Allies and the Me 262 occurred on July 25, 1944, when a de Havilland Mosquito photo-reconnaissance aircraft was intercepted by one at 29,000ft (8,845m) over Munich. The Me 262 belonged to an experimental unit known as EK 262 based at nearby Lechfeld. The Mosquito pilot, Flight Lieutenant A. E. Wall, took evasive action and shook off the 262 three times, eventually reaching cloud cover, but not before his aircraft had been damaged. He went on to make an emergency landing in Italy.

Although most Me 262 fighter sorties were flown against the American daylight bombers, RAF bomber crews also had several encounters with the jets, and with Me 163 rocket fighters. On February 8, 1945, for example, an Me 262 was shot down by two gunners in a Halifax of No. 427 (RCAF) Squadron engaged in a daylight raid on Goch, while the gunners of another Halifax of the same squadron claimed an Me 163 as probably destroyed.

For the RAF, the most serious conflict with the jets came on the night of March 30, 1945 and the next day. One German night-fighter squadron, 10/NJG 11, was equipped with Me 262s, and on this night its commander, Oberleutnant Walter, shot down four Mosquitoes on the approaches to Berlin. The following morning, Halifaxes of No. 6 (RCAF) Group—operating over Hamburg without fighter cover because they had arrived over the target ten minutes late—were attacked by 30 Me 262s, and eight Halifaxes were shot down.

Another revolutionary aircraft in Luftwaffe service during the closing months of the war was the Arado Ar 234 Blitz (Lightning). Two versions—bomber and reconnaissance—were produced; the bomber version of the Ar 234 equipped KG 76 from October 1944,

flying its first operational missions during the Ardennes offensive in December. The jet bombers were very active in the early weeks of 1945, one of their most notable missions being the ten-day series of attacks on the Ludendorff bridge at Remagen, captured by the Americans in March.

Top-scoring Me 262 ace Heinz Bär, who destroyed 16 enemy aircraft while flying the jet fighter, had this to say about the aircraft:

"The P-51 Mustang was perhaps the most difficult of all Allied fighters to meet in combat. The Mustang was fast, manoeuvrable, hard to see and difficult to identify because it resembled the Bf 109 closely in the air. These are my general impressions of Allied aircraft, and of course, the quality of the Spitfire needs no elaboration. They shot me down once and caused me at least six forced landings.

"The edge in performance and armament given us by the Me 262 was decisive in fighter combat. This assumes, of course, that the Me 262 was functioning correctly on both engines. In the jets, we were in real trouble if we lost one engine, and it was a petrifying experience also to be low on fuel, preparing to land, and find that Allied fighters had followed you home."

" Encounters with jets

It was during the Arnhem operation in September 1944 that the Me 262 fighter-bombers of KG 51 began to appear in numbers. Sergeant Walter Langham of the Glider Pilot Regiment recalls an attack by a solitary Me 262:

"[The Me 262] strafed us in the wood. It was the first jet plane we had ever seen, and luckily there was only one, as several of us stood up to get a better view!"

Jim Rosser, a flight lieutenant and back on operations after a spell as a production test pilot, was now flying Spitfire IXs with No. 66 Squadron from Lille/Wambrechies. Below, he describes his encounter with a 262. He was on patrol at 15,000ft (4,575m) over Venlo in Holland when he sighted a 262 a few thousand feet lower down.

"I don't think anyone had actually managed to shoot down a 262 at that time, and I thought this was my big chance. I went down after him, flat out, but he saw me coming and opened the taps. Smoke trails streamed from his turbines and off he went. I hadn't a hope of catching him, so I gave up and rejoined the formation.

"The incident had an interesting sequel. Years after the war, when I was stationed in Germany, I met a colonel in the Federal German Luftwaffe. We had a few drinks and got talking, and it turned out that he had flown 262s. We compared dates, places and times, and by one of those extraordinary coincidences it came to light that he had almost certainly been the pilot of 'my' 262. He said that if I had kept after him, it was on the cards I would have got him. His fuel was very low, and he couldn't have maintained full throttle for more than half a minute. So there it was; I was shot down near Arnhem a few days later, so I never did get another chance to have a crack at a jet."

Wing Commander "Johnnie" Johnson, who in September 1944 was commanding No. 144 Wing of the 2nd Tactical Air Force, an all-Canadian Spitfire IX Wing based at Grave, Belgium, also had experience with the Me 262. He was inspecting the airmen's accommodation when he encountered the aircraft:

"[My] visit was rudely interrupted by the roar of powerful engines and the whine of an aircraft in a steep dive. As we ran out of the mess tent, we were in time to see the unfamiliar, sleek silhouette of a Messerschmitt 262 climbing steeply away after its dive-bombing attack. A cloud of smoke rolled into the air and I drove quickly to the scene. The bombs dropped by the enemy aircraft were of the canister type, and the containers burst at a pre-selected altitude a few feet above the ground. Small fragmentation bombs were then scattered over a wide area, and these had found their mark in 416 Squadron's dispersal."

ABOVE "Johnnie" Johnson and his Labrador, Sally. Johnson's callsign was "Greycap", a reference to the Canada goose, as he commanded a Canadian Spitfire Wing.

LEFT The Messerschmitt Me 262 was deployed too late to influence the air war. Its operations were hampered by attacks on its airfields and by fuel shortages.

BELOW The Daily Mail produced this *World War Atlas* in response to popular demand. It was updated at regular intervals.

The attack killed five airmen and destroyed a Spitfire. Others were saved when Canadian pilots taxied them to safety, away from exploding fuel and ammunition.

"During the following days we were often attacked by the 262s, and more airmen were killed and more Spitfires damaged. The enemy jets came in very fast from the east, and in order to protect our airfield we carried out standing patrols at the favourite attacking height of the intruders. But our Spitfires were too slow to catch the 262s, and although we often possessed the height advantage, we could not bring the jets to combat.

" . . . the complete superiority of the Messerschmitt 262 was well demonstrated to us one evening when we carried out a dusk patrol over Grave. Kenway [the Ground Controller—author] had told us that the jets were active over Holland, but although we scanned the skies we could see nothing of them. Suddenly, without warning, an enemy jet appeared one hundred yards ahead of our Spitfires. The pilot must have seen our formation, since he shot up from below and climbed away at high speed . . . as he soared into the darkening, eastern sky, he added insult to injury by carrying out a perfect, upward roll."

On December 10, 1944, the French pilots of No. 145 Wing had their first encounter with Me 262s. Two flights, one each from Nos. 329 and 345 Squadrons, took off to dive-bomb a German HQ on the right bank of the Rhine, near Nijmegen, and the Spitfires were attacked by four of the jets as they approached the target. The 262s made one pass, causing no damage, but they forced the Spitfire pilots to jettison their bombs. The Spitfires were escorted by Tempests, which pursued the Me 262s into the clouds.

At the end of the war, the Allies found hundreds of Me 262s intact on their airfields, or dispersed in forest clearings. The potent jets had finally been defeated not in air combat but by attacks on their bases, and by lack of fuel.

Spitfire Mk XIV

The Mk XIV was the first Griffon-engined Spitfire to be put into large-scale production, although it was intended as an interim aircraft pending the introduction of the Mk XVIII. Remarkably, with a modest increase in width and height, the engine's capacity was augmented by some 10 liters, and its power by around 1,000hp; however, the aircraft was nearly 3ft (1m) longer than the Mk I Spitfire due to the longer engine and nose cone spinner, and a broader rudder.

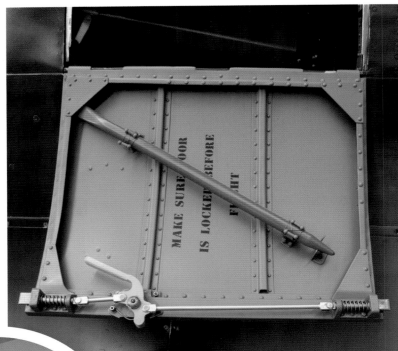

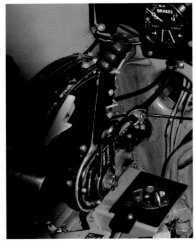

The Griffon drove a five-blade constant-speed Rotol propeller, and the aircraft was armed with two 20mm cannon and two .5 or four .303 Brownings, and could carry one 500lb (227kg) bomb or rocket projectiles. Developments included a retractable tailwheel (inset); in this case a "scallop" cutaway, a recent modification, allows the doors to be closed while the wheel remains down. The crowbar (top right) was used to smash the canopy in the event of an emergency.

Spitfire Mk XVI

The Spitfire Mk XVI was essentially a Mk IX fitted with an American Packard-built Merlin 266 engine in place of the British Rolls-Royce-built Merlin 66. Externally, the Mk XVI was identical in appearance with late production Mk IXs, but there were several internal technical differences; for example, the supercharger gear on the Mk XVI was electro-hydraulically operated compared with electro-pneumatic operation on the Mk IX.

The radio (right) had four preset frequencies, selected by push buttons. The throttle handle (black, opposite, on the left beneath the radio) could be twisted to range the gyro gunsight; the wheel on the throttle pivot was used to set the friction of the mechanism so it would neither move with vibration nor be too stiff to adjust freely. Opposite, top center is the "engine group," with oil pressure and temperature, radiator temperature, and boost control indicators, and rev counter at the top.

High-altitude Spitfires

In 1941 the Spitfire Mk VI made its appearance. This was the first Spitfire to be developed for high-altitude interception, and the first to be fitted with a pressurized cockpit. The prototype was a Mk I, R7120, which was taken off the production line and partially dismantled. Two airtight bulkheads were installed in the fuselage, the forward one being placed as close as possible to the rear of the fuel tanks and the rear one immediately behind the perspex window aft of the pilot's seat.

ABOVE The Spitfire Mk VI had extended wingtips, a pressure cabin and a four-blade propeller. This is the prototype, X4942, which had no cannon fitted.

BELOW Fur-lined boots were essential for the pilot of a high-altitude Spitfire; these "escape" boots could be converted into shoes to disguise their military origins.

The sliding hood was replaced by a specially designed hood of strengthened perspex that was clamped down on to a sponge rubber seal before take-off; and the pilot's side door was blanked off. Despite some initial difficulty in making the cockpit completely airtight, the pressurization system worked well, producing a pressure equivalent to that of 28,000ft (8,540m) altitude while the aircraft was at 40,000ft (12,200m).

Fitted with a Merlin 47 engine of 1415hp, R7120 went to RAE Farnborough for pressurization trials in June 1941. In the meantime, a second aircraft, X4942, had been converted from a Mk VA. Both aircraft were fitted with the extended wingtips that were to be a feature of all the high-altitude Spitfires, increasing the wing area from 242 sq ft (22.49 sq m) to 248.5 sq ft (23 sq m). This was a notable recognition feature, and the type appeared in the Air Ministry aircraft recognition lists as "Experimental Aircraft No. 152". One hundred Mk VI Spitfires were ordered, the first entering service with No 616 Squadron at King's Cliffe, Northamptonshire, in April 1942.

The second high-altitude Spitfire variant was the Mk VII, which also had a pressurized cockpit and was powered by a Rolls-Royce Merlin 60 engine, a two-stage, two-speed, inter-cooled powerplant that took development of the Merlin to its ultimate level. Like the Mk VI, the Mk VII was a limited production, high-altitude interceptor, only 140 examples being produced.

A flight of four high-altitude Spitfires, Mks VI and VII, was assigned to Skaebrae in the Orkneys for the defense of the Fleet Anchorage at Scapa Flow, a task shared in 1943–44 by Nos. 312 and 602 squadrons.

On February 20, 1944, Pilot Officer Ian Blair and another pilot, Flight Lieutenant Bennett, took off to intercept an unidentified high-flying enemy reconnaissance aircraft that was approaching the anchorage. Blair was flying Spitfire Mk VII MD114; his number two was flying a Mk VI; as Blair writes opposite, the unidentified aircraft turned out to be a Messerschmitt 109G.

"I was on standby when a 'scramble' was received [Blair reported]. I immediately took off with my No. 2 and as soon as airborne received a vector of 085, which indicated a hostile approaching from the direction of the Norwegian coast. My aircraft, a Mk VII H.F. Spitfire had a very good rate of climb, 2,200ft [671m] per minute at over 25,000ft [7,620m]. Soon a vapour trail was observed approaching from the east, further height was gained, and at about 38,000ft [11,582m] the hostile below decided to turn back towards the Norwegian coast. Using my height advantage I commenced a dive in pursuit. The Spitfire accelerated very quickly and soon the hostile was rapidly being overtaken. I had to throttle back so as not to overshoot; my No. 2 failed to do the same and overshot me in the dive.

"Once in the attacking position he opened fire, but his guns failed to operate. I quickly closed to 180 yards [165m] and fired a burst. Closing to 140 yards [128m] I opened fire again and the starboard wing of the E/A finally broke off in a shower of debris. The E/A crashed into the sea, no signs of the pilot. I set course for base. My No. 2 called me on the R/T saying that I appeared to have a glycol leak. I immediately gained some more height and slowed the aircraft down, trying to get the radiator temperatures down in an effort to conserve the coolant.

"My No. 2 stayed with me and we set course for Skaebrae, having sent the usual 'Mayday'. I was unable to make Skaebrae, and decided to set down on the nearest land which was Stronsay, a small island in the Orkney group. I picked my spot, which was a soft peat bog, and executed a good landing. I called my No. 2 on the R/T to let him know all was well.

"I suffered a cut on the bridge of my nose and subsequently two black eyes. I walked about 20 yards [18m] to a crofters cottage, and when the old lady opened the door and saw me standing there, although she could only speak Gaelic, she knew what was required of her and called the local doc who arrived very quickly.

"I had fired a total of 216 rounds of 20mm and 673 rounds of .303. The removal of the Spitfire from the island took three weeks. Later in the afternoon, Pierre Clostermann collected me from Stronsay Island in the unit Tiger Moth. The Control Centre at RAF Kirkwall was excellent. The RN C-in-C personally sent for me, to thank me and to receive a person-to-person account of the operation."

Page 4 DAILY RECORD, Wednesday, February 23, 1944

Kesselring's 4

Scot's 500 m.p.h. Dive To Bring Down Raider

TWICE IN THE NEWS

STREAKING down in a 500 m.p.h. power dive, a young Glasgow R.A.F. Spitfire pilot yesterday shot down, in two seconds, with blazing cannon fire, an intruding German long-range ME 109, which fell into the sea off the coast.

The Spitfire tracked down the enemy at 32,000 feet, dived after him all out, and "killed" at 4000 feet.

The Spitfire was so close to the enemy plane when it was destroyed that bits of the doomed aircraft flew back and damaged the Spitfire's radiator—but the pilot got home safely.

Hero of this split-second kill is Pilot Officer Ian Blair (26), who is a married man.

Pilot Tells of Chase

"I was sitting on the 'drome when I received the word 'scramble, enemy aircraft approaching coast,'" Blair said.

"I took off and climbed full out. It was about 32,000 feet when we levelled off and I received the signal bandit ahead.'

"By then we could see his vapour trails in the sky. He saw us and dived to the starboard on a southerly course, going all out.

"I opened up everything I'd got and went into a power-dive after him.

"We were now about 4000 feet diving hell ... seaward. My speed was so ... to throttle back to ... ave him a two- ... ing broke off and ... ed over and over ... atched it burning ... e on the water.

Pilot Officer Ian Blair, of 407 St. Vincent Street, Glasgow, was previously in the news when, though without previous flying experience, he brought home a bomber the pilot of which had been killed.

CLOSTERMANN
le Grand Cirque

1 volume illustré FLAMMARION

ABOVE An excerpt from a cutting from Scotland's *Daily Record* newspaper—dated February 23, 1944—telling the story of Ian Blair's exploits in shooting down a marauding Messerschmitt 109 over Scapa Flow.

LEFT French pilot Pierre Clostermann wrote a fanciful account of the incident in his book *Le Grand Cirque*, a best-seller that was translated into English as *The Big Show*.

BELOW Spitfire Mk VII MD114 DU-G, taken at Skeabrae in 1944; Ian Blair piloted this aircraft.

Russia's Spitfires

The first Spitfire operations from Russian territory had taken place in September 1942, when a pair of PR. Mk IVs of No. 1 PRU deployed to North Russia to give PR support for two squadrons of Handley Page Hampden torpedo bombers, which were deployed there for offensive operations against enemy shipping. The Hampdens were later handed over to the Russians, as were the Spitfires. On October 4, the Soviet ambassador in London presented a request for the urgent delivery of Spitfires in order to relieve the critical pressure on the Stalingrad front; this was approved by Winston Churchill, and, early in 1943, 137 Spitfire Mk VBs drawn from Middle East stocks, plus 50

in spares, were handed over to the Russians at Basra in Iraq. These aircraft, armed with two cannon and two machine guns, were deployed with units of the 220th and 268th Fighter Divisions in time for them to take part in the major Russian counterattack that led to the encirclement and destruction of the German Sixth Army at Stalingrad. A few were assigned to the Moscow air defense region, where they had some successes against German reconnaissance aircraft.

In addition to the Mk Vs, the Russians took delivery of 1,188 Spitfire Mk IXs before the end of the war, plus five PR.Mk IVs and two PR.Mk XIs. They fought on every front, but their main area of operations was in the north, where they performed sterling service in the air defense of Leningrad and in the air battles over Karelia.

Purely for political reasons, none of the official Soviet Air Force historians documenting the World War II made mention of the Spitfire, or for that matter any other Allied aircraft (with the possible exception of the Bell P-39 Airacobra) serving on the Eastern Front.

However, one pilot who testified to the presence of the Russian Spitfires was Finnish air ace Eino Luukkanen, who encountered some while on patrol over the Gulf of Finland in a Brewster Buffalo fighter.

"Foul weather. Day after day of low cloud, rain and dank mist kept the squadron grounded at Rompotti, our spirits as grey as the skies sitting on the tops of the surrounding trees. The days passed in dreary

ABOVE A page from the *Daily Mail World War Atlas*, showing operations in the Caucasus. Many Spitfires were assigned to the Kuban region, where fierce battles took place.

RIGHT Spitfires being made ready for a ferry flight to the Soviet Union from an airfield in Persia. They already bear the red star insignia of the Soviet Air Force.

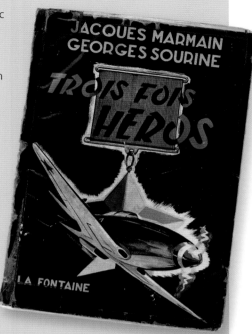

LEFT The survival chances of the Arctic convoys to Russia increased greatly when aircraft carriers became available to escort them. Here, carriers and their Seafires assemble in Scapa Flow.

RIGHT One of the first books published in the West detailing the exploits of Soviet fighter pilots was this example, by French authors.

BELOW The Hawker Hurricane, seen here under camouflage in the snow, was the first British fighter supplied to the Soviet Union.

succession, the tedium fraying both nerves and tempers, but at last, on October 30, 1942, after nearly a month of kicking our heels on the ground, the ceiling lifted and we took off into a grey dawn on an offensive patrol with five aircraft . . .

"I scanned the sky thoroughly and above the Inkeri shoreline, near Oranienbaum on the Russian side, and well above our altitude I counted eight tiny black specks. I called my companions, pointing out the Russians above us, and suggested that we might take on two each!

"We began climbing towards the enemy formation, the needle of the altimeter slowly unwinding. Eight . . . nine . . . ten . . . 11,000ft [3,353m]. At this altitude we could see that six of the Russians were I-16s, but the other two fighters were not so readily identifiable. Twelve . . . 13,000ft [3,658 . . . 3,692m], and it was obvious that the Russians had spotted us. There was no longer any chance of bouncing them, so, with throttles wide open, we tore into the Ivans, each selecting a target. I fired one short burst at an I-16 and pulled up into an Immelmann [a stall turn, devised by the World War I German ace Max Immelmann, designed to bring a fighter down on an opponent's tail—author]. The sky was immediately a fantastic melee of frantically twisting and turning aircraft. The intercom was a babble of excited voices, oaths, warnings, and counter-warnings. The third flight was operating on the same wavelength and had evidently taken a large gaggle of Russians somewhere near Seiskari. Everyone was shouting at the same time. Above me, an I-16 clawed into a vertical stall, stood on its tail, for a fraction of a second, and then fell away into the forest below. Almost at the same moment tracers flickered past my cockpit. Instinctively, with throttle wide open, I pulled the Brewster into the tightest of shuddering vertical turns, and the I-16 that had managed to get on to my tail flashed past and was gone.

"Out of the corner of my eye I spotted one of our Brewsters far below with a Spitfire on his tail. So that was what the two unidentified fighters had been—Spitfires. There was no mistaking the curved wings of the graceful British fighter, and this was the first time we had encountered the type in Russian hands. I yawed the tail of my Brewster to make sure that no Ivan was stealing up on me, and then, stick over and well forward, I plunged down in a near-vertical dive. I fired one long burst into the cockpit of the Spitfire, which immediately flicked over on its back and dived straight into the sea near the village of Karavalda, on the Gulf."

Spitfires over Burma

During the long retreat through Burma to the Indian frontier before the relentless Japanese advance of 1942, it was the Hawker Hurricane and the Curtiss P-40, the latter flown by the American Volunteer Group the "Flying Tigers," that had borne the brunt of the enemy's onslaught. More than a year later, the Hurricane was still the RAF's principal fighter and ground attack aircraft in the theater, and although it continued to prove its worth in the close support role, it was hard put to hold its own in air combat with its main opponent, the Nakajima Ki 43 Hayabusa (Peregrine Falcon), known as "Oscar" to the Allies; nor did it have the necessary performance to catch the enemy's troublesome Dinah reconnaissance aircraft, which were going about their business virtually as they pleased.

RIGHT Items that formed part of an aircrew escape kit for operations in the Middle East and Far East, including a written appeal for assistance and the offer of a reward.

BELOW Also included in the escape kit was a compass rose and a few days' worth of emergency rations, together with essentials such as salt tablets.

It came as a considerable relief when the first Mk VC Spitfires arrived in the theater in September 1943 and were issued to three Hurricane squadrons, Nos. 136, 607, and 615. The last two deployed to Chittagong, and within a month they had shot down four Dinahs, greatly reducing the enemy's photographic intelligence on the Allied dispositions on the Arakan front. On December 31, No. 136 Squadron, operating from Ramu, scored a major success when its pilots destroyed 12 Japanese bombers and fighters of a force that was attempting to attack shipping off the Arakan coast.

By January 1, 1944, there were six Spitfire squadrons on the Eastern Air Command's Order of Battle, equipped with either Mk VCs or Mk VIIIs, and with their aid the Allied Air Commander, South-East Asia—Air Chief Marshal Sir Richard Peirse—set about achieving complete air superiority over western Burma. In January the Spitfires claimed 24 enemy aircraft for the loss of seven Spitfires in air combat, and in February they claimed 12 more, with a further 6 probably destroyed and 56 damaged.

On March 9, 1944, three Japanese divisions cut off the vital supply routes to Kohima and Imphal, bases that lay 40 miles (64km) inside India, and were consequently of great importance. As far as air operations were concerned, Kohima was a battle fought by ground-attack aircraft; in 16 days, four Hurricane fighter-bomber squadrons flew 2,200 sorties against the Japanese, while four Vultee Vengeance squadrons struck at the enemy's supply dumps and base camps. The isolated Kohima garrison, which was eventually relieved on April 20, 1944 after one of the bloodiest battles of the Burma campaign, was entirely supplied by air.

The same Spitfire squadrons that had fought over the Arakan now took it in turns to operate from within the besieged area, using six airstrips. Their primary task was to provide cover for the transport aircraft bringing in essential supplies. The idea was to keep three Spitfire Mk VIII squadrons available at Imphal at any one time, with a fourth in immediate support, and the scheme worked well. In general, the Spitfire pilots took advantage of the Mk VIII's superior performance at altitude to position themselves above enemy fighters, attack at speed out of the sun, then climb away hard out of range. The Japanese Oscars—the only fighter type encountered at Imphal—were lighter and more maneuverable than the Spitfire, had greater endurance, and were generally present in greater numbers, so the Spitfire pilots avoided turning combats whenever possible.

In March 1944 the Spitfires of Nos. 81 and 136 Squadrons, taking their turn at Imphal, destroyed ten Oscars and two Dinahs, claiming three Oscars probably destroyed and five damaged. No. 81 Squadron lost six Spitfires, two in a strafing attack on the ground. No. 81 Squadron shot down three more Oscars and a

Dinah in April and, together with No. 615 Squadron, claimed five Oscars as probably destroyed. A further 23 aircraft were claimed to have been damaged; only two Spitfires were shot down during the month, and another damaged.

The air defense task in May was shared between No. 81 and 607 Squadrons; No. 607 claimed eight Oscars, and between them the two squadrons shared eight more probably destroyed and 29 damaged for the loss of eight Spitfires, three of which were destroyed when a Dakota transport crashed into them as it landed.

In June there was a marked decrease in enemy air activity, only six enemy fighters being destroyed by Nos. 607 and 615 squadrons. Only one Spitfire was lost in air combat, although three of 615 Squadron's aircraft were wrecked in a storm.

The siege of Imphal lasted 80 days. It ended in late June 1944, and during that time the Japanese Army Air Force managed to shoot down only two Dakotas and one Wellington supply aircraft, so effective were the Spitfires.

The Japanese had been decisively defeated on the Imphal Plain, and the Allies now turned to the offensive, the beginning of a great rout which would end, in July 1945, with the Japanese surrender in Burma.

TOP A folding chair, canvas bucket and canvas washbasin; the somewhat primitive trappings of squadron life in the Far East.

ABOVE A jungle survival booklet issued by the Air Ministry. Whereas the Japanese treated the jungle as an ally, to most westerners it was a deadly enemy.

Hurricanes and Spitfires versus Oscars

One RAF pilot who had firsthand experience of air combat with the Nakajima Oscar fighter was Flying Officer (later Wing Commander) Gordon Conway, who flew both Hurricanes and Spitfires in Burma with No. 136 Squadron. During 1943 it was the Hurricane that held the line, as Conway recalls:

"The last few days of March 1943 brought a raid a day, during which [Nos.] 135 and 79 squadrons intercepted 33 bombers at 25,000ft [7,620m] without fighter escort. The escort had lost their bombers under a cloud layer, and while we had a series of inconclusive scraps at 30,000ft [9,144m] over base with the fighters, the squadrons down south destroyed 11 of the unescorted bombers.

"The fighting in April followed this pattern, starting with more raids against our airfields. Our squadron was involved each time. On the first raid we had visual contact with the fighter and bombers, but we were still climbing when they bombed from 27,000ft [8,230m]. In the afternoon, on a second scramble, my aircraft was still having its guns checked and was not ready in time for the first scramble . . . I later got off alone and joined up with a flight of 67 Squadron at 21,000ft [6,401m], just as half a dozen Oscars jumped them. I saw a big red spinner coming up fast behind, called the break and was peppered in my starboard wing and aileron; I can still recall the surprisingly loud

RIGHT A leaflet issued by the city of Durban, South Africa, welcoming Allied servicemen in transit to the Far East.

BELOW Spitfires of No. 132 Squadron in October 1943. This unit departed for the Far East in December 1944, arriving at Bombay (Mumbai) in January 1945.

"Khaki and Blue we welcome you"

Durban is glad to see you

bang as he hit me. I flicked to starboard as the Oscar dived underneath, hit my attacker in the fuselage and tail and claimed my first 'damaged.'

"On the 22nd of May they hit us with 25 bombers at 20,000ft [6,096m], escorted by 15-plus Oscars. Both 67 and ourselves intercepted; 67 claimed two destroyed, two probables and one damaged, while we claimed five destroyed, four probables and three damaged . . . I got into the fighter screen and claimed one destroyed and another probable. A week later the Japs repeated this raid, using 15-plus bombers at 18,000ft [5,486m], with 20-plus fighters at 22,000ft [6,706m]. Joe Edwards was leading, and as he dived on the top fighters, another fighter from a different flight turned on to his tail in front of my sight. I gave this Oscar a long burst of cannon, closing from astern, and he literally fell apart. He seemed to stop in mid-air, his port wheel came down followed by his flaps, and with pieces flying off all around he flicked and spun vertically into the sea just by the airfield. We claimed five, one and two, while 67 claimed three probables and one damaged. So ended a good month in which our only casualties were two pilots, both of whom escaped with slight injuries . . . In six months we [Nos. 136 and 67 squadrons] had destroyed 14 enemy aircraft, probably destroyed 10 and damaged 18 for the loss of four pilots. Down south, 79 Squadron had destroyed 17 enemy aircraft; 135 had claimed over 20, but at the great cost of 13 of their own pilots . . . "

Later in the year, No. 136 Squadron converted to Spitfires, and while flying these aircraft Gordon Conway increased his personal score to seven Japanese aircraft destroyed.

BELOW No. 159 Squadron operated Consolidated B-24 Liberators, which were used by the RAF's long-range bomber force based in Bengal.

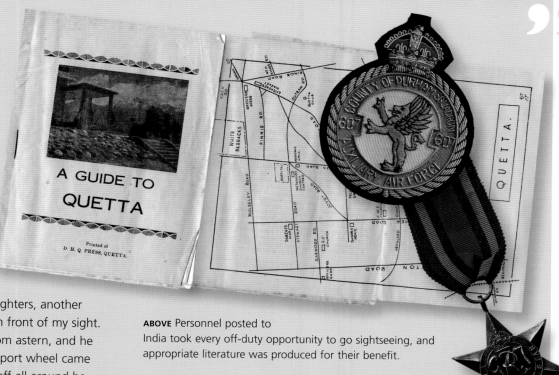

ABOVE Personnel posted to India took every off-duty opportunity to go sightseeing, and appropriate literature was produced for their benefit.

RIGHT & ABOVE A Burma Star awarded to Leading Aircraftman Robert Anable, who served with No. 607 Squadron and later with No. 159; No. 607 Squadron's badge was a winged lion.

In 1944, the responsibility for the air defense of Imphal was in the hands of No. 221 Group under Air Commodore S. F. Vincent. The official RAF history describes the situation:

"As soon as the decision to stay and fight had been taken, Vincent called his airmen together in the large bamboo canteen at Imphal and explained the situation. Their temper and spirit rose with every word he uttered. Orders were given that every man should carry arms; emergency radio networks were set up to take the place of the ordinary telephone system should it break down; the ground crews and other administrative services on the airfields were formed into self-supporting 'boxes,' of which the garrison was required to hold out until overrun. Retreat from them, as from Imphal, was not even considered. At night, until the decision to remove most of the fighters to other airfields outside the plain was taken, pilots and ground crews guarded their own aircraft and lived in foxholes nearby. One Spitfire box looked like a honeycomb. Each section of pilots, armourers, fitters, riggers, electricians, wireless technicians and maintenance crews was responsible for its own dugout, and all were arranged to guard the perimeter. Pilots, armed, stayed by their aircraft . . . a very strict blackout and absolute silence were maintained from dusk to dawn. Then, with the bright light of day, the fighters and fighter-bombers took off to fly and fight, for now more than ever it was essential to hold the mastery of the air."

Hold it they did, and their deeds contributed in no small measure to the final setting of Japan's sun.

Seafires in action: The Indian Ocean and Pacific

Although the British aircraft carriers that operated in the waters of the Far East were equipped mainly with American aircraft, the Supermarine Seafire was also to make its mark in this theater of war. The first to arrive, in October 1943, was a flight of Seafire IIs, which operated alongside Grumman Wildcats and Fairey Swordfish in No. 834 Squadron on the escort carrier HMS *Battler*. It formed part of a trade protection group, hunting Japanese and German submarines that were attacking shipping in the area from their base at Penang, in Malaya. In 1944, the group was strengthened with the deployment from European waters of the escort carriers *Shah*, *Begum*, *Ameer*, and *Atheling*. The latter carried two fighter squadrons, No. 890 with Wildcats and No. 889 with Seafires. The No. 889 Squadron's operational career with the Seafire was short lived; in April 1944, having lost several of its pilots in accidents, it disbanded. It reformed in June 1945 with Grumman Hellcats.

In March 1945, the 21st Carrier Group—comprising the escort carriers *Stalker*, *Attacker*, *Emperor*, *Hunter*, and *Khedive*—began operations in the Bay of Bengal, bringing with them ten new fighter squadrons, three of which were equipped with Seafires. These were No. 807 (HMS *Hunter*), 809 (HMS *Stalker*), and 879 (HMS *Attacker*). Between April 30 and May 2, 1945, the Seafires and Hellcats flew 180 combat sorties during Operation Dracula, the Allied amphibious landings in the Rangoon area; no air combat took place, but the Fleet Air Arm fighters strafed Japanese position near the beachhead. This was followed on May 5 and 6 by attacks on enemy shipping among the islands off the long southern coast of Burma and on airfields in the Tenasserim area.

During this period, 6 Seafires, which had been operating in the fleet defense role, were written off in landing accidents and

LEFT The destroyer HMS *Nizam* pictured from a Fairey Swordfish, one of the aircraft deployed on a Royal Navy escort carrier in the Indian Ocean.

BELOW A naval task force in the Pacific could put up a formidable amount of anti-aircraft fire, as seen in this photograph.

Nos. 887 and 894, both on board HMS *Indefatigable*. After assembling at Sydney under the command of Rear-Admiral Sir Philip Vian, the fleet reached Ulithi Atoll in the Caroline Islands on March 19, 1945, where—designated Task Force 57 (TF 57)—it formed part of the US Fifth Fleet. As well as the carriers *Illustrious*, *Indomitable*, *Indefatigable*, and *Victorious*, TF 57 included a powerful screening force of battleships, cruisers, and destroyers.

On March 28 the British warships sailed to take part in Operation Iceberg, the landing on Okinawa. TF 57's mission was to attack six enemy airfields in the Sakishima Gunto island group, which lay to the southwest of Okinawa. During these operations, the task force's American fighters—Corsairs and Hellcats—shot down 28 enemy aircraft, but once again the Seafire squadrons were restricted to Fleet CAP.

On April 1, 1945, Japanese aircraft appeared over the fleet in strength, and on that day the Seafires made their first combat claims in the Pacific. Sub-Lieutenant R. H. Reynolds of No. 894 Squadron, who had already destroyed two Blohm und Voss Bv 138 flying boats over the Atlantic, destroyed three Zeros and so became the Royal Navy's only Seafire "ace."

In June 1945 the fleet carrier HMS *Implacable* joined the British Pacific Fleet at Manus anchorage, in the Admiralty Islands. She replaced HMS *Indomitable*, which departed for a refit. *Implacable* brought with her two more squadrons of Seafire Mk IIIs, Nos. 801 and 880. Also, among her stores, she carried American auxiliary fuel tanks that had been "liberated" from a USAAF depot in New Guinea in exchange for several cases of Scotch. With these slung under their bellies, the Seafires were able to extend their combat radius by 50 per cent, enabling them to take part in offensive operations at last.

At dawn on August 15, 1945, several days after the dropping of the atomic bombs on Hiroshima and Nagasaki, Grumman Avengers of No. 820 Squadron were intercepted by Zeros during an attack on targets in the Tokyo area. The Japanese fighters were immediately overwhelmed by the Seafires of Nos. 887 and 894 Squadrons, which shot down eight of the enemy, incurring no loss.

Two hours later, all offensive operations against the Japanese home islands were suspended.

ABOVE A Seafire XV hooks the wire on the escort carrier HMS *Pretoria Castle* in August 1945, at the very end of the Pacific War.

RIGHT A silk escape map issued to Allied aircrew serving in the Pacific Theater. The map could be worn as a scarf.

13 more were damaged, underlining the type's unsuitability for carrier operations. The principal problem was the Seafire's narrow-track undercarriage, but in general the aircraft was by no means as robust as its American counterparts.

Another problem with the Seafire was its short combat radius, which restricted it to the role of combat air patrol (CAP). One of its few chances to engage the enemy in combat in the Indian Ocean came on July 27, 1945, when seven Japanese aircraft came in low over the sea toward the ships of the 21st Carrier Squadron in the Bay of Bengal. Three were shot down by CAP Seafires, two more were hit by AA fire and blew up, and another slammed into the side of the minesweeper *Vestal*, which exploded and sank. The seventh aircraft narrowly missed the carrier *Ameer*, which received slight damage in the explosion. It was the 21st Carrier Squadron's first and only experience of a kamikaze suicide attack.

Seafires also served with the British Pacific Fleet, which had sailed from Trincomalee, Ceylon, for Sydney in January 1945, striking en route at the Japanese oil refineries at Palembang in southern Sumatra; with it went two Seafire Mk III squadrons,

Flying the Seafire

The handling qualities of the Seafire Mk IB, IIC, and III were so similar to those of the Spitfire VA, VB, and VC, from which they were derived, that it was not considered necessary to produce a new set of Pilot's Notes to cover the "navalized Spitfire." An addendum was all that was deemed necessary, dealing with obvious items such as deck take-off and landing:

"Deck take-off: Warming up should not be unduly prolonged, because radiator temperature immediately before take-off must not exceed 100°C. The drill of Vital Actions is the same as that for normal take-off, except that flaps should be lowered 18 degrees. On aeroplanes in which Mod No. 63 [to give more than one flap setting] has not been incorporated, this flap setting is obtained as follows:

a. Lower flaps fully, have flight deck crew insert wooden blocks, and then raise flaps.
b. After take-off lower flaps fully at a safe height and then raise flaps.

"The wings of the Seafire III are of the folding type and must, therefore, be checked for locking and correct spread, as follows, before starting up:

i. Before entering the cockpit see that the small access door under each wing tip is closed.
ii. See that the round red indicator rod, just inboard of each main folding joint, is flush with the wing upper surface.

"Deck landing: On approaching the carrier before landing, reduce speed to 120 knots IAS and lower the arrester hook. Check that the indicator light shows green. The lowering of the hook should preferably be done before breaking formation, where applicable, as an additional check can then be made by pilots of other aeroplanes. See that the cockpit hood is locked open and check brake pressure (at least 120lb/sq in [84kg/sq m]).

"The drill for vital actions is U, P, Hook and Flaps:
U—Undercarriage down (Check green lights)
P—Propeller control fully forward
Hook—down (Check green light)
Flaps—down

"Speed for preliminary approach: 70 knots IAS. Speed for final approach: 65–70 knots. The nose of the aeroplane should be kept high during the approach, but in order to improve vision ahead, the final approach should be slightly 'crabbed.' The airspeed indicator, however, must be watched carefully."

As for the Seafire's notorious deck landing accident rate, Lieutenant-Commander John Moore, RNVR, a naval officer with much experience of carrier flying, had this to say about landing a Seafire on an escort carrier: "From 5,000ft [1,524m] the deck looks smaller than a playing card; a Seafire, at its normal landing speed, flies the whole length of the ship in four seconds. That doesn't give the pilot much time to correct an error of judgment. Moreover, if the ship is pitching, the after end of the flight deck may have a rise and fall, between trough and crest, of more than 20ft [6m]. The pilot may have been making a perfect approach until the deck fell away beneath him, or came up to meet his wheels. In such circumstances you cannot blame him if the impact smashes his undercarriage or throws the aircraft over the side."

OPPOSITE TOP A Royal Navy pilot and his Seafire. Landing the Seafire on a carrier required considerable skill because of the narrow-track undercarriage and long nose, which obscured the view ahead.

OPPOSITE BOTTOM A Seafire smashes into a Fairey Firefly (right) and a Grumman Avenger after a bad landing on HMS *Indefatigable* in the Pacific, 1945.

ABOVE Near miss: a Kamikaze suicide aircraft, hit by anti-aircraft fire, plunges into the sea near the escort carrier USS *Sangamon* in August 1945.

BELOW The crests of Seafire squadrons that served in the Far East. No. 801 Squadron saw action in the Pacific and No. 809 in the Indian Ocean. No. 899 served as an operational training unit in Australia.

Once in its natural element, the Seafire was a match for any other fighter in its class. Japanese pilots were impressed by the Seafire's agility, as this account by Lieutenant Kuroe of the Imperial Japanese Army Air Force reveals. He encountered the Seafire when, in May 1944, the British escort carriers penetrated into the Bay of Bengal and approached Akyab Island. The Japanese were alerted and a force of bombers escorted by Zeros went out to attack the warships, which were about 100 miles (160km) off the coast of Burma.

"I led the second wave of eight Zero fighters and eight light bombers. The first wave had found no Allied fighter escort, so when I arrived over an hour later I expected no fighter opposition. I was greatly surprised, therefore, to find the enemy fleet covered by Seafires. We attacked the ships, but none of our bombs hit the target; then the Seafires struck back at us, and five of our bombers and two fighters were shot down.

"It was then I did something stupid. Instead of staying with the other fighters and bombers I went chasing off after a Seafire. He took evasive action and I followed him all the time. I chased him for more than 13 minutes, but then discovered that another Seafire was also chasing me. He got me in a bad position and attacked. Afterwards, I found 30 bullet holes in my aircraft. My fuel tank was hit, my undercarriage damaged, and I was unable to alter the pitch of my propeller. It was my turn to run now, and I made for an emergency landing strip. I landed all right, but the business with the Seafire gave me a nasty fright."

Life on a British aircraft carrier

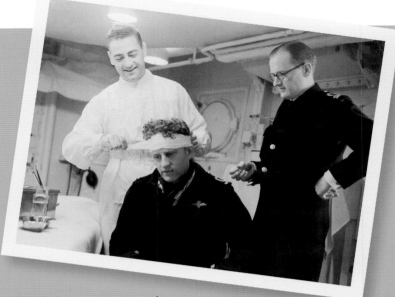

Life on a British aircraft carrier was by no means uncomfortable, and in some ways the conditions on an escort carrier were better than those on one of the large fleet carriers, especially if the escort vessel was American built. One account describes the amenities on an American-built carrier:

"The Sick Bay is a doctor's paradise, for it is fitted up on the lines of a fashionable New York clinic, with nothing spared and nothing stinted . . . The Sick Bay is situated forrard [sic]; as you go aft, you pass the officers' cabins and bathrooms, the Wardroom Mess with its own galley and pantry, and reach the crew's mess decks and canteen. This canteen is the delight especially of young sailors, for it contains machinery for making fizzy iced drinks and ice-creams in a variety of flavour . . . American ships, of course, are 'dry'; they have no daily rum issue. The fizzy drinks perhaps serve as some compensation. Our sailors, when they took over the ship, also took over a supply of Coca-Cola; and they were just beginning to get to like it when the supply ran out."

Aft of the canteen was the main galley, where food for the escort carrier's 500-strong crew was cooked three times a day. The food was served on the cafeteria system, with an individual tray for each man. The system saved labour, and ensured that the food was always served hot. It also ensured that each man got his fair share, something that did not always happen on Royal Navy warships, where so-called "cooks of messes," who were not cooks at all, drew the whole of the food for their respective messes from the galley.

Close to the galley was the bakery, where the ship's baker produced 500lb (227kg) of bread per day, together with rolls and cakes if he had the time. As in all warships equipped with a

ABOVE First-aid drill on an escort carrier. These American-built ships had the benefit of excellent medical facilities.

LEFT Despite the amenities enjoyed by the crew, life on board an escort carrier could be tough. Here, HMS *Nairana* rides out an Arctic storm in 1944.

bakery, the bread was always white, for the simple reason that the cheap brown flour produced in wartime would not keep for long periods at sea.

"Everywhere in the ship one comes across evidence of the peculiarly American delight in gadgets: gadgets that really work and really save labour. For instance, there is the laundry. It is unusual for a ship as small as an escort carrier to have a laundry; indeed, until recently not even battleships possessed such a luxury. However, the Americans had provided space for one . . . at sea in wartime, when men are ordered to sleep in their clothes, the matter of laundering becomes really important; and if the ship goes into the tropics, where they wear 'whites,' it will be even more so."

The provisions carried by a typical American-built escort carrier, such as those that served with the British Eastern Fleet in the Indian Ocean, were sufficient to feed the ship's company for nine months. The carrier typically stored more than 20 tons of flour, grown and milled in Canada; 5,000lb (2,268kg) of canned meat from Montevideo; and 15,000lb (6,804kg) of frozen meat from the USA. She was equipped with three refrigerating rooms, one for meat, one for fruit and vegetables, and one for butter, eggs, and cheese. Her "dry stores"—sugar, tea, coffee, salt, and so on—would have filled a small warehouse.

In addition to its provisions and naval stores, an escort carrier also had to maintain tools and spares for its Swordfish and Seafires, running into thousands of items: radio equipment, oxygen bottles, pumps, flying kit and parachutes—the latter packed and aired in their own room in the forward part of the ship—weapons, munitions, fabric, dope, batteries, lamps, first-aid kits, and emergency rations.

For the crew in their off-duty periods, there was plenty of opportunity for open-air sport on the carrier's flight deck, something denied to sailors on the cluttered decks of other warships.

"While the weather remained bad, they worked off steam by organising hockey matches on the flight deck, Seafires versus Swordfish, which were played in the dog watches and were more dangerous to life and limb than most flying operations. It was during one of these games, on the fourth evening out, that the loudspeakers suddenly blared and the Quartermaster's voice was heard:

"B Flight and aircraft handling parties fall in at the forward end of the hangar at the hurry . . . squadron commanders and duty aircrews to report to the Air Staff Officer in the Air Operations Room at the hurry . . . range a strike of two Swordfish and one Seafire at the after end of the flight deck immediately . . . hands to flying stations. Stand by to fly off aircraft." It was a timely reminder that there was a war on.

LEFT This booklet was issued by the Ministry of Information in 1942, a few months after HMS *Ark Royal* was sunk by a submarine in the Mediterranean.

BELOW A game of deck hockey is briefly interrupted by the sudden appearance of a Fairey Swordfish, making a low pass over the players.

Spitfires for sale: The post-war years

Spitfire production continued for some time after the end of World War II, although the orders placed during the conflict were gradually tapered off in order to prevent mass unemployment. By the end of 1946 there were only two first-line Spitfire units left in the United Kingdom, No. 63 Squadron at RAF Middle Wallop and No. 41 Squadron at Wittering. No. 63 Squadron would retain its Spitfire LF.16Es until 1948, when it reequipped with Gloster Meteor F.3 jet fighters. No. 41 relinquished its Spitfire F.21s for de Havilland Hornets, also in 1948. However, the Spitfire got a new lease on life in 1946, when the Auxiliary Air Force (which was to become the Royal Auxiliary Air Fore in 1947) was reestablished. Of its 20 squadrons, 13 received Spitfires, the others arming with Mosquitoes. Similarly, various types of Seafire equipped the squadrons of the Royal Naval Volunteer Reserve until 1951, when they were replaced by the Hawker Sea Fury.

In Europe, the Spitfire formed the main equipment of several air forces that were reconstituted following the defeat of Germany. In 1946 two Belgian-manned Spitfire squadrons, Nos. 349 and 350, were transferred from the control of the Second Tactical Air Force to the Belgian Government, together with 51 Spitfire Mk IXs and 21 Mk XVIs; Belgium also took delivery of 132 Mk XIVs, delivered between 1948 and 1951. Denmark received 41 Spitfire Mk IXs and a Mk XI, while the Royal Netherlands Air Force received 55 Mk IXs and the Royal Norwegian Air Force, whose Second TAF Spitfire squadrons had made a significant contribution during the war, received 47 Mk IXs.

ABOVE Converted Seafire XV UB403 (formerly SR642) of the Union of Burma Air Force, one of 20 such aircraft delivered.

In 1945, 73 Spitfire LF.Mk IXs were ferried to Prague to form the backbone of the reconstituted Czech Air Force, while France received 172 Mk IXs, many of which were used operationally in Indo-China and North Africa. The Armée de l'Air also took delivery of 70 Mk Vs, which were used mainly for training, while the Naval Air Arm, the Aéronavale, received a number of Seafires, Mk IIIs, and Mk XVs. Italy, which had operated some Spitfire Vs as part of the Co-Belligerent Air Force on the side of the Allies in 1944–45, was limited by postwar treaty to an air force of not more than 200 fighters, and about 110 of these were Spitfire IXs.

When Greece was liberated at the end of the war, the operational component of the Royal Hellenic Air Force comprised Nos. 335 and 336 Squadrons, whose Spitfire Mk Vs had formed part of the Balkan Air Force. A third Spitfire squadron, No. 337, was formed soon afterward, and in 1947–49 the Mk Vs were replaced by 74 Mk IXs, followed by 55 Mk XVIs. Yugoslavia, which had operated one Spitfire squadron, No. 352, in Italy and the Balkans, continued to use its Mk Vs for some time after the war.

Syria took delivery of ten Spitfire F.22s in 1950, and these remained in service until 1953, when they were replaced by Gloster Meteor F.8s. Portugal, an early overseas customer, followed its initial purchase of 15 Spitfire Mk IAs with 50 Mk VBs, most of which remained in first-line service until 1952, when they were replaced by Republic P-47D Thunderbolts. Of the other neutral countries, Sweden purchased 50 PR Mk XIX Spitfires in 1955, and these—designated S.31s and operated by a single unit, F11 at Nyköping—were used for reconnaissance work over the Baltic and the Gulf of Bothnia.

Finally, the Irish Air Corps received 12 denavalized and refurbished Seafire Mk IIIs and six Spitfire Mk IXs, the latter all trainer conversions.

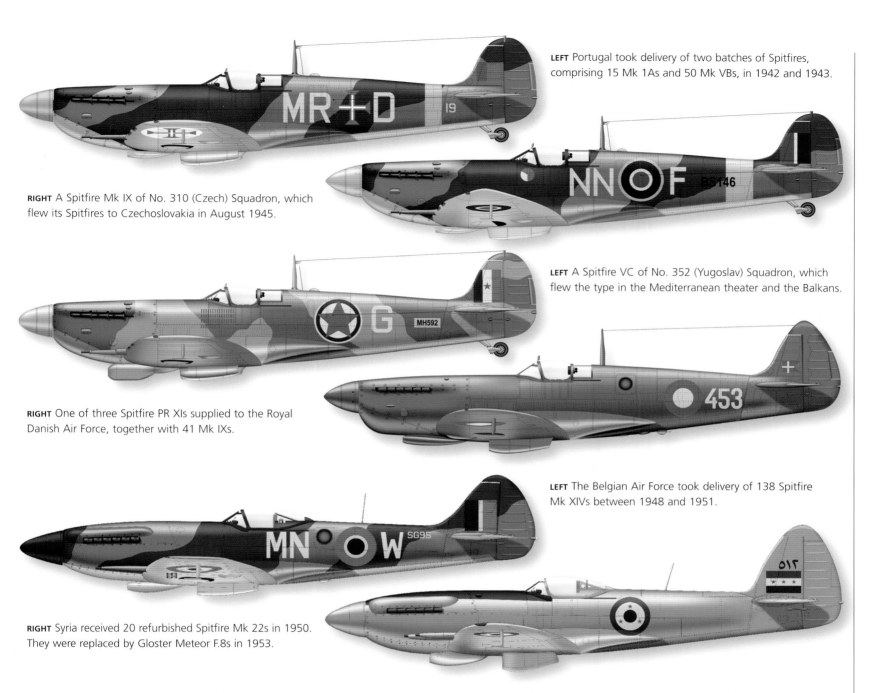

LEFT Portugal took delivery of two batches of Spitfires, comprising 15 Mk 1As and 50 Mk VBs, in 1942 and 1943.

RIGHT A Spitfire Mk IX of No. 310 (Czech) Squadron, which flew its Spitfires to Czechoslovakia in August 1945.

LEFT A Spitfire VC of No. 352 (Yugoslav) Squadron, which flew the type in the Mediterranean theater and the Balkans.

RIGHT One of three Spitfire PR XIs supplied to the Royal Danish Air Force, together with 41 Mk IXs.

LEFT The Belgian Air Force took delivery of 138 Spitfire Mk XIVs between 1948 and 1951.

RIGHT Syria received 20 refurbished Spitfire Mk 22s in 1950. They were replaced by Gloster Meteor F.8s in 1953.

In the Far East, 12 denavalized Seafire Mk XVs were supplied to the Union of Burma Air Force in 1951, while the Royal Thai Air Force received 30 FR.Mk.XIVs from 1948. They were replaced by Grumman F8F Bearcats in the mid-1950s.

There remained Egypt and Israel, two nations that were to become locked in bitter conflict following the establishment of the State of Israel in 1948. It would be the only war in which Spitfire fought Spitfire.

LEFT Formerly a Seafire III, this aircraft was one of 12 that underwent the "Type 506" de-navalization by Vickers, removing the arrestor hooks, etc.

Israel's Spitfires in action

Although most nations seeking to rearm after World War II had no trouble purchasing arms from Britain or the United States, the new State of Israel enjoyed no such luxury. Surrounded by hostile Arab neighbors—who made no secret of the fact that they planned to destroy the infant State of Israel as soon as Britain's mandate on Palestine came to an end and British forces withdrew—the Israeli government launched a desperate search for arms, with combat aircraft high on the priority list. The main threat came from the Egyptians, whose assets included a mixed bag of 40 Spitfire Mk IXs and Fiat G.55s, 15 Harvards, 5 Hawker Furies and 25 Dakotas, all adapted to carry small bomb loads.

In March 1948, the embryonic Israeli government began negotiations with the Czech Defence Ministry for the purchase of a small number of surplus fighter aircraft. These were Avia C.210s (designated S.199s for export), which were basically Messerschmitt Me 109G-14s built from component parts left behind when the Germans withdrew in 1944.

On May 15, 1948—the day the State of Israel came into being—two Spitfire LF.Mk IXs of the Royal Egyptian Air Force attacked Dov airfield in Tel Aviv. One was hit by ground fire, and its pilot made a belly landing on the beach at Hertzlia. Although badly damaged, the aircraft was salvaged and, with the use of spare parts left behind by the RAF, it was made airworthy again. It was the Israeli Air Force's first Spitfire.

For a month after Israel's inauguration, the Egyptian Spitfires were able to roam over the country unmolested. On May 22, 1948, a lone Spitfire from Egypt appeared soon after dawn over Ramat David airfield, and, after circling several times, dropped two bombs and make a couple of strafing runs, destroying two aircraft on the ground. Unfortunately for the Egyptians, the aircraft were RAF Spitfire FR.18s, for at that time Ramat David was still occupied by Nos. 32 and 208 Squadrons. Two

LEFT The insignia of the Royal Egyptian Air Force, which also used Spitfires in the Arab-Israeli war of 1948–49.

BELOW LEFT Israeli Air Force Spitfire LF.IXs of No. 101 Squadron preparing for a sortie from Hatzor airstrip in the Negev during the War of Independence, 1949.

BELOW An Egyptian Air Force Spitfire LF.IX shot down during the Arab-Israeli war. The Israelis used it for spare parts.

hours later the airfield was again attacked by Egyptian Spitfires, which destroyed a Dakota on the ground and damaged seven more aircraft. This time, the RAF was on the alert and four FR.18s were airborne; they shot down two of the three Spitfires involved in the attack and the third was brought down by anti-aircraft fire. The next day, the Egyptian authorities apologized to Britain for the "regrettable navigational error" made by their pilots.

The first of 23 S.199s arrived in Israel on May 20, in crates. They were assembled and formed into the Israeli Air Force's first fighter squadron, No. 101. They saw action for the first time on May 29, attacking Egyptian army units south of Tel Aviv. Although the S.199 was a dreadful aircraft, overweight and difficult to handle, to the Israelis it was a godsend, and on June 3 it scored its first aerial victory.

That evening, two Egyptian Dakotas escorted by four Spitfires approached Tel Aviv on a bombing mission. They were intercepted by an S.199 flown by a 27-year-old ex-RAF pilot called Mordechai ("Modi") Alon, who shot down both Dakotas and drove off the Spitfire escort. Alon, who would be appointed to command No. 101 Squadron, was later killed in a landing accident on October 16, 1948.

In June 1948, Israeli representatives in Prague concluded negotiations for the purchase of 50 Spitfire IXs that the Czech Air Force was in the process of phasing out. The Spitfires were ferried to Israel by air, using long-range external wing tanks taken from S.199s in addition to their auxiliary belly tanks. The transfer began on September 24, 1948, and the Spitfires were gradually absorbed into No. 101 Squadron. On October 21, 1948, John Doyle—a former RCAF pilot—shot down an Egyptian Spitfire over the Negev and damaged two more, scoring the first air combat victory by an IAF Spitfire.

By July 1949, when the Israeli War of Independence ended, No. 101 Squadron had 21 Spitfires, with 26 more being assembled after arriving by sea from Czechoslovakia. The Israeli Air Force ultimately received 56 ex-Czech Spitfires in total, enabling a second squadron, No. 105, to be established in 1950. In the

ABOVE A Spitfire Mk IXE of No. 101 Squadron, Israeli Air Force, in typical markings of the 1948–49 period.

LEFT Pilots in the Middle East needed tinted lenses such as these, designed for the Mk VIII goggles, and equiped with an anti-misting cloth.

following year a contract was signed with the Italian government for the purchase of 30 more Mk IXs, although they were not delivered until 1953. At the beginning of that year No. 101 Squadron converted to F-51D Mustangs, handing over its Spitfires to a newly formed unit, No. 107 Squadron, which went on to disband in March 1954. All the surviving Spitfires were now centralized in No. 105 Squadron. In 1955, 30 refurbished aircraft were sold to Burma, and in February 1956 the remaining Spitfires were withdrawn from use when No. 105 Squadron also disbanded.

Ironically, not all of the IAF's Spitfire victims during the War of Independence were Egyptian. On January 3, 1949, three RAF Spitfire FR.18s of No. 208 Squadron and a Tempest of No. 213 were shot down by Spitfires of Israel's No. 101 Squadron, the allegation being that the British aircraft had crossed into Israeli air space. One of the 101 Squadron Spitfire pilots was Ezer Weizmann, later to become president of Israel.

Ultimate Spitfires

More than 20,000 Spitfires of all types were produced before, during, and after World War II; it was the only Allied fighter to be in production when the war started and remain in production when it ended.

The squadrons of the Second Tactical Air Force in Germany retained their Spitfire IXs, XIVs, and XVIs for some time after the end of hostilities, while the fighter-reconnaissance FR.18s were retained by the Middle East and Far East squadrons. The last Spitfire variants were the Griffon-engine Mks 21, 22, and 24, which bore very little resemblance to Reginald Mitchell's original design; the Griffon-engine versions of the Seafire were the Mks XV, XVII, 45, 46, and 47.

In the United Kingdom, besides the Mks 21, 22, and 24 that equipped the Royal Auxiliary Air Force in the late 1940s, Spitfires continued to serve on second-line duties with anti-aircraft cooperation units, meteorological flights, and training establishments. Many were retained in storage at maintenance units in case of emergency, a situation that lasted until 1953, when the Korean War ended.

In the Middle East, No. 208 Squadron—which, as described on pages 154–155, fell afoul of the Israeli Air Force—retained its Spitfire FR.18s until 1951, when they were replaced by Gloster Meteor FR.9s. Still farther east, Nos. 28 and 60 Squadrons at Sembawang, Singapore, had 16 FR.18s and PR.19s, and in 1948 they went to war against the communist terrorist guerrillas who were attempting to seize control of Malaya. The Spitfires, deploying north to form the nucleus of an air-strike task force at Kuala Lumpur, carried out their first air strikes on insurgent camps in July 1948 and had mounted 83 more by the end of the year.

In May 1949 the Spitfires of No. 28 Squadron were redeployed to Hong Kong, their place being taken in Malaya by the Hawker Tempest F.2s of No. 33 Squadron. In September of that year, the air-strike force available for operations in Malaya comprised 17 Spitfires, 16 Tempests, 8 Beaufighters and 10 Sunderland flying boats. The Spitfires FR.18s of No. 60 Squadron, the last in first-line service with the RAF, were withdrawn in January 1951, having flown 1,800 operational sorties against the terrorists, and the squadron rearmed with de Havilland Vampire FB.5s. Spitfires continued to provide photo-reconnaissance coverage in Malaya until the end of 1953, the task being fulfilled by the PR.19s of No. 81 Squadron at Seletar, together with the Squadron's PR Mosquitoes.

On June 30, 1950, with the British government's backing for United Nations action in Korea secured following the communist invasion of the south, the aircraft carrier HMS *Triumph* arrived in Korean waters from Hong Kong, accompanied by two cruisers,

BELOW LEFT A Seafire Mk 47. The type saw action for a brief period during the early months of the Korean war, operating from HMS *Triumph*.

BELOW Pilots operating in Malaya were provided with items necessary for survival in jungle terrain, and useful phrases for communicating with the local population.

two destroyers, and three frigates, and on the following day the USS *Valley Forge* and her escorts also took up station in the Yellow Sea, the Allied force operating under the designation of Task Force 77.

It was the British force that opened the naval war off Korea when, at dawn on July 2, 1950, the cruiser HMS *Jamaica* and the sloop *Black Swan* engaged six North Korean MTBs, which were presenting a threat to the aircraft carriers, and sank five of them. At 05:45 the next morning, the carrier aircraft flew their first strikes against targets in North Korea. Twelve Fairey Firefly fighter-bombers of No. 827 Squadron and nine rocket-armed Seafire 47s of No. 800 Squadron were launched by HMS *Triumph* to attack Haeju airfield, with railways and bridges as secondary targets. During the next few weeks the Seafires flew more ground attack missions, but in the end they were relegated to Combat Air Patrol, partly because of their restricted combat radius and partly because they could easily be confused with the Russian Yak-9 fighters, which were used by the North Korean Air Force. In fact, one was shot down in error by the gunners of a B-29 Superfortress; luckily, the pilot was rescued.

Meanwhile, in August 1949, the Spitfire FR.18s of No.28 Squadron at Hong Kong's Kai Tak airfield had been joined by the F.Mk 24s of No. 80 Squadron, deployed from Germany. On Battle of Britain Sunday, 1951—the Sunday on which the RAF's victory in 1940 is commemorated annually—No. 80 Squadron flew low in salute over the Hong Kong War Memorial; it was the last time that a Spitfire squadron performed this tribute.

However, it was not quite the end of the Spitfire saga. In 1944, Supermarine had flown a redesigned version of the Spitfire

ABOVE LEFT Carrier aircraft attacking a target in North Korea. Enemy transport was a top priority.

ABOVE One of the Spitfire LF.IXs acquired by Israel from Czechoslovakia.

LEFT The prototype Supermarine Seafang, which was to have replaced the Seafire in Royal Navy service.

BELOW The Supermarine Attacker jet fighter brought the Spitfire line to an end. It served with the Royal Navy and the Pakistan Air Force.

XIV with a laminar-flow wing, an aircraft so different from the Spitfire that it merited a new name, Spiteful. Seventeen aircraft were completed, but none entered RAF service. A navalized version, the Seafang, was also flown, but it was abandoned in favor of the turbojet-powered Supermarine Attacker.

At last, the long and distinguished Spitfire line had been overtaken by the jet age.

The Spitfire variants at a glance

SPITFIRE VARIANTS

Spitfire Prototype (K5054/Type 300): First flight March 5, 1936.

High Speed Spitfire: Modified Mk I airframe, first flight November 10, 1938.

Spitfire Mk I (Supermarine Type 300): Entered service August 4, 1938; 1,566 built.

Spitfire Mk II (Type 329): Basically a Mk I built at the Castle Bromwich factory and fitted with Merlin XII engine; 920 built.

Spitfire Mk III (Type 330): Two aircraft built; did not enter production.

Spitfire Mk IV (Type 337): First Griffon-engined Spitfire. First flight November 27, 1941; one prototype only.

Spitfire PR.Mk IV (Type 353): 229 aircraft converted from Mk VA/B airframes.

Spitfire Mk V (Type 349): Major production version. First deployed march 1941; 6,479 built.

Spitfire Mk VI (Type 350): High-altitude version with Mk V airframe and pressurized cockpit; 100 built.

Spitfire Mk VII (Type 351): High-altitude variant with Merlin 61 engine; 140 built.

Spitfire PR. VII: Armed version of the PR.IV. Service modification; not a production aircraft.

Spitfire Mk VIII (Type 359): Unpressurized version of the Mk VII intended for low-level air superiority role; 1,658 built. Mk VIII Trainer (Type 502); two conversions.

Spitfire Mk IX (Type 361): Mk V airframe with Merlin 61 engine. First deployed June 1942; 5,665 built. Mk IX Trainer (Type 509); 21 conversions for supply to Ireland, The Netherlands and India.

Spitfire PR.X (Type 362): Only 16 built for service with Nos. 541 and 542 squadrons.

Spitfire PR.XI (Type 365): Reconnaissance adaptation of the Mk IX; 471 built.

Spitfire Mk XII (Type 366): First production Griffon-engined Spitfire; 100 built.

Spitfire PR. XIII (Type 367): Low-level tactical reconnaissance version of Spitfire Mk V; 18 built.

Spitfire Mk XIV (Type 379): Based on a Mk VIII airframe; first Griffon-engined variant to enter large-scale production; 957 built (527 fighters, 430 fighter-recce).

Spitfire Mk XVI (Type 361): Version of Mk IX with Packard Merlin 266; 1,054 built.

Spitfire F/FR Mk XVIII (Type 394): Last (by date of introduction) Griffon-engined Spitfire variant with elliptical wing; 100 completed as fighters, 200 for the fighter-reconnaissance role.

Spitfire PR.XIX: Last of the PR Spitfires, and the only PR mark with a Griffon engine; 225 built.

Spitfires Mks 21, 22, and 24: Last variants of the Spitfire, all with Griffon engines and laminar-flow wings. Production: 122 Mk 21, 278 Mk 22, 54 Mk 24.

Spitfire Floatplane: Four prototypes (one Mk I and three Mk V conversions) of a floatplane version of the Spitfire were built, but the variant did not enter production.

SEAFIRE VARIANTS

Seafire Mk Ib (Type 340): Naval conversion of Spitfire Mk VB; 166 produced.

Seafire Mk IIc (Types 357 and 375): Naval variant of Spitfire VC; 402 produced.

Seafire Mk III (Type 358): Basically a Mk IIc with folding wings. Major Seafire production version; 1,220 built.

Seafire F.XV (Type 377): Basically a navalized Spitfire Mk XII with Griffon engine; 390 built.

Seafire F/FR. XVII: Developed version of the Seafire F.XV; 232 built.

Seafire F/FR.45: Navalized version of the Spitfire F.21; 50 built.

Seafire F/FR.46: Navalized Spitfire F.22; 24 built.

Seafire F/FR.47: The ultimate Seafire; 90 built. Saw action in Malaya and Korea.

THE SPITFIRE SQUADRONS

Royal Air Force: Nos 1, 2, 4, 5, 6, 11, 16, 19, 20, 26, 28, 32, 33, 34, 41, 43, 54, 56, 60, 63, 64, 65, 66, 67, 69, 71 (Eagle), 72, 73, 74, 80,81, 82, 87, 91, 92, 94, 94, 111, 118, 121 (Eagle), 122, 123, 124, 126, 127, 129, 130, 131, 132, 133 (Eagle), 134, 136, 140, 145, 152, 153, 154, 155, 164, 165, 183, 184, 185, 186, 208, 213, 222, 225, 229, 232, 234, 237, 238, 241, 242, 243, 249, 253, 256, 257, 266, 268, 269, 273, 274, 275, 276, 277, 278, 287, 288, 289, 290, 302 (Polish "Poznanski"), 303 (Polish "Warsaw-Kosciusco"), 306 (Polish "Torunski"), 308 (Polish "Krakowski"), 310 (Czech), 312 (Czech), 313 (Czech), 315 (Polish "Deblinski"), 316 (Polish "Warszawski"), 318 (Polish "Gdanski"), 322 (Dutch), 326 (French GC 2/7 "Nice"), 327 (French GC I/3 "Corse"), 328 (French GC I/7 "Provence"), 329 (French GC I/2 "Cigognes"), 331 (Norwegian), 332 (Norwegian), 335 (Hellenic), 336 (Hellenic), 340 (French "Ile de France"), 341 (French GC 3/2 "Alsace"), 345 (French GC 2/2 "Berry"), 349 (Belgian), 350 (Belgian), 352 (Yugoslav), 501, 502, 519, 520, 521, 527, 541, 542, 543, 544, 548, 549, 567, 577, 587, 595, 600, 601, 602, 603, 604, 607, 608, 609, 610, 611, 613, 614, 615, 616, 631, 667, 680, 681, 682, 683, 691, 695, 1435.

Commonwealth and Dominion Spitfire Squadrons: Nos 1 (SAAF), 2 (SAAF), 3 (SAAF) 4 (SAAF), 7 (SAAF), 9 (SAAF), 10 (SAAF), 11 SAAF) 40 (SAAF), 401 (RCAF), 402 (RCAF), 403 (RCAF), 411 (RCAF), 412 (RCAF), 414 (RCAF) 416 (RCAF), 417 (RCAF), 421 (RCAF), 430 (RCAF), 441 (RCAF), 442 (RCAF), 443 (RCAF), 451 (RAAF), 452 (RAAF), 453 (RAAF), 457 (RAAF), 485 (RNZAF)

The following 16 squadrons of the Indian Air Force were also armed with Spitfires: Nos 1, 2, 3, 4, 6, 7, 8, 9, 10, 12, 14, 15, 16 Fighter and No 1 PR Squadron (later renamed 101 Squadron)

USAAF Spitfire Squadrons: 2nd, 4th, 5th, 12th, 107th, 109th, 153rd, 307th, 308th, 309th, 334th (formerly No 71 Eagle Sqn), 335th (formerly No 121 Eagle Sqn), 336th (formerly No 133 Eagle Sqn)

Operational Royal Navy Seafire Squadrons: Nos 800, 801, 802, 803, 804, 805, 806, 807, 808, 809, 833, 834, 842, 851, 879, 880, 883, 884, 885, 886, 887, 889, 894, 895, 897, 899, 1831, 1832, 1833

Glossary

A&AEE: Aeroplane and Armament Experimental Establishment.

AFDU: Air Fighting Development Unit.

Airframe: The structure of an aircraft, minus the engine.

Air speed: The speed of an aircraft relative to the surrounding air, normally expressed in knots.

Aeroplane (Airplane): Powered heavier-than-air craft supported in flight by fixed wings.

Aileron: An aerofoil, usually fitted near the wingtips, used for causing an aircraft to roll around its longitudinal axis.

Altimeter: Instrument that measures altitude, or height above sea level.

Angle of attack: The angle between the wing (airfoil) and the airflow relative to it.

Bf: Bayerische Flugzeugwerke (Bavarian Aircraft Factories).

Ceiling, service: The height at which the rate of climb has fallen to a certain defined limit (for example 100ft [30.5m] per minute).

Cockpit: The portion of the fuselage designed to accommodate the pilot.

Control column: The lever by which the ailerons and elevators are operated. (Coll: "stick").

Cowling: The metal cover enclosing an engine installed in the airframe.

Drag: The resistance produced by an aircraft as it moves through the air.

Dope: A chemical preparation for the purpose of protecting, tautening and strengthening the canvas covering of an airframe.

Elevator: A horizontal control surface used to control the upward or downward inclination of an aircraft in flight. Usually hinged to the trailing edge of the tailplane (horizontal stabilizer).

Erk: RAF slang for an airman, a member of ground crew.

Flap: Device fitted to the trailing edge of an aircraft's wing that provides extra lift when lowered.

Fuselage: The main structure or body of an aircraft, to which the wings and tail unit are attached.

Ground speed: The speed of an aircraft over the ground, influenced by factors such as wind direction and speed.

Gyro gunsight: A type of gunsight in which target lead (the amount of aim-off in front of a moving target) and bullet drop are allowed for automatically by means of a gyroscope mechanism.

IFF: Identification Friend or Foe; an electronic pulse emitted by an aircraft to identify it as friendly on a radar screen.

Kampfgeschwader: A Luftwaffe bomber wing, usually comprising 75 aircraft.

Ki-gass: A priming system for the Merlin engine.

Knot: One nautical mile per hour, equivalent to 1.15mph (1.85 km/h).

Laminar Flow: The flow of air in layers, which progressively accelerate, over an aircraft's wing. The bottom layer, which remains stationary, is called the boundary layer.

Leading edge: The forward edge of a streamlined body or aerofoil.

Liquid-cooled engine: An engine, such as the Rolls-Royce Merlin, that is cooled by liquid rather than air, as in a radial engine.

MG: Machine gun.

Observer Corps: A cadre of volunteers, trained to man posts throughout the UK and report approaching enemy aircraft.

Order of Battle: The disposition and composition of a military, air or naval formation's operational units.

Port: The left-hand side as seen by the pilot looking forward.

Radar: Radio Direction And Ranging (also known as RDF).

Radial engine: A reciprocating type, internal combustion engine configuration in which the cylinders point outward from a central crankshaft like the spokes on a wheel.

Range: The maximum distance an aircraft can fly under given conditions without refueling.

Reflector sight: Type of gunsight in which illuminated information on target range, wing span, etc. is projected on to a glass screen mounted on top of the instrument panel.

Rudder: Movable vertical surface or surfaces forming part of the tail unit. Used to yaw the aircraft.

Specification: An official document detailing all the requirements for a new type of combat aircraft, or modifications to an existing one.

Stalling speed: The airspeed corresponding to the maximum lift coefficient of an aircraft. An aeroplane is said to stall when its airspeed drops below that necessary to support it in the air.

Starboard: The right-hand side as seen by the pilot looking forward.

Stuka: *Stürzkampfflugzeug* (literally: diving fighting aircraft—dive-bomber).

Turbojet engine: Jet engine that derives its thrust from a stream of hot exhaust gases.

Supercharger: A device that compresses the air back to sea-level equivalent pressures, or even much higher, in order to make an aero-engine produce just as much power at cruise altitude as it does at sea level.

Sweep: Name for an offensive cross-Channel operation by several RAF fighter squadrons.

Taxying: The movement of an aircraft on the ground, under power and fully controlled.

Trailing edge: The rear edge of a streamlined body or aerofoil.

Trimming tab: A small additional aerofoil, fixed to rudder, elevators and ailerons, to give these extra "bite."

Ultra: The collation and dissemination of high-grade intelligence gleaned from various sources, including Enigma.

VHF: Very High Frequency.

V-1: *Vergeltungswaffe* (Vengeance Weapon) 1; properly designated Fieseler Fi-103.

Yaw: The action of turning an aircraft in the air around its normal (vertical) axis by use of the rudder.

Zeke: Original Allied code-name for the Japanese Mitsubishi A6M Zero fighter.

Bibliography, Picture Credits, and Acknowledgments

BIBLIOGRAPHY

Air Ministry: *Pilot's Notes for Spitfire* (HMSO, 1943)
Andrews, C.F. and Morgan, E.B.: *Supermarine Aircraft since 1914* (Putnam, 1981)
Baker, E.C.R.: *The Fighter Aces of the RAF* (Kimber, 1962)
Bekker, Cajus: *The Luftwaffe War Diaries* (Macdonald & Co, 1967)
Bishop, Edward: *Their Finest Hour* (Purnell, 1968)
Bowyer, Chaz: *Supermarine Spitfire* (Arms and Armour Press, 1980)
Bowyer, Michael J.F.: *The Spitfire 50 Years On* (PSL, 1986)
Breche, Yves and Buffotot, Patrice: *Historique de Groupe de Chasse II/2 "Les Cigognes" 1914–1945* (Service Historique de L'Armée de l'Air, 1981)
Brown, David: *The Seafire: The Spitfire That Went to Sea* (Greenhill Books, 1989).
Caidin, Martin: *Me 109* (Purnell, 1968)
Caine, Philip D.: *American Pilots in the RAF: The WWII Eagle Squadrons* (Brassey's, 1993)
Clostermann, Pierre: *The Big Show* (Chatto & Windus, 1951)
Francillon, René J.: *Japanese Aircraft of the Pacific War* (Putnam, 1970)
Friedheim, Eric and Taylor, Samuel W.: *Fighters Up* (Nicholson and Watson, 1944)
Halley, James J.: *The Squadrons of the Royal Air Force* (Air-Britain, 1980)
Haughland, Vern: *The Eagle Squadrons: Yanks in the RAF, 1940–1942* (Ziff-Davis Flying Books, 1979)
Henshaw, Alex: *Sigh for a Merlin: Testing the Spitfire: 2nd Revised edition* (Crécy Publishing, 1999)
Hodgkinson, Colin: *Best Foot Forward* (Odhams Press, 1957)
Hough, Richard and Richards, Denis: *The Battle of Britain* (Hodder & Stoughton, 1989)
Hunt, Leslie: *Twenty-One Squadrons: The History of the Royal Auxiliary Air Force 1925–1957* (Garnstone Press, 1972)
Jackson, Robert: *Air Aces of WWII* (Crowood Press, 2003)
Jackson, Robert: *Dunkirk* (Arthur Barker, 1976)
Jackson, Robert: *Fighter Aces of World War II* (Corgi, 1978)
Jackson, Robert: *Hawker Hurricane* (Blandford Press, 1987)
Jackson, Robert: *Spitfire—The Combat History* (Airlife, 1995)
Jackson, Robert: *Spitfire—The History of Britain's Most Famous World War II Fighter* (Parragon, 2003)
Jackson, Robert: *The Forgotten Aces* (Sphere, 1989)
Jackson, Robert: *The Guinness Book of Air Warfare* (Guinness Publishing, 1993)
Jefford, Wng Cdr C.G.: *RAF Squadrons* (Airlife, 2001)
Johnson, Gp Capt J.E.: *Wing Leader* (Chatto & Windus, 1956)
Lee, Air Chief Marshal Sir David: *Flight From the Middle East* (MoD AHB, 1978)
Lee, Air Chief Marshal Sir David: *Eastward* (HMSO, 1984)
Lee, Air Chief Marshal Sir David: *Wings in the Sun* (HMSO, 1989)
Masters, David: *So Few* (Eyre & Spottiswoode, 1943)
Moore, Lt Cdr John: *Escort Carrier* (Hutchinson, 1943)
Morgan, Eric B. and Shacklady, Edward: *Spitfire—the History* (Key Publishing, 1987)
Nowarra, Heinz J.: *The Focke-Wulf 190—a Famous German Fighter* (Harleyford, 1972)
Price, Alfred: *The Spitfire Story* (Jane's Publishing Company Ltd., 1982)
Quill, Jeffrey: *Spitfire: A Test Pilot's Story* (Arrow Books, 1983)
RAF Historical Society: *Photographic Reconnaissance in WWII* (1991)
RAF Historical Society: *The RAF and the Far East War, 1941–1945* (1995)
Ramsey, Winston G. (Ed): *The Battle of Britain Then and Now* (After the Battle Publications, 5th Edition, 1989)
Robertson, Bruce: *Spitfire—the Story of a Famous Fighter* (Harleyford, 1961)
Shores, Christopher and Brian Cull with Nicola Malizia: *Malta: The Spitfire Year* (Grub Street, 1991)
Smith, J.R. and Kay, Anthony L.: *German Aircraft of the Second World War* (Putnam, 1972)
Sturtivant, Ray and Balance, Theo: *The Squadrons of the Fleet Air Arm* (Air-Britain, 1994)
Toliver, Col Raymond F. and Constable, Trevor J.: *Fighter Aces of the Luftwaffe* (Schiffer Publishing, 1993)
Vader, John: *Spitfire* (Purnell, 1969)

PICTURE CREDITS
Page number and position are indicated as follows: L = left; TL = top left; C = center; CL = center left; CR = center right; B = bottom; BL = bottom left, etc:

Author's collection: 10BL; 12–13; 13C; 16TR; 19TR; 21TR; 36C; 37BL; 38BR; 38BL; 39T; 41BL; 42TL; 43BL; 44BL; 44BR; 48TR; 59TR; 61BC; 64TL; 67TR; 66BL; 68B; 71TR; 70BL; 77BR; 82C; 83BL; 82TR; 85TL; 85CR; 90BL; 92BR; 93TL; 92BL; 93BR; 94BC; 95BL; 101BR; 103BC; 110BR; 110L; 114TR; 115BR; 116C; 117B; 121TL; 121BL; 124TR; 124C; 126BL; 128C; 129CR; 136L; 137TR; 137BL; 141C; 143BL; 143TL; 145C; 144BR; 144C; 147BL; 147BC; 147BR; 148BL; 149C; 154BL; 157TL; 157TR. **Peter Arnold:** 15BL; 19BL 22BL; 23C; 23BR; 25TR; 29B; 29B; 31C; 34–35; 37BR; 41T; 43T; 45BR; 49TL; 50T; 53; 53; 53; 53; 53; 53; 53; 53; 53; 53; 53; 53; 53; 53; 53; 53; 53; 53; 53; 52TR; 58BL; 58BL; 65R; 72TR; 72BL; 72BL; 75T; 77TR; 89B; 89B; 111L; 119TR; 120B; 120B; 122T. **Ian Blair:** 135BR. **Bletchley:** 98TR; 99T; 99C. **Austin Brown:** 126TR; 127CR; 128BL. **Bundesarchiv:** 42B; 57BR. **Cody:** 98TR; 99T; 99C. **Gavin Conroy:** 78B; 79; 80T; 105. **Crown Copyright:** 11TL. **Bill Dady, Claveworks Graphics:** 153TR; 153TR; 153TR; 153TR; 153TR; 153TR. **Daily Record:** 135TR. **John Dibbs:** 80B; 106; 107; 131. **Elephant Book Company LImited:** 17C; 20–21; 22BR; 25–26; 26; 28C; 30BL; 32TR; 36BL; 45CL; 46B; 47C; 48BL; 49BC; 51C; 55B; 61T; 61T; 67TL; 67C; 73B; 78T; 80C; 84BL; 85CR; 93C; 94C; 97C; 101T; 102R; 103T; 104; 109C; 115C; 114C; 119T; 123B; 123B; 123B; 122B; 122B; 125BR; 125L; 127T; 130; 132; 133; 134B; 140BR; 141T; 140BL; 142R; 143TR; 155C; 155C; 156BR. **Matthew Freudenberg:** 54BR. **Free French Association:** 116BC; 117TR. **Getty:** 137TL; 146TR. **IWM:** 20C; 40C; 149BR; 148TR; 32B. **Phil Jarrett:** End papers, full title; foreword; introduction; 8–9; 11B; 12TR; 12BL; 17BR; 19TL; 22TR; 29T; 33C; 32BL; 37TL; 45TL; 47TL; 47TR; 50BR; 51TL&C; 51B; 55TL; 55TR; 56BL; 59TL; 59CL; 59CR; 62–63; 65BC; 69C; 71C; 73TL; 74TR; 75BL; 76TR; 83C; 86–87; 88BL; 88TR; 91TC; 94TR; 96BR; 97TR; 96TR; 100TR; 108BR; 109B; 108BL; 111TR; 112–113; 119BC; 121BR; 129TL; 135C; 134TR; 138–139; 142BL; 145TL; 146BR; 147T; 150–151; 152TR; 153BL; 154BR; 155TR; 157BR. **NARA (The National Archives and Records Administration):** 90BR. **Nostalgic Aviation.com:** 57T. **Dan Patterson:** 27. **Col Pope:** 104. **RAF Radar Defence Museum:** 28T; 33TR. **Solent Sky Museum:** Half title; 15TR; 14BL; 14TR; 17TL; 17TL; 17BL; 18BR; 20TR; 31TR; 50BL; 56C; 89TR; 95CR; 118BR; 156BL; 157C. **TopFoto:** 122CR; 123R. **US Navy Historical:** 74BL. **Robert A Watkins / Disney:** 68T. **WW2Images.com:** 41BR; 49BR; 60TR; 84BL; 117TR. **Via Bruce Zigler:** 68T.

Jacket and front cover illustration: *Achtung Spitfire* by Roy Grinnell, altered by permission of the artist. (website: www.roygrinnell.com)

AUTHOR AND EDITORS' ACKNOWLEDGMENTS:
The author and editors wish to thank the following for their help in preparing this book: Susannah Jayes, additional picture research.

Museums
RAF Manston Spitfire & Hurricane Memorial Trust
The Memorial Museum, The Airfield, Manston Road, Ramsgate, Kent, CT12 5DF, England.
Tel: 01843 821940 (www.spifirememorial.org.uk).

Solent Sky Museum
Albert Road South, Southampton, Hampshire, SO14 3FR, England.
Tel: 02380 635830 (www.spitfireonline.co.uk).

Tangmere Military Aviation Museum
Tangmere, Nr Chichester, West Sussex, PO20 2ES, England.
Tel: 01243 790090 (www.tangmere-museum.org.uk).

Royal Air Force Museum Cosford
Shifnal, Shropshire, TF11 8UP, England.
Tel: 01902 376200 (www.rafmuseum.org.uk/cosford).